RICHARD STEARNS ⟩ PRESIDENT, WORLD V̵̵̵̵̵̵̵US
RUSADE FOR CHRIST // JERRY WHITE ⟩ IN̵̵̵̵̵̵ S //
SRAEL L. GAITHER ⟩ RETIRED NATIONAL CON̵̵̵̵ MIS
CHAIRMAN OF THE BOARD, PRISON FELLOW̵̵̵̵ IES
SA // ELISA MORGAN ⟩ PUBLISHER, *FUL̵̵̵̵ . //
MELINDA DELAHOYDE ⟩ PRESIDENT, CARE NET // DAVID MCKENNA ⟩ FORMER PRESIDENT, SPRING
ARBOR UNIVERSITY, SEATTLE PACIFIC UNIVERSITY, ASBURY THEOLOGICAL SEMINARY // C. JEFFREY
WRIGHT ⟩ CEO, UMI (URBAN MINISTRIES, INC.) // MARK G. HOLBROOK ⟩ PRESIDENT/CEO, EVANGELICAL
CHRISTIAN CREDIT UNION // STEVE HAYNER ⟩ PRESIDENT, COLUMBIA THEOLOGICAL SEMINARY
⟩ JOSEPH KRIVICKAS ⟩ CHAIRMAN, GORDON COLLEGE CENTER FOR NONPROFIT STUDIES AND
HILANTHROPY // DAVID J. GYERTSON ⟩ SENIOR FELLOW, ENGSTROM INSTITUTE // JOHN C. REYNOLDS
⟩ EXECUTIVE VICE PRESIDENT, AZUSA PACIFIC UNIVERSITY // TED W. ENGSTROM ⟩ PRESIDENT
MERITUS, WORLD VISION INTERNATIONAL / PAST PRESIDENT, YOUTH FOR CHRIST INTERNATIONAL

NONPROFIT

///////////////////////////

**ESSENTIAL INSIGHTS FROM
15 CHRISTIAN EXECUTIVES**

///////////////////////////

PROFIT
LEADERSHIP
IN A FOR-PROFIT WORLD

This book is dedicated to the late Ted W. Engstrom, for whom the Christian Leadership Alliance's Engstrom Institute (EI) was named. Throughout his life Ted modeled the Christian leadership principles honored in *Nonprofit Leadership in a For-Profit World*. The quintessential Christian ministry leader, he served as president of World Vision International and Youth for Christ International and in a myriad of other leadership roles. He modeled a lifelong pursuit of honoring God through excellence in leadership and management. As the EI Christian Leadership series develops—this book being the first of that series—Ted's legacy will endure.

This book is also dedicated to the memory of Lisa Krivickas, wife of editor Joseph Krivickas, who passed away in 2009. She was a passionate advocate and inspiration for the development of this book. In the last months of her life, Lisa suggested that the CLA ask some of the Engstrom Institute's dearest partners, ministry leaders from across the nation, to collaborate on this defining book on Christian leadership. We are indebted to her vision for sharing the wisdom in this book with Christian leaders.

C**O**NTENTS

PREFACE

///

Nonprofit Leadership in a For-Profit World is released in association with the Engstrom Institute and with a plan for many more books in the EI Christian Leadership series. The Engstrom Institute is the knowledge resource center of the Christian Leadership Alliance (CLA), an association of more than ten thousand leaders of Christian nonprofits nationwide. Our resources reflect CLA's mission to equip Christian leaders to achieve organizational excellence as they work on the front lines serving those in need.

Nonprofit Leadership in a For-Profit World asks how nonprofit leadership co-exists with the for-profit world and, even more importantly, how the nonprofit and for-profit worlds can influence one another toward achieving excellence. It also asks what the next generation of Christian nonprofit leadership should look like. How can the current generation of Christ-centered leaders ensure they are fully equipped for all that God has planned for the next (and perhaps last) chapter of the redemption narrative?

For this book we contacted several of today's most effective and insightful Christian leaders. We asked them to share intimate, transparent, and trans-forming attitudes, principles, and practices they believe are required if the next generation of Christian leaders is truly to walk worthy of their high calling in Christ Jesus (see Ephesians 4:1). As a guide, we asked them to respond to but not be limited by the following questions:

) If you could give a "last lecture" to the next generation of those called to lead faith-based nonprofits, what would be the most important lessons you would share?

- If you could invest the next year of your life in the next leader of your most treasured faith-based nonprofit organization, what would be your emphasis?
- If you could lead your organization into the future, what would you do differently and why?
- What do you believe to be the most important legacy God has allowed you to leave as a faith-based nonprofit leader?

In offering this resource to the public, the authors and publisher hope that it will help meet the needs of thousands of Christian nonprofit organizations, as well as the thousands of churches with ministry outreaches.

// HOW TO USE THIS BOOK //

This book is formatted in a way to help you become more effective in both your individual and team leadership responsibilities. We believe that the threads offered by each author produce a rich tapestry of tones and images that are informational, transformational, and inspirational for your leadership journey.

At the end of each chapter is a "My Leadership Bookshelf" section where the contributors share what for them, at this stage in their leadership, are the most influential books. Our goal was to help you sort through the myriad of offerings and find a core collection.

We also include two sets of questions with each chapter, designed to help you relate our contributors' insights and experiences first to you personally and then to your leadership team. The questions are designed to bring motivations to the surface, to highlight theoretical/theological understandings, and to suggest practical applications. Consider these as tools for executive coaching—questions that you likely would be asked if you had the opportunity to sit personally with these mentors.

We included a biography of each of the authors in their chapters. We worked at finding a mix of leaders to represent the diversity in race, gender, age, mission, organizational size, leadership style, and perspective that makes up our faith-based nonprofit membership within the Christian Leadership Alliance.

Chapter 1, "A Mentor's Mentor," was constructed from some of the foundational insights of the late Dr. Ted W. Engstrom, for whom the Engstrom Institute of the Christian Leadership Alliance is named. His dedication to Christ-centered leadership, and lifelong investment as a mentor and friend to many of today's senior Christian CEOs, has made him a father of contemporary Christian leadership thought and practice.

After you read chapter 1, we encourage you to read the editor's overview at the beginning of each of the chapters, asking the Holy Spirit to guide you to those contributors that best speak to your needs at this moment. The chapters are arranged alphabetically by author (except for the final chapter), so there is no inherent rationale for their order based on topics. Let your reading be a series of divine appointments and sovereign encounters led by the Holy Spirit's tutoring.

// ACKNOWLEDGMENTS //

As editors, we (Dr. David J. Gyertson and Joseph Krivickas) would be remiss if we did not first honor God for providing the vision for this project. We also thank Dr. Robert Andringa for his vision for the Engstrom Institute, as well as for his passionate support for the development of this book and the Christian Leadership series. We deeply appreciate the vision and leadership that Frank Lofaro, president and CEO of the Christian Leadership Alliance, provided in helping to develop this resource. And we are indebted to Jan Sokoloski for her administrative support and coordination of the various contributors, as well as the development of their biographies. We would also like to thank Dale Reeves and his team at Standard Publishing for their support and leadership in helping to bring this book to press. Finally, we salute the distinguished authors, all accomplished Christian nonprofit leaders, who have given of their time and wisdom to make this book a reality.

1

///

A MENTOR'S MENTOR

ADAPTED FROM THE WRITINGS OF TED W. ENGSTROM

Perhaps no single individual has influenced so many of today's senior Christian leaders as Ted W. Engstrom. He mentored hundreds of Christian CEOs, helping us focus on best practices with practical advice—but always with a penetrating, sobering call to personal integrity and spiritual maturity. Most of us who have contributed to this volume have been influenced deeply by his life, his insights, and his loving challenges. For those he mentored, there was a consistent and focused call to excellence in all we did professionally, as well as personally and spiritually. He demanded logical thinking in our decision making but always underscored the critical nature of spiritual wisdom and discernment. Even at our most lucid moments, he reminded us that the wisdom we needed was from on high.

Dr. Ted, as he was affectionately known to so many, also served as a "watchman on the wall" (see Isaiah 62:6), challenging us to be ever vigilant for the dangers that lurked in our leadership. He stands as a mentor's mentor whose intimate conversations shaped a generation of Christian leaders around the world. We include some of his insights here on his major themes of excellence, decision making, and vigilance as the foundation for what you will hear from our contributors to this volume. Ted served as president and president emeritus of World Vision International and was former president of Youth for Christ International. This chapter is adapted from articles in the *Christian Leadership Letter* that Ted, along with Ed Dayton, wrote during their time in leadership at World Vision.[1]

// CHRISTIAN EXCELLENCE //

In 1961, John W. Gardner, who was then head of the Carnegie Corporation and was subsequently to move on to prominent roles of leadership in the Department of HEW and Common Cause, wrote a book with the simple title *Excellence: Can We Be Equal and Excellent Too?* (W. W. Norton & Company, 1995). In this book Gardner was attacking the idea that it is almost undemocratic to excel at something over your fellow man.

Gardner was on the right track. We need to excel. And yet Christians also fall into this trap of believing that no one should be better than someone else. We become uneasy with the idea of having the best, being the best, or doing that which is outstanding. In our thinking we all too often do not mind "excellence" if the Lord is given the credit: "The Lord has really blessed the ministry" or "The Lord really gave him great gifts." But we may become suspicious if someone is praised directly for doing an excellent job.

There are some very real tensions here, and they work themselves out in strange ways:

- ❶ I once visited a beautiful chapel on a new church campus. In contrast to three obviously expensive chandeliers was a hand-drawn Sunday school attendance chart taped on the foyer wall. They paid $1,500 for the chandeliers, but the best they could do to communicate what was happening to people was a crude graph.
- ❶ Another time, World Vision was criticized for purchasing first-quality plumbing for a new building, a long-term investment that has paid good dividends but that seemed to some to be "too good."
- ❶ In contrast is the pride we exhibit when a Christian makes the big time in athletics or politics. For some reason, it is all right to praise man for excellence in the secular realm!

Part of our problem is just defective theology. Most of us cannot live with the biblical (paradoxical) truth that God is doing it all—he is in all and through all (Colossians 1:17; 3:11)—and the parallel truth that is just as completely incomprehensible: man is the one who has not only been given complete responsibility for his actions but is *commanded* to act. All of this is part of our tension in theology and life. We constantly struggle with the concept of operating a business that is also a ministry. They do not conflict—both are vital.

But we are called to excellence. And we are called to set standards of excellence for ourselves and others. In Philippians 1:10, Paul prays that we may have the ability to "discern what is best" ("approve things that are excellent," *KJV*). "Be perfect . . . as your heavenly Father is perfect" (Matthew 5:48) is the standard. But where do we begin? Does a call to excellence mean a call to excellence in everything?

Colossians 3:17 admonishes us: "Whatever you do, whether in word or deed, do it all in the name of the Lord Jesus, giving thanks to God the Father through him." No higher standard could be found. And yet most of us must admit that there are large segments of our lives where this is not our experience. What's the answer? How do we as Christian leaders apply these criteria?

Let's start with some definitions.

EXCELLENCE IS A MEASURE

Excellence demands definition. One of the trite replies of our day, when asked how we like something or how well something is going, is "Compared to what?" But excellence is like that. It assumes a standard. And conversely, excellence assumes inferiority. It assumes there's a way of doing or being something that is:

- less than the best.
- less than what it could be.
- less than worthwhile.

EXCELLENCE ASSUMES A GOAL, AN OBJECTIVE

Excellence demands that we think beyond dreams, beyond concepts; that we think into reality in terms of what we can be, what we should be.

EXCELLENCE ASSUMES PRIORITIES

It not only has to do with doing one thing well but also is concerned with a choice between goals. There are some goals that are less worthy, less honoring to God, goals that fall short of all that God intends us to be. It is not that there is one right way for all men, but rather that a potential for excellence in some area lies in all men. We are called to live a life in which we need to do many things, but within which we are called to do some of those things with excellence. Certainly we are to excel in prayer. Or perhaps we are to excel in one book of the Bible or to exercise one gift to its fullest potential. (Some of us have great gifts, but we are too lazy to unwrap them.)

EXCELLENCE IS A PROCESS MORE THAN AN ACHIEVEMENT

Life is a process—management is a process. There are times in history when we can look at an individual or event and pronounce it excellent, but it is continually pressing on that marks the man dedicated to excellence.

Paul said, "One thing I do: Forgetting what is behind and straining toward what is ahead, I press on toward the goal to win the prize for which God has called me heavenward in Christ Jesus" (Philippians 3:13, 14).

EXCELLENCE SHOULD BE A STYLE OF LIFE

Know yourself. What is your style? What can it be? People are tremendously different: outgoing vs. introspective, thinkers vs. doers, leaders vs. followers, logical vs. intuitive, and teachers vs. learners. Some are ahead of their time—some are behind. Some are musical geniuses—some are not. Some are great preachers—some are not. Some are conceivers of grand ideas—others are men of small detail. But for each of us, excellence demands that we be true to the best that God has placed within us. Our style of life should be one of excellence. The Christian can adopt nothing less as his or her goal.

EXCELLENCE HAS TO DO WITH MOTIVATION

Excellence is not achieved easily. The first 80 percent of an excellent solution comes easy. The next 15 percent is hard. And only the highly motivated person reaches beyond to the 100 percent. There is a joy in such achievement that is an all too rare experience for most of us. One of the mysteries of living is that the goal that is easily achieved brings little inner satisfaction or reward. Old victories will serve old age, but before I reach that, I must forget what lies behind and press on to the goal.

Think big! Believe a big God! Remember that God is greater!

EXCELLENCE ASSUMES ACCOUNTABILITY

Excellence assumes accountability, either to our own inner standard or the standard of the group. Oh, how we Christians have so often missed that!

// RESPONDING TO THE GOAL OF EXCELLENCE //

Sort your goals. You can't do everything. You can't be everything. And that's all right!

Of those goals you believe you must push toward, decide which have top priority. Do those with excellence.

Decide who you are and what you are. Or approach it this way: decide how God made you and what he wants you to be. Do that with excellence. It was said of Jesus, "He has done everything well" (Mark 7:37). Can we ask less of ourselves?

As we seek Christian excellence, keep it in perspective. Some things are more excellent than others. Philippians 1:10 was quoted earlier. If we back up and quote verses 9-11, Paul tells us how we will be able to judge that which is excellent: "This is my prayer: that your love may abound more and more in knowledge and depth of insight, so that you may be able to discern what is best and may be pure and blameless until the day of Christ . . . to the glory and praise of God."

// DECISION MAKING //

Many years ago a Christian leader wrote a letter to some of his followers in Corinth, reflecting back on his decision not to visit them: "When I planned this, did I do it lightly? Or do I make my plans in a worldly manner so that in the same breath I say, 'Yes, yes' and 'No, no'? But as surely as God is faithful, our message to you is not 'Yes' and 'No.' For the Son of God, Jesus Christ, who was preached among you by me and Silas and Timothy, was not 'Yes' and 'No,' but in him it has always been 'Yes'" (2 Corinthians 1:17-19).

Paul faced all the demands for making a decision. The situation demanded action. He was under a time pressure. He lacked complete information. There was uncertainty, which suggested a risk in making a decision. There were possible costly consequences if he made the wrong decision. On the other hand, there was the possibility of good benefits from an effective decision. Lastly, there was the possibility of two or more alternative actions.

The need for a decision comes at any time of the day, and decisions come in all sizes. Good decision making is the hallmark of effective leadership in an organization. But good decision making in Christian organizations requires an additional spiritual dimension that can give the Christian executive the confidence needed to move ahead with a decision while others stand and vacillate. Pray about the alternatives. Then seek God's promised wisdom (James 1:5).

There is a close relationship between decision making and problem solving. Usually both start with a statement like "Something needs to be done!" Here are the steps in the process.

IDENTIFY AND DESCRIBE THE SITUATION

Good managers know that many times just their ability to understand a situation is half the solution. Gather as many facts as possible. There will never be enough, but within the time demands of the decision, organize the available data. Data gathering is a skill that needs to be developed. What are the key sources of information? Who should you call in? But remember, at this point you're asking for data, not opinions on what decisions should be made.

LINE UP ALTERNATIVES

From the data you have gathered, list possible alternatives in some way that will permit you to view them one at a time. If you are working with a group, it is very helpful to write the data (problem description) on one piece of newsprint and then to list the alternatives on another. There will be cases when a decision is either yes or no, go or don't go. However, try not to be satisfied with only two alternatives. Get wise counsel. Ask other people for possible alternatives based on the data that you have.

COMPARE THE ALTERNATIVES

Since we can never completely predict the future, almost every alternative will include some level of uncertainty. Find a way to compare alternatives against one another. Some of the things that you might want to compare are the risk involved (see below), the cost of the alternative, the people available to implement the decision, the past effectiveness of using this type of alternative, the amount of time that this alternative will require, and how it will be received within the organization.

A list of assumptions that you are making for each one of the alternatives may be the key to determining which is best. It is surprising how often people arrive at the same conclusion for different reasons. Therefore, a side benefit of listing your assumptions is your ability to communicate to others (and yourself!) the base upon which you are building your reasoning. How much time you take in this process will, of course, be dictated by the urgency of the decision you face.

CALCULATE THE RISK

The major difference between problem solving and decision making is that in problem solving we assume that there is a right solution. The problem has an answer. But decision making almost always includes an element of risk. We do not have enough information. We are not sure of the future. We don't have enough time to gather all the data. Therefore, try to develop your own method of rating the risk of each of the alternatives. Perhaps something as simple as a grading scale of 1 to 10 will be of help. Look back to your previous assumptions and see if they help you in assessing the penalties for making the wrong decision. Many times the correct alternative is self-evident as we compare and rate the risk of each of the various alternatives. But there are many times when it is difficult to choose between alternatives. What do we do now?

Sometimes you can combine alternatives. This can be done by taking parts of two different alternatives or perhaps trying both of them. For instance, one might be a short-range solution to the need that you face, while another might be a longer-range solution. Do not be afraid of a compromise. Inflexibility in decision making tends to destroy effective leadership. Often the best you can do is to make the best of a series of bad situations. But intuition or hunches will play a major role in selecting the "best" alternatives. And be sure to seek God's wisdom.

IMPLEMENT THE DECISION

How a leadership decision is announced and implemented is just as important as the decision itself. If it is not a major-impact decision that requires an immediate announcement, consider the timing of the announcement. Perhaps it should be postponed until just the right set of circumstances presents itself. When you make an important decision, take a little bit of time before announcing it. Sleep on it. God may have other plans!

The manner in which the decision is announced is of tremendous importance. If it is presented as "I'm sorry, but this is the best we can do in this lousy situation," then you can expect the same response in your subordinates as they communicate the decision throughout the organization.

The individuals to whom the decision is announced can make a big difference in its reception. Many times it is a good idea to privately lay some groundwork ahead of time with those who are going to have to implement (or will be affected by) a major decision.

Once a decision is made, don't look back or second-guess yourself. Expect commitment to the decision—on your part and on the part of those who will be working on it. Don't seek popularity in decision making. Leadership can be a lonely business. Be constant in applying the consequences of your decision. Don't vacillate.

WHEN THINGS GO WRONG

As every veteran leader knows, "If there is a possibility of anything going wrong, it probably will." What may have been a very good decision three weeks ago, in the light of subsequent events or new data, may appear to be a very poor one. This means that important decisions should have a built-in feedback process that will let you know as soon as possible if things are going sour. At this point it is not a question of who's at fault, but how to turn things in a more positive direction. In a sense you are faced with a new decision: what to do with a bad one you may have made! It may be that the decision was right but the planning was poor. Perhaps the wrong individuals were given the assignment to implement. Perhaps a new and better alternative has appeared, one that is distracting people from the original course of action.

Go through the same process of decision making that you went through before: identify and describe the situation, line up alternatives, compare the alternatives, calculate the risk and select the best new alternative; then implement a new and revised decision.

It is here that the Christian executive has the tremendous advantage over his secular counterpart. Each one of us as children of God can be assured that God is working all things together for good on our behalf (see Romans 8:28). Those of us who are privileged to work as part of the organizational life of his body can assume that this also applies to the organizational task. This does not mean that we should be casting blame for failure on the Lord. Nor should we discount our own role in any successes. It does mean that that extra spiritual dimension can produce decisions that can turn the world upside down.

// PITFALLS TO AVOID //

It has been well said that an organization begins with a person, becomes a movement that develops into a machine, and eventually becomes a monument. How do these things happen?

Organizations (and their leaders) succeed or fail for many different reasons. When an organization is young, and the future is bright and exciting, it is easy to think there are no pitfalls in the road. But the mature organization is not without its hazards either. In many ways the dangers that a mature organization faces are much more subtle and are often the result of success rather than failure. In what follows, I have attempted to list ten pitfalls for the Christian organization. You can use this as a checklist to help discover whether you may be facing any of these dangers and to determine a strategy for avoiding them.

1. SETTLING FOR THE STATUS QUO

How easy it is for the Christian agency to be willing to settle for the status quo, to simply keep things as they are. But it is impossible for any organization to stand still; it will either progress or regress. God's work demands that we move forward. This is true in our personal lives, and it is just as true in our organizational life. Once we settle for maintaining things as they are now, we begin to slide toward ineffectiveness, a slide that becomes steeper the farther we go. One clue indicating that we are settling for the status quo is that we have very little internal tension within the organization. This naturally leads us to the next danger.

2. ELIMINATING CREATIVE TENSION

The organization that "has it made" tends to resist creative tensions. They like to settle for peace and calm. Creative people have new ideas. They want to change things, to make them better. But new ideas bring with them a conflict of interest, and conflict of interest brings internal tension. When a new idea is offered, too often what we hear is "You have done things wrong," rather than "Here's a better way." The result of eliminating creative tension is that we often fail to face up to the situation around us. An example of this might be how we handle the world economic scene. If we do not go through the struggle of creatively addressing ourselves to the tensions that a troubled economy is going to create in our ministries at home and abroad, many organizations will find themselves in deep difficulty down the road.

3. NOT PLANNING IN DEPTH

Almost every organization does some planning, but if we fail to plan our ministries in depth, as well as breadth, danger lies ahead. In other words, it is too easy for us to look for quality and quantity as a primary result of our planning, rather than quality and meaningfulness in the program and ministry God has placed before us. These need to be placed in priority. Quality is far more important than quantity. Size must always be secondary to the effectiveness of the ministry that we perform under God.

Discriminating between breadth and depth is not easy. That is why there is a real danger here. We may have a great desire to expand our ministry throughout and beyond our community or to the rest of the world, but if the quality of the ministry that we are performing at the place we have begun is not being continually strengthened, then we may discover that we have overextended ourselves.

4. FAILING TO LISTEN

A very subtle danger for experienced Christian leaders is a failure to really hear and listen to younger colleagues, to give them a role in participatory leadership. Younger staff members have a great deal to contribute. Often we are so certain that we have "been there" before, we do not listen. This is even more true of our usual attitude toward younger *women* staff members. Those who are older and who provide leadership need to have an open heart to what younger colleagues may say as God speaks to them. After all, it is self-evident that tomorrow's leadership rests with them. If we want to ensure the continuation of a solid ministry, then we need to invest ourselves in the developing leadership. Part of the investment is to have the will and time to listen.

5. RELYING ON PAST SUCCESSES

How easy it is to place our confidence in what the organization has done in the past, or even what it is doing now. It is easy to bask in the accolades of others who tell us what a great job we have done. But our dependency is not on what we have accomplished in the past or what we are doing now. Rather, it should be on what God is doing now. How wonderful it is to cast ourselves on him and believe that he is leading us on a daily basis.

How do you do that? It is a paradox. On the one hand, we are responsible for God's work. On the other hand, God is doing it all. But when we place our confidence in what we have done in the past and fail to balance this with complete confidence in what God will do in the future, danger lies ahead.

6. DEPENDING ON PERSONAL EXPERIENCE

This is a corollary to depending on the organization's experience. Too many of us are ready to depend on our own brainpower, expertise, and experience rather than to depend on God himself. Obviously, God has gifted those in the church, and these gifts need to be utilized and sharpened. But it is "'not by might nor by power, but by my Spirit,' says the LORD Almighty" (Zechariah 4:6). There is a danger of our attempting to take back what we have given to the Lord, to take our lives back into our own hands.

7. NEGLECTING THE HIGHEST GOOD

Here is a danger of which we are all aware but too seldom face. It is the danger of becoming so busy in what are genuinely good and fine works for the Lord that we neglect the highest good, which is our worship of God through all our service. We need to saturate our hearts with God's Word. How easy it is to become so busy about his business that we forget God's desire for us to know him. We need to remember that it should be, to quote Oswald Chambers, "my utmost for his highest."

8. FORGETTING UNITY

Christian organizations have the promise of a special kind of unity. We are related to one another as the different parts of the body of Christ. This relationship is not an option—it is nonnegotiable. The maintenance of this type of Christian unity takes skill and perseverance. Too easily we forget that the way the world knows that we are Jesus' disciples is by the love that we have for one another. And the world will believe that Jesus is the Christ when they see that we have the same type of oneness that he had with the Father. Jesus prayed that all believers "may be one, Father, just as you are in me and I am in you. May they also be in us so that the world may believe that you have sent me" (John 17:21).

Unity is not the absence of healthy conflict caused by creativity and differences of opinion. Unity finds its first dimension in the allegiance we have to our Savior. It finds its expression in our recognition that each of us has gifts that help us to function as parts of his body. Part of our task is to affirm one another's gifts and to respect one another's roles. This is a primary task of Christian leaders.

9. LOSING THE JOY OF SERVICE

How quickly those who are in the work, who are on the front lines of service, can lose the real joy of that service. The further we proceed in positions of leadership and authority, the greater servants we should become. The highest role of leadership is that of servant. Jesus said that he himself "did not come to be served, but to serve" (Matthew 20:28). Christian leaders, like all leaders, need to be undergirded with authority and privileges of office. However, if these are seen as being the just due of the individual rather than the benefits of the office, we can become dangerously close to believing that we are the ones who should be served. The servant role ought to mark us. It is in this kind of ministering service that there is the deepest joy, gratification, and satisfaction.

10. FORGETTING THE BOTTOM LINE

Accountants like to call our attention to the bottom line, the final statement of what is left over after outgo has been balanced off against income. Every organization needs to know what its bottom line is. The bottom line in Christian service is the complete honoring of Christ and the offering to the world the knowledge of the Savior. Everything must head toward that goal and objective.

Which of those pitfalls is your organization most prone to fall into? Now is a great time to take stock of what dangers might be ahead for you. Knowing the bumps in the road ahead can make all the difference in avoiding them.

MY LEADERSHIP BOOKSHELF

Ted W. Engstrom was a prolific writer whose insights on principles and practices of Christ-centered leadership have stood the test of time. You are encouraged to peruse his many writings on a wide range topics. We suggest, particularly, the following that remain readily available.

The Essential Engstrom edited by Timothy J. Beals (Authentic Publishing, 2007) is the best collection of Ted W. Engstrom's thinking on a wide range of topics, practices, and principles gleaned from a lifetime of writing, speaking, and observations.

The Making of a Mentor: Nine Essential Characteristics of Effective Christian Leaders by Ted W. Engstrom and Ron Jenson (Authentic and World Vision, 2005) presents the foundation for mentoring the next generation of

Christian leaders by using Jesus as a model to discuss qualities such as self-discipline, encouragement, gentleness, and confrontation.

////// PERSONAL REFLECTIONS AND APPLICATIONS //////

1. Reflect on Colossians 3:17, which admonishes us: "Whatever you do, whether in word or deed, do it all in the name of the Lord Jesus, giving thanks to God the Father through him." The chapter suggests that much of our ability to achieve excellence is hindered by our "defective theology." What aspects of your own Christian beliefs and experiences—upon inspection—may involve defective assumptions and could be hindering your commitment to excellence?

2. Work through the points used to encourage excellence (p. 15), and establish a strategy for implementing each in your personal and professional life. How will you monitor your progress? Who will you invite to hold you accountable for presenting your calling to God as a sacrifice that reflects your best efforts empowered by the Holy Spirit?

3. Many times we are paralyzed or, at the very least, hobbled in decision making because we fail to exercise the basic steps needed to describe the situation, consider and compare alternatives, do a sufficient risk assessment, implement the decision, and anticipate challenges. Use that outline to assess a recent decision you made. What steps did you do well? Which ones were missed or addressed insufficiently?

4. Discernment is one of the most important dimensions of effective living and serving as an intentional Christian. Review the ten pitfalls (p. 22) and rank them from most significant to least significant in their impact on your leadership service. Develop a strategy for addressing the three most significant in both your personal and professional life. Now rank the ten from most important to least important for your organization. What does this

ranking reveal about changes that may be needed for your organization to be more effective?

///////// TEAM REFLECTIONS AND APPLICATIONS /////////

1. How do you measure how effective your organization is in its commitment to excellence? Is there a corporate culture committed to excellence at every level of your organization? How do you measure, recognize, reward, and facilitate excellence as a leadership team? Are there any historical influences, company policies/practices, or theological assumptions that keep your organization from achieving its highest capacity and results for Christ's glory?

2. Use the list of decision-making steps (p. 18) and discuss how you see and experience decision making in your ministry setting. Develop a checklist based on these steps to apply to the next five major decisions you make as a leadership team. Openly discuss the strengths and weaknesses you discover. How could these steps be used as a training opportunity to improve decision making throughout your organization?

3. One of the realities we sometimes forget is that, given the spiritual nature of our mission as a Christ-honoring organization, we are in a continuous conflict with Satan, the enemy of God's work and plans. Several tactics were suggested that our enemy uses to deflect, diminish, and if possible, defeat our work together. As a team, review that list of ten pitfalls (p. 22) and openly discuss which ones seem to be the most problematic for your work together. What steps can be taken and attitudes changed to address these pitfalls for your team? Remember, "Knowing the bumps in the road ahead can make all the difference in avoiding them."

TED W. ENGSTROM
PRESIDENT EMERITUS, WORLD VISION INTERNATIONAL /
PAST PRESIDENT, YOUTH FOR CHRIST INTERNATIONAL
///

The late Dr. Ted W. Engstrom, president emeritus of World Vision International and past president of Youth for Christ International, was an influential evangelical leader whose impact spanned much of the twentieth century and continues.

A gifted preacher, astute manager, and the author of more than fifty books, Engstrom has been described as "a giant in American evangelical circles for more than half a century." He died in 2006 at the age of ninety, leaving a remarkable legacy through his mentorees, writings, and personal example.

Engstrom is recognized for his focus in two fundamental areas as he contributed to American evangelical culture in the twentieth century. First, he introduced standard business practices and management principles to churches and other faith-based institutions, groups which often went awry because they paid too little attention to the bottom line. Second, he combined social outreach with evangelism, contending that service to mankind was as important as preaching salvation in Christ.

As executive vice president and later president and chief executive officer of World Vision International, Ted W. Engstrom helped turn a small Christian agency focused on war orphans into one of the world's largest and most extensive relief and development organizations. He served as vice president for nineteen years and president for two, retiring in 1987.

Engstrom combined his business acumen with his passion for Christian service. He coauthored the best-selling *Managing Your Time* and wrote *The Making of a Christian Leader* and *The Fine Art of Mentoring*.

It was during his tenure at Zondervan in Grand Rapids, Michigan, that Engstrom became the local director of Youth for Christ International. In 1947, the Grand Rapids chapter of Youth for Christ invited a then little-known evangelist named Billy Graham to do a crusade. Directed by Engstrom, it was

Graham's first citywide crusade. As executive director of Youth for Christ International and later president, Engstrom himself visited more than sixty nations and preached at Youth for Christ rallies in most of the world's major cities.

Ted W. Engstrom chaired or was a member of numerous boards, including Focus on the Family, Azusa Pacific University, the Evangelical Council for Financial Accountability, and Taylor University (his alma mater). He and his wife of sixty years, Dorothy, were parents of three children and were longtime members of Pasadena's Lake Avenue Congregational Church.[2]

2

///

STRENGTHENING THE INNER CORE OF LEADERSHIP

MELINDA DELAHOYDE

I n this chapter, Melinda takes her extensive experiences and commitments in Christian leadership and challenges us to consider the inner core of our living and leading. Just as in physical conditioning, where a strong midsection is important to overall health and fitness, so also is the condition of our spiritual and emotional core essential to effective leadership. Focusing on building reserves of character, integrity, and strength, she prepares us for the demanding and varied challenges of leading in today's often unpredictable and stress-filled environments. She asserts that at the center of our core must be the person and presence of Jesus Christ, who enables us to do all things through him (Philippians 4:13), fortifying us for our sacred calling.

While we have provided some summary questions and thoughts for you and your team to consider at the end of this chapter, please be sure to pause as you go and reflect on Melinda's challenges to listen, ask, believe, and seek. Pray as you read, asking God to strengthen your inner core for every opportunity and challenge of the leadership calling you have embraced.

Several years ago I read an assessment of essential leadership characteristics. In this study of successful leaders, the question being addressed focused on the one character trait common to all effective leaders. There were many traits the leaders held in common—discipline, vision, communication skills . . . One in particular caught my attention. What all leaders possess, the one most important characteristic they all share is a deep core of inner strength. Somewhere inside of each of them is a reserve of courage, discipline, and fortitude that enables them to face the consistent, continual challenges and problems that are synonymous with leadership.

It is that core that matters most. Those inner reserves of character, integrity, and strength enable a leader to rise up in difficult times, to cast a vision for hope and transformation when catastrophe strikes, to call a team back to trust in the mercy and power of God as they navigate uncharted waters. For those leaders whose lives and callings are centered in Jesus Christ, the core is the place where God develops biblically based leadership—working from the inside out.

No doubt skills, training, and experience are essential for effective leadership. In the management of an organization, excellence in board governance, fiscal oversight, and sound policies and procedures go hand-in-hand with building successful leaders—particularly in this time of increased scrutiny of nonprofit organizations. Yet if we focus on the external without first developing that inner core of values, disciplines, and practices, the results can be tragic.

It is this arena of building an inner core of leadership traits into which God continually draws me. It is what I continue to learn every day and want to share with the next generation of kingdom leaders. It is where I find great joy, grace, peace, and encouragement in leadership. It is this kind of biblical leadership—centered in God and joined with a pursuit of excellence in all things—that will transform lives.

// BEGINNING WITH GOD—LEADING FROM HIS PRESENCE //

One of the most important questions we face as leaders in the faith-based world is "What does it mean to truly lead from a biblical perspective?" How does God communicate his presence and his plans to an organization? What is the difference in theory and in practice between a secular and biblical model of leadership? It is not difficult to put a Christian veneer over a corporate type of management model. We do that every time we begin with our plans, strategies, and tactics and then, when we are finished, present those plans to God for his blessings. We do not do this intentionally. I know of many times when I have honestly and earnestly sought God's blessing on what I naturally assumed was his vision and plan. It seemed so clear to me. Of course, I presumed, my plans were what he had in mind. However, God's "school of leadership" does not work that way.

In her book *Strengthening the Soul of Your Leadership,* Ruth Haley Barton recounts the example of Gary Haugen and the way in which God prepared the ministry, International Justice Mission (IJM), for new initiatives. From his times alone with God, he was impressed with the conviction that God had a greater work for the ministry, but they were not ready to take this on. His plan for preparing the organization for new ventures was unique. Each day would begin with thirty minutes of individual prayer for each employee. The time was known as 8:30 Stillness. They would be paid to come in thirty minutes early to pray.

When Barton interviewed Gary and asked what he and the staff had gained from the practice, he said: "Humility—because we discover that it is so difficult . . . to just be with God and that is very humbling! Wisdom—that does not necessarily come in the times of silence but comes in moments when you need it. . . . And peace. The kind of urgent, painful things we deal with on a daily basis can make us anxious and frustrated, but the practice of being quiet in God's presence brings us back to a place of trust in God."[1]

God has done an amazing work through IJM, but the pathway is unique. Gary Haugen responded to God's leading and the conviction he gave him on how to prepare for the work God had for them. This is a great example of how to lead from the presence of God and not from our own plans and ideas.

There is a deeper dimension of biblically based leadership that begins with seeking God's presence in our lives and our organization and then flows to the "doing" necessary to bring results. I do not understand how it all works, and I do not always practice this kind of leadership. I cannot write it down in a one-page executive summary. But I know it is true, biblical, best-practices leadership—and something I want to continually strive for.

God got my attention on this issue many years ago when I was asked to create a major donor program for our ministry. It was a great job. There was no program in existence, and it could only get better! I immediately created a plan complete with marketing materials, segmented donor lists, high-touch components, and goals and timetables. This was my background, and I knew what I was doing. Yet as I looked at the completed plan, I was flooded with a sense of inadequacy. I felt that I could not do this, and in desperation I went to prayer. Actually, I just sat there, unable to pray. Four words came to me, and I wrote them on an old church bulletin I found in my Bible. I refer to that church bulletin often. The four words were *listening, asking, believing,* and *seeking.*

The success of this program did not hinge on my gifts and abilities. God was drawing me to him and his presence in this job. These four words formed a verbal road map for me in beginning to understand how God communicates his presence and plans to an organization.

LISTENING

Have I taken the time to wait quietly, to just be with God, listening for his voice? This habit of waiting and listening in prayer lets me step back from my plans and ideas and wait for God. What a foreign concept this is to our Western minds and our definition of take-charge leadership. However, it is clearly the path God laid out for leaders throughout biblical history. Moses spent years in isolation just so God could prepare him to listen. Joseph, one of God's most gifted servants, endured years of humiliation and servitude so he could learn to say that God meant it for good. It is the path he has for us. Am I listening and waiting?

ASKING

Am I asking God what he wants me to do? Am I seeking what he has for our ministry? What direction does God impress on my heart and mind? Is there a new work that he has for us? Is he opening a pathway of service? God wants to answer these questions. It is his vision, his plan, his kingdom. So much of our responsibility as leaders is simply to stand there with him and be faithful. When I am listening to God, and genuinely desire his will, the focus is where it should be—on God and not on my abilities to accomplish the task God has given.

BELIEVING

Do I believe that God is able to perform what he is calling us to do? Do I believe that he is at work supplying the needs for the task? God provides the provision for what he envisions. But this is more than just the material resources that he provides. Amy Carmichael in *Edges of His Ways,* quotes from Doctor Way, "You have not to do it in your unaided strength: it is God Who is all the while supplying the impulse, giving you the power to resolve, the strength to perform, the executive of His good-pleasure."[2] In his classic devotional *My Utmost for His Highest,* Oswald Chambers speaks often of not limiting the ministry of Jesus by taking into account only our meager talents, gifts, and abilities: "When we get into difficult circumstances, we impoverish His ministry by saying—'Of course He cannot do anything,' and we struggle down to the deeps and try to get the [living] water for ourselves."[3] Do I have a heart and mind of faith in the direction God is giving the ministry? Am I going to trust him not only at the beginning of the task, but throughout the tough times when the challenges come?

SEEKING

Now is the time to seek the best resources available to achieve the results we desire. This is the time to gather the experts, collect the data, convene the strategic planning team, and build the case for support. This is when God takes those gifts and abilities and links them to his plans and purpose. This is the pursuit of excellence in what he gives us to do. It is the place where God bonds together our life in him and the work he has given us to do in the kingdom.

// FOLLOWING JESUS' LEADERSHIP TEMPLATE //

For the past several years, I have served on the board of an international leadership development ministry, MentorLink. Their mission is to build Christian leaders around the world whose lives and ministry reflect the values of Jesus Christ. The core of the organization is a set of five transformational values that form the basis of their training for leaders. Mentoring is the delivery system for imparting these values into the leaders' lives.

These are the MentorLink values[4] (and my description of each):

- Building God's Kingdom—Having a personal understanding of the kingdom of God and a perspective that seeks the glory of Christ and the promotion of his kingdom worldwide.
- The Living Gospel of Grace—Leadership based on the finished work of Christ: living and leading in humility, openness, and love; treating others with acceptance, forgiveness, and honesty.
- Leading as a Servant—Leading others through authentic relationships, integrity, and service and giving oneself to meet the needs of others and equipping them to succeed.
- Operating in Teamwork and Community—Leading as part of a team that cooperates together to carry out God's work; influencing through relationships, mutual accountability, and delegation.
- Accomplishing Intentional Multiplication—Multiplying leadership growth through the mentoring of gifted leaders who are willing and able to expand God's ministry far beyond anyone's individual capabilities.

Those are also the essential values of leadership in God's kingdom. They produce the kind of leader that transforms organizations, ministries, churches, and cultures. They are also the values that keep us from falling. A life that is centered on God's kingdom and his agenda is a life that does not end up splattered on the front pages of the national tabloids for all to see. It is a life of challenge, sacrifice, and discipline. But it is also a life of deep joy in Christ and in his calling, vision, and work.

It is a life that leaves a legacy of faith, grace, and service. It is the life God has for all of us as leaders. All around us we see examples of great and gifted men and women whose public witness has been decimated by their private lives. And as a result, followers of Jesus are often viewed unfavorably by many in our society. Francis Schaeffer, Billy Graham, and Chuck Colson are all examples of leaders who remained, or are remaining, great witnesses and servants of the kingdom.

Consider the magnificent opportunity that is before our next generation of emerging kingdom leaders. The "muscular Christianity" that transformed nations and cultures, the faith that brought Christ to China and India—that persuasive, winsome combination of strength, truth, faith, humility, compassion, and love—is still ours if we will let God have our lives and our leadership. He has not changed. The God who inspired the great reformers and missionaries is our God. Let him mold and lead you, implanting his values for leadership in you. Let his presence be your guide in all he gives you to do.

God's call to leadership is not a pathway to career development. It is a total surrender to serve him, to live the leadership values of his Son and to be used to serve in his kingdom.

If I could say only one thing to our emerging leaders it would be this: Forget being in the right place at the right time. Don't worry about making the right connections or networking your way to the top. Surrender your life, your career, your education, and your résumé to God.

I see gifted young leaders who are so brilliant, articulate, and sophisticated in every way. However, what seems so often lacking is passionate surrender to God and the resulting humility and call to serve—wherever and however God chooses. I would gladly take one young leader with this call to passionate surrender over twenty of the most articulate, well-educated, well-connected emerging leaders and work with that one to develop the needed skills and training. He already has the most important quality: following God first.

// LEADERSHIP FROM THE INSIDE OUT—THINGS I WISH PEOPLE HAD TOLD ME //

So much of our preparation for leadership focuses on an external set of skills, expertise, and experiences that we acquire through the years to prepare us for the work God gives us to do. These external skills are essential leadership qualifications that help create leaders who know how to pursue excellence in ministry. Then there are the intangible things you learn through experience that you wish others had told you. These are the things that often cannot be communicated in the classroom. They only come to you through the daily experiences in leadership. These "nuggets" help you deal with issues such as the personal demands, the need for courage, and the inherent loneliness of leadership.

LISTEN TO THAT INNER VOICE

I am not talking about some mystical, subjective experience you have with God. I am speaking about a very practical decision-making tool, a conviction that clarifies and crystallizes your direction on issues and decisions you have to make. This is the set of convictions that will enable you to make the difficult calls, make the decisions that demand courage and faith, and take the direction in ministry that will call for faith and perseverance.

This inner voice comes as a leader spends time in prayer and listening to God. It is often confirmed through Scripture, external circumstances, and wise counsel from those with more experience. It is that aha moment that comes when the pieces fit together and the path seems clear. Here is an example:

At Care Net, one of our key strategic initiatives is planting pregnancy resource centers where there are few or none of those but many abortion providers. The dynamics of implementation are difficult. My first thought (and not my best one!) was to gather information for a master plan—the demographics, abortion rates, number of abortion providers, etc. It made perfect sense to me to start here. We know how to start pregnancy centers. We should go where the abortions are being performed. I was doing what I so often do. I began with the plan and not with listening to God.

The first question to ask was, where was God leading us to plant a pregnancy center? Where was he working to open up hearts and minds of urban leaders and pastors? Where was he building trust with those leaders in the community? I cannot overestimate how important the issue of trust and partnerships is when it comes to bringing a pregnancy center to a community. Building that trust, and allowing God to speak to pastors and leaders about the truth of abortion, must take place before any center can exist. These cities are abortion strongholds, and only God can open up the way for a prolife ministry to women and children.

I began to pray and ask God where we were supposed to go, and our entire team started praying. I must admit, this seemed so simplistic, so unsophisticated at times. What if God did not answer?

Several cities came to mind, but one was impressed on all of us. Detroit is the one city where we had no contacts. After we felt we had heard from God, we began thinking about the need. There is no pregnancy center in downtown Detroit. The poverty and abortion rates are miserably high. Detroit was where we all believed God was calling us. We had no idea how that would happen, since we had no connections to churches or other ministries in the community.

And then the phone rang. A large church had just moved to new property in the heart of Detroit. The pastor was greatly burdened with the need for a pregnancy center, and he knew of Care Net.

"Will you come help us?" he asked.

When our urban director came to that church, the pastor stood up and told how God had burdened his heart. He had spoken to the congregation about Care Net, and now we were there.

We are now working with a committed steering committee with the support of a church in the heart of Detroit. We have no illusions about the difficulty of building a pregnancy center there. It is pioneering work—a spiritual battle with constant challenges. However, our internal conviction as an organization is clear to all of us, and that clarity and the evidence of God's leading will see us through these difficulties. It is that kind of clear voice, that inner core conviction, that God wants to build in you. Listen to and lead from that voice.

DO THOSE THINGS THAT ONLY YOU CAN DO

The pressing needs of a ministry organization are constantly bearing down on its leader. The pull is always toward the details, the crisis of the day that must be solved, the phone calls and e-mails begging to be answered, and the last-minute meeting that must be attended. In the midst of the daily press of the tyranny of the urgent, keep asking yourself: *Am I doing the things that only I can do?* I ask myself this question at least once a day.

If you have been hired to lead, then there are certain tasks that only you can fulfill. Are you stepping back from the details of the day to think about the bigger picture of the organization, the external landscape, the partnerships that can be developed, the relationships that only you can build, and the new strategic opportunity that is developing for the ministry? It is this type of high-level thinking that only the key leader can do. If you are not doing those things that only you can do, they are not getting done.

This is much more difficult than it sounds. For many of us, the calls and requests begin the moment we walk through the door. They are usually about very important issues. We feel like we are being sucked into a giant wind tunnel with no return! So ask the question again: *Am I doing what only I can do?* Sometimes the answer is yes. Are we short-staffed and short on resources? Maybe the thing that only you can do in that situation is to step back and build your resource development plan so that you can hire the team you need to move forward with the mission. You may not think of yourself as a fund-raiser, but if you are leading a nonprofit organization, you *are* a fund-raiser; and that may be the one thing that only you can do to build the ministry.

FEEL THE FEAR, BUT ACT WITH COURAGE

Some people are born fearless. They inspire, motivate, and encourage everyone they encounter with their boundless optimism and their amazing ability to take hold of life. I am not one of those people. Some mornings I wake up feeling like Gideon—afraid, inadequate for the tasks at hand. I am just amazed when I open my devotional and read all the wonderful promises. Could they really apply to me?

Fear is a natural part of leadership. As leaders we are asked to take risks, to bear responsibility for staff members, to think outside the box—far beyond our comfort zone of things we know we can do well. Fear is natural. That is why God spends so much time talking about it in the Bible.

The phrases "Be strong and courageous" and "Do not be terrified" highlight God's message to Joshua as he became commander of Israel (Joshua 1:1-9). These were God's words to a man who had shown monumental courage throughout his life. But Gideon is my favorite. The angel of the Lord addressed him as a "mighty warrior," even though Gideon expressed fear that the Lord was not with him and demeaned himself as "the least in my family" (Judges 6:11-15). Could someone's self image be more at odds with the way God viewed him?

That is the point. We may feel fearful, but the important issue is how we act. We act with courage in the midst of natural fear. We do what Moses, Joshua, Gideon, Esther, and every other leader in the Bible did.

Bruce Wilkinson shares a story of his own crisis of fear in his well-known book *The Prayer of Jabez.* He tells of being paralyzed by fear after God had dramatically expanded the borders of ministry. The fear took the form of feeling he absolutely could not be the man for this job. A pastor he spoke with about this problem assured him this was exactly what he should be feeling. That feeling, that he could not do what God had called him to, was precisely what led him to absolute dependence on God. As Wilkinson states it, "It's a frightening and utterly exhilarating truth. . . . As God's chosen . . . we are expected to attempt something large enough that failure is guaranteed . . . unless God steps in."[5]

No leader in the Bible was ever told that his personal gifts and abilities were sufficient for the task God had given him. No matter how extravagantly gifted the person, his faith, hope, and courage were in God. Naturally, God uses our gifts and strengths; but our dependence is on him, and our courage to act flows from this trust and dependence. Dependence on and trust in God combine as a best practice of biblical leadership.

// THE LEADER AND THE TEAM—THREE QUESTIONS I ALWAYS ASK //

I love building a team. I am naturally drawn to teamwork, partnerships, and collaborations. There is something wonderful about seeing a group of gifted people gather around a task that no one person could accomplish alone. Not only do I naturally gravitate to teams and partnerships, I used to think it was fairly easy to put a team in place. Experience has taught me some difficult lessons about myself as well as building a team. Now before I embark on a team project, I stop and ask myself three questions. And if I answer them honestly, I'll be saved hours of frustration and also move our team and task forward.

1. DO I HAVE PEOPLE'S TRUST?

When I took over as Care Net's president, the area that I tackled first was building our team. It had been a period of tough transitions, and our team needed encouragement. Frankly, this seemed like the easiest part of the job to me. I had a long history with the ministry, and I expected people to implicitly trust my leadership. It never occurred to me that I would have to build trust with our team. I just assumed that they would share my plans and goals for the organization, and in many ways they did. But I had to slow down, step back, and listen carefully. I had to take the time to understand staff concerns and questions. I had to do this not just as a way of getting to the goal I had set, but because what they were telling (and *not* telling) me was very important information for building our future. And these people were important parts of that future.

I was coming to the job with an eye to focusing on the task at hand, the strategic priorities, and the measurable outcomes for the organization. The staff was wondering what kind of leader I would be. Would I listen and respect their opinions, or was I always right? Was I a person who would do what I said I would do? Was I a person of integrity?

One year later trust had been built to the point that two senior staff members felt they could trust me and our COO enough to tell us that they thought our plan for building operational excellence within our national network of pregnancy centers was flawed. They did not think the tasks we had assigned to them were what they were supposed to be doing—and they were right! They told me that they had prayed hard before they told us what they really thought. I am so glad they trusted me enough to speak the truth. As a result of their honesty, we were able to take Care Net down a much better pathway and provide many more resources for building operational best practices for our centers.

2. DO OTHERS SEE ME THE WAY I SEE MYSELF?

I can almost guarantee that the answer to that question is no. I think of myself as a fun-loving, laid back, open-minded kind of leader with few rules and lots of flexibility. Even though our grown children have often assured me this is not the case, I persist in believing it. That is, until the evening of the staff party after our national conference last year. The staff, led by our fearless COO, held a "roast" in my honor. This was a forty-five-minute roast complete with PowerPoint, a master of ceremonies, props, and costumes. There were multiple testimonies to my concern for the dress code, manners, and professionalism in the workplace. And did I mention the dress code?

It was obvious that even though I thought of myself as laid back and relaxed, I really came across as driving our staff toward the highest levels of professionalism in the workplace in dress, manners, and work product. Again, they were right. I do believe in creating a professional workplace; but in a very funny way, they showed me that I really do not come across the way I think I do and I am not as open-minded and laid back as I might want to believe.

This question can be answered from another, more encouraging perspective. Rarely do we see the gifts God has given us as others see them. Sometimes we have no idea of the way God uses us to encourage and build up our staff. Sometimes we are unaware of the way God uses us in his kingdom. There can be such freedom in this realization.

I enjoy public speaking and often have opportunities to share with groups. I used to memorize my speeches almost word for word. I wanted to get the message just right. The problem was that I always went totally blank when I got to the podium. Sometimes I could not remember later what I had actually said, and I never could have repeated the same speech twice.

Yet God used the words to encourage others. Finally, I got the message. Instead of focusing on my perfect memorization and delivery of each word of a speech, why not let God give me the thoughts, outline, and examples? Obviously, God was working in spite of my obsessive methods and doing what he wanted to do through my words. I could relax and focus on letting him guide me through a speech. Of course, I gave thought and preparation to the topic, but I let go of my control and let God use this gift in a much greater way. I do not memorize my speeches anymore. I spend much more time actually listening for what God wants me to say to a particular group of people. The focus is on him and not me. It feels like a great burden has been lifted.

3. AM I A SERVANT?

We need to ask ourselves whether those who work with us would answer yes to this question when referring to our lives. When the Engstrom Institute held its first CEO Forum several years ago, the keynote address was given by Bill Pollard, former CEO of ServiceMaster. I will never forget the speech—or the title: "The Debt We Owe to Those Who Work with Us." That was strong language. I had never thought about a debt that I owed to our team. Let's be honest.

What I really think sometimes is that they should be glad to be part of such a great ministry, doing such a significant work in the kingdom. Why would I owe them a debt?

Yet here was a highly respected leader telling this group of CEOs to see ourselves as indebted to those who work with us. Think of what an upside-down concept of leadership we are talking about here. ServiceMaster makes its profit by providing services, some of which are the most menial and undervalued services in society, involving cleaning up other people's messes. We look on those who perform these services as, literally, servants. In reality, we are to serve them.

This is such a great example of Jesus' leadership style. I need to ask myself whether I am that kind of servant leader for our team.

- Is each person on our team, regardless of job description, respected and valued?
- Am I willing to go the extra mile when there is work to be done, just as I expect them to pick up the pace and get the job done?
- Do I listen to their thoughts and opinions and put in place feedback mechanisms to regularly gather their input?
- Do our policies and procedures as well as our organizational culture reflect genuine care for the well-being of those who work with us?
- Am I seeking to serve or be served by those whom I work with?

Do not underestimate the power both of our egos and the status that comes with the position, no matter how modest our ministry.

Think back to the transformational values of leadership in God's kingdom on page 36: I am to honor Christ and to equip those who serve with me to use the gifts God has given them. I am to serve and not be served.

True, godly leadership is the ability to find those inner reserves that rise up within us to meet the challenges and delights of serving God's kingdom. We cannot create those reserves—they come from listening, asking, believing, and seeking.

My prayer is that God will build a new generation of leaders with a passionate surrender to his call, his service, and most of all to his Son. May you, by his grace, be strengthened in the inner core of your leadership to see his kingdom come on earth as it is in Heaven.

MY LEADERSHIP BOOKSHELF

Spiritual Leadership: Principles of Excellence for Every Believer by J. Oswald Sanders (Moody Publishers, 2007).

Strengthening the Soul of Your Leadership: Seeking God in the Crucible of Ministry by Ruth Haley Barton (IVP Books, 2008).

Harvard Business Review (www.HBR.org)—particularly their collection of theme-based books that are compilations of articles from the Review on a specific topic (such as leading through change or women in leadership).

////// PERSONAL REFLECTIONS AND APPLICATIONS //////

1. Do you find yourself asking God to bless your plans, or are you usually blessed by *his* plans? Which is the more normal route for you to take? Why? Think over the times when you know you heard from God about his particular plan for your leadership. Are there any patterns, practices, and disciplines at the core of how God leads your leadership?

2. Being blessed by his plans depends on your ability to hear his still, small voice. How often are you able to "be still, and know" that he is God (Psalm 46:10)? Make use of the International Justice Mission's 8:30 Stillness discipline somewhere in your business day—before work begins, during a coffee break or a lunch hour—and exercise your spiritual core of listening for God's voice.

3. Make use of MentorLink's five core values (p. 36) as a tool to self-diagnose the condition of your leadership core. What elements are strongest and

which are weakest in your own life? What specific leadership exercises can you deploy to be strengthened in your inner being (see Ephesians 3:16)? Note that all five values are essential components for a thorough leadership workout.

4. What are the things that only you can do in and for your organization? If staff and circumstances permit, delegate everything else to focus on the distinctive functions God has equipped you to do at such a time as this.

5. One of the most difficult exercises for proactive, talented leaders is to recognize and then pay attention to the biblical truth that God's strength is made perfect in our weakness (2 Corinthians 12:9). Take time to enlist some trustworthy help to catalog both your strengths and weaknesses. How do these work in tandem to ensure that your whole body, soul, and spirit are preserved blameless (1 Thessalonians 5:23)? How might God use your weaknesses as a means to create a leadership lifestyle known for humility, trust, and faith?

///////// **TEAM REFLECTIONS AND APPLICATIONS** /////////

1. As a leadership team, can your group be trusted and depended on? Are you known as serving leaders?

2. What tools do you use to determine how your leadership team is perceived by those who do the work of your ministry? by those who sacrificially support your ministry?

3. Discuss the implementation of the International Justice Mission's practice of 8:30 Stillness. Is it something you should try as an entire organization for a thirty-day period? At the very least, make it a thirty-day practice for your leadership team and then openly discuss the results.

4. If it is true that "God provides the provision for what he envisions," what core programs and commitments of your organization seem to be under-resourced? Is it possible that God did not order these and, as a result, has no responsibility to "pay for them"? If so, have a courageous discussion with your team about how you will determine God's will for these efforts and the steps you will boldly take to address what you agree to as his purposes.

5. Can your organization as a whole be described as a grace-filled place of service and ministry? What steps can be taken to create a core of grace so that the people who serve, and those they serve, are experiencing an inner core of leadership that reflects the amazing grace of God's love and direction?

MELINDA DELAHOYDE
PRESIDENT, CARE NET
///

A lifelong leader in the pregnancy center movement, Melinda Delahoyde was appointed President of Care Net (www.care-net.org) in 2008. She has worked with Care Net from its inception, serving in various roles both on staff and on Care Net's board of directors, including chairman of the board.

Care Net and its network of almost twelve hundred pregnancy centers offer hope to women facing unplanned pregnancies by providing practical help and emotional support.

Care Net also plays a key role in reaching women in crisis through its 24/7 Option Line call center and Web site, and in planting pregnancy centers in urban communities. The ultimate aim of Care Net and its network of pregnancy centers is to share the love and truth of Jesus Christ in both word and deed.

Before coming to Care Net, Delahoyde led the educational outreach for Americans United for Life. She originally joined Care Net to serve as the director of special projects before becoming a member of the board of directors.

An accomplished writer, she is the author of *Fighting for Life* (Crossway Books, 1984); coeditor of *Infanticide and the Handicapped Newborn* (Brigham Young University Press, 1982); and contributing author to three additional books, including one with Christian philosopher Francis A. Schaeffer. She has authored numerous articles on life and bioethics published in a variety of periodicals, including *The Religion & Society Report, Moody Monthly,* and *Christian Life.* A frequent spokesperson in the media on pregnancy centers and the emerging culture of life, she was a featured panelist on the Annenberg Media Channel in a series on Ethics in America.

She graduated from the University of California–Irvine with a BA in philosophy and received an MA in philosophy of religion from Trinity Divinity School (IL).

Melinda Delahoyde and her husband are from Raleigh, North Carolina, and have four children.

3

///

LIVE, LOVE, AND LEAD

STEVE DOUGLASS

One of the hallmarks of Campus Crusade for Christ is its commitment to the fundamentals and foundations of the Christian faith. Their goal, inherited from their founder, Bill Bright, is to introduce people to the lordship of Christ by focusing on the simple but profound and eternal truths of the gospel. From the use of the Four Spiritual Laws to the compelling and moving imagery of The JESUS Film, Campus Crusade is known for its effectiveness at getting to the heart of true Christian discipleship. Crusade has trained millions of serious, intentional, and proactive Christians to live like Jesus.

Steve follows in this great tradition as he presents the foundational and profound truths of Christ-honoring leadership. From his vast global experiences as a team member with Bill Bright, and now as the organization's chief executive, Steve challenges us to live, love, and lead. He cautions that no single formula is adequate and no simple design able to fully circumscribe the vast dimensions of effective Christian leadership. With that caution, Steve chooses to keep it simple, presenting a focused summary of what helps him to "live a life worthy of the calling" in Christ Jesus (Ephesians 4:1). To live for Jesus and to love like Jesus produces a leading like Jesus that transforms lives here and for eternity.

Keep it simple! How many times have you heard that? Most people agree that it sounds good. But how can a leader do that? After all, life and leadership are complex. In studying for my masters in business administration, my classmates and I read, analyzed, and discussed about one thousand case studies. Each situation was unique. Each solution had elements customized to the situation. In each case there was a leader whom we were "advising." It would have been so nice to say, "Just always do this."

I have been involved in full-time ministry for forty years. I imagine I have been confronted with tens of thousands of decisions to make and problems to solve. Each had some distinctive uniqueness. How can a person cope with all that?

Are there some simple patterns of leadership attitudes, behaviors, and communications that can guide in most situations? Over time I have discovered the answer is yes. In fact, through the years I have found there are a relatively small number of processes that can apply to the vast majority of the situations I have faced—whether it be solving problems, making decisions, planning for or leading change.

If this were a book and not a chapter, I would elaborate on several of them. However, what seems best for this setting is to suggest a foundational process—a basic guide for you as a leader. If I could sit down with you over a cup of coffee, I would start here. If I were encouraging you to be sure to engage in the simplest and most profound things as a Christian leader, it would be these concepts. In my opinion, if you aspire to exert a positive, biblical influence on those around you, these things must be central to who you are, how you relate, and what you do.

// SOURCES FOR CHRISTIAN LEADERSHIP CONCEPTS //

Where do these concepts come from? First, they come from the Scriptures. From examining Jesus' life and listening to his words, we can see important patterns emerge. And from reading the apostle Paul's New Testament letters we see that some concepts represent essence and others provide instructions for effective practices.

Second, these concepts come from watching leaders come and go, succeed and fail, have great impact and not. It was my privilege to serve God next to Bill Bright, the founder of Campus Crusade for Christ, for over thirty years. He exemplified Christian leadership concepts extraordinarily well.

By now you might think I am peddling some magic elixir. I am not. There are certainly many concepts, lessons learned, and studies done that will be very helpful to you. If you aspire to be an increasingly effective leader, you must continue to learn and add to your repertoire of leadership knowledge and skills. What I share with you here is basic to being the leader God intends for you to become. If you do not keep growing in your application of these foundational truths, you will be less effective than you could have been.

So what are they? There are just three concepts—three words—actually, just three syllables: live, love, lead.

// LIVE //

"Live a life worthy of the calling you have received" (Ephesians 4:1). Love God and what he says. Abide in Jesus and follow him. Appropriate the power of the Holy Spirit to do these things. Jesus said the greatest commandment is to love God "with all your heart and with all your soul and with all your mind" (Matthew 22:37, 38). He also said we should abide in him and that apart from him we can do nothing (John 15:5). All of these, and much more, represent the essence of the message that all Christians are to live a life that is distinctively holy and pleasing to God. How many sermons have you heard, or even preached, on that?

"OK," you may be saying, "I know I need to live the Christian life. Tell me something new." Well, I am not trying to tell you something new; I am trying to *emphasize* something that is absolutely basic. The life we live, and that people around us see, is the basic foundation for our ability to influence. There is no clever leadership skill that can overcome the practice of sin on the part of a leader.

Sometimes this is obvious. When some prominent Christian leader is found to be unfaithful to his wife or guilty of financial impropriety, he loses most, if not all, of his ability to influence people for God. Hardly a month goes by when I do not hear about a new example—which illustrates why I'm emphasizing this point.

Some years ago I knew a particular Christian leader well. I admired the progress he was seeing in his areas of responsibility. He was a dynamic motivator and an articulate spokesperson. He was creative and energetic. He seemed to be respected by all who knew him. But then it came to light that he had a mistress. He had been unfaithful to his wife for some time. In a short period of time, his opportunity to lead was destroyed. He lost his ministry, and his marriage was in serious trouble. To the best of my knowledge, he has never since been a leader in a Christian organization.

Let me quickly say, there but by the grace of God could any of us go. There is no room for pride or pointing of fingers here. But the issue is that Christians want to follow men and women of God. They do not want to follow those who consistently refuse to walk with and obey God.

Through the years I saw people disagree with some of the decisions Bill Bright made. However, what caused those people to follow him was often not his rationale for a decision or direction; they followed him because they could say, "I may disagree with his decision, but I know he walks with God. And if he is wrong, I know God can change his mind." There is no substitute for your credibility as a leader. And there is no greater element of credibility in a Christian context than a quality walk with God.

Now you might be asking, "But doesn't a closer walk with God naturally occur as a person takes on additional leadership responsibilities for God?" From my experience, the answer is no. For one thing Satan, the enemy of your soul and ministry, has a greater incentive to cause leaders to fall away from their close walk with God—and he seems to work aggressively toward that end.

Additionally, the nature of leadership responsibilities can work against a closer walk with the Lord. Leaders tend to be busy, focused, and confident. Those factors can hurt their walk with God. Why? Because . . .

IT IS EASY FOR A BUSY LEADER NOT TO FIND TIME TO SPEND WITH GOD

A crucial ingredient to an effective walk of faith is time. The same principle applies to any relationship—family, friends, and coworkers. A strong, productive relationship takes time. The busier I became in my ministry responsibilities, the more tempted I was to cut my devotional time short. After all, I needed to get to work. I was serving the Lord!

I had to take some specific steps to fight that tendency. One was to start journaling. I am an achievement-oriented person. So having physical evidence of my times with God helped motivate me to keep them. Also I listen to the New Testament on an MP3 player as I walk in the morning. On the way out I listen to Scripture. On the way back I pray for the people in my life. This gives me a significant addition to my morning devotional time.

IT IS EASY FOR A FOCUSED LEADER TO BASICALLY IGNORE GOD DURING THE DAY

The busier I get, the more focus is necessary for me to complete my priorities. With that focus comes the exclusion of other things—which may be fine unless one of those "other things" is God. David is a real model for me in this. No doubt he often was distracted by many priorities. Yet David said in Psalm 16:8, "I have set the LORD always before me. Because he is at my right hand, I will not be shaken." David learned to think about God all the time. And the result was peace in spite of circumstances.

The question I would ask you is, "Is the Lord right there beside you? Are you conscious of his presence throughout the day?" If so, you will involve him often, taking problems to him.

I was in a small group discussion. Sitting next to me was Sally (not her real name), a recent college graduate who had just broken up with her longtime boyfriend. Although the discussion question was not about relationships, she just blurted out, "I feel so lonely," and shared some specifics. I found myself saying, "Let's skip the rest of our discussion and pray for Sally. After all, the

Lord is here and can help Sally with this." Since I consciously sensed his presence, it was easy to involve him.

A CONFIDENT LEADER CAN THINK TOO HIGHLY OF HIS OR HER ABILITIES

A number of years ago, when I was giving a familiar talk at a training session for some of our new staff, I became aware that I was just "grinding it out." I had not prayed much in preparation. In fact, I thought I knew the talk so well that I really did not prepare at all. It was a disaster. Afterward I asked a new staff member what she thought of my talk. She confirmed, "I thought you sort of ground it out."

I rushed back to my room, fell to my knees, and prayed, "Lord, I don't want to rely on any knowledge or expertise I may have in giving a talk. I want your message and to deliver it in your power."

I learned a valuable lesson. Confidence is only valuable when it has as its foundation a dependence on God. Only in his power can we be rightly confident.

// LOVE //

The second foundational concept to successful Christian leadership is to love others. Jesus himself prioritized this right behind the greatest commandment to love God: "And the second is like it: 'Love your neighbor as yourself.' All the Law and the Prophets hang on these two commandments" (Matthew 22:39, 40).

That last sentence is rather stunning. There are a lot of commandments from God given in the Law and the Prophets. Do these two great commandments fully summarize the essence of them? Take the Ten Commandments (Exodus 20:1-17) as a short list. The first four relate to loving and honoring God. The final six give some specifics on what it means to love your neighbor as yourself.

Paul also seems emphatic about the significance of the second greatest commandment: "The entire law is summed up in a single command: 'Love your neighbor as yourself'" (Galatians 5:14).

There is no question that loving others is crucial to living the Christian life successfully, but why is it so crucial to leadership? At the core of the answer to that question is the word *heart.* Time after time I have heard people advise leaders about communicating: "Show your heart!" Why is that such good advice? Because followers are far more likely to trust a leader who they know loves them, particularly when they are receiving difficult news or new direction.

Recently I was preparing to videotape a message to Campus Crusade for Christ leaders concerning a major reorganization. It affected a significant percentage of our leadership team. As with anything that moves people to new positions, it could sound like many had not done a good job or were not valued anymore. It was so important that I not say the wrong thing, I decided to teleprompt the message. Those around me advised against it. They felt it might come across wooden and not show my heart. So I thought I would at least work from extensive notes so I could stay away from the potential problems that could be created by a wrong statement.

I started the taping, got into it a few minutes, and felt awful about how it was coming across. I started again, and the same thing happened. The small group of us in the taping room stopped and prayed. What God seemed to say was to throw away the notes, look straight at the camera, share about my love and concern for my listeners, and show them how our reorganization will help them and their people be even more needed and fruitful in the years to come. It was amazing! God seemed to give the right words; but more importantly, I sensed that my heart of love for them came through.

People do sense our hearts and, in particular, whether we love them. I think that was a significant reason for why Jesus so quickly gained the attention of the Jewish people. Yes, he did miracles such as healing the sick and casting out demons. However, if you take a step back from the specifics, in addition to illustrating his supernatural power, those miracles demonstrated his heart of love.

Part of why Jesus' compassion stood out was because of the *lack* of compassion of the Pharisees. In Matthew 23:1-4 we see an example of what Jesus had to say about their absence of love for their people. In verse 4 we read: "They tie up heavy loads and put them on men's shoulders, but they themselves are not willing to lift a finger to move them."

Love really communicates to those around us. It usually exerts much more influence than we may realize.

Paul and Sharon Townsend were serving with Wycliffe Bible Translators a number of years ago in Guatemala, when guerrilla warfare broke out. They stayed and used their truck to help families—sometimes to get the bodies of murdered loved ones in order to bury them. As a result, the people truly loved them. One young man, whose family the Townsends had helped, joined the guerrilla forces. As the Townsends' names came up to be assassinated by the guerrillas, he moved their names to the bottom of the list several times. He had sensed and been moved by their genuine love.

Love puts us in a position to influence people significantly. Let me share an example that I heard from Dr. Ed Hill, a pastor in south central Los Angeles for many years. He was one of my favorite preachers. He often spoke of his mama, who loved him dearly and raised him to aspire to fulfill the potential God had given him. When Ed graduated from high school, it would have been normal to go to work instead of to college. That was what all his friends did. But his mama insisted that he go to college. As he was boarding the bus in his hometown to travel to college, Mama put five dollars in his hand and said, "Oh, Ed, I'll be praying for you."

By the time the bus got to the college, Ed only had two dollars left. (I guess he stopped for lunch somewhere.) And when he entered the hall where he had to register, he saw the sign that said, "$80 Registration Fee—Due Today—Cash." A voice began speaking into his ear: "Ed, you don't have enough money. Don't get in line." But in his other ear he heard, "Oh, Ed, I'll be praying for you." So he got in line and eventually made it to the front.

As the young woman ahead of him was folding her receipt and leaving, the first voice said, "Ed, you fool, get out of line while there is still time!" But again his mama's voice prevailed: "Oh, Ed, I'll be praying for you."

Just then a gentleman came up to Ed and asked, "Are you Ed Hill?"

"Yes," he replied.

"Well, that's good, because we have been waiting for you. We have for you a full scholarship—all tuition, all room, all board, and spending money besides!"

And in Ed's ear he heard, "Oh, Ed, I'll be praying for you."

Mama loved Ed. She prayed for him. Ed knew that well. So when the time came for her to exert some specific influence on him, he listened. And as a result, he became one of the great preachers of the second half of the twentieth century.

I trust you see what a significant foundational element love is to being a good leader. Learning to love deeply is a lifelong process, whether it is on the job, in marriage, with children, or with friends. In a few paragraphs I cannot be very thorough as to how to love those you lead. However, I can offer one concept that seems helpful. It stems from the interaction Jesus had with Peter in John 21:15-17.

Jesus was reinstating Peter, after his denial, for a future leadership role in the early church. It occurs to me that Jesus could have dwelt on Peter's failures and assured him of forgiveness. He might even have used Peter's problems as an example to the other disciples, showing how frail and prone to fall we all are. Instead, Jesus talked about the need to feed and otherwise care for his sheep—those who would follow him in the years to come. Jesus knew Peter was called to lead. And what he was telling Peter was that the people who would become a part of the church would have needs. It was important, therefore, for Peter to sense those needs and make sure they were met.

That is good advice for us as leaders today. If we are called to lead people and want them to sense our heart of love for them, they also must sense that we know their needs. And they must see us seeking to meet those needs as best as we reasonably can.

We may meet the need for affirmation by offering encouraging words. But we may choose to meet more complex and persistent needs through the help of others. We see an example of that in Acts 6:1-7. Some people's needs were not being met. The twelve apostles arranged for others to meet the need. The proposal pleased the people, and the gospel spread.

By whatever method, people need to sense that we love them. That is a cornerstone element of successful Christian leadership.

// LEAD //

Own the task. Take the initiative. Get involved. Be intentional. These represent much of what is required for implementing effective leadership. That is how Nehemiah led. The book of Nehemiah is a great text for leadership initiative. Nehemiah heard about a serious problem. He sat down and wept. He mourned, fasted, and prayed. And when the perfect opportunity arose to speak up and take action, he did so.

After doing some research, he developed a strategic plan. He motivated and involved the key stakeholders. He supervised appropriately. He overcame opposition. And by God's grace, he saw the task through to completion. At the end he made sure the people gave God the credit, confessed their sins, and worshipped God.

Nehemiah had to be just one of many Jewish people who came to know about the humiliation and the disrepair of the city of Jerusalem. No doubt some others even had a position of leadership in the Jewish community. Nehemiah did not. Yet from his deeply burdened heart, he took the initiative—and the rest is history.

You see, leadership is not primarily a position—it is a mind-set that's proactive. So often people think they have to be appointed to an official leadership position to lead. They do not. In fact, if they are not already leading in some fashion before being appointed, I question their qualifications for the job.

Today, as in Nehemiah's day, just-in-time leadership occurs when someone volunteers to meet a need. In November 1980, there was a terrible forest fire in the mountains just above San Bernardino, California. At that time the main part of the headquarters of Campus Crusade for Christ was in the foothills of those mountains, at a place called Arrowhead Springs. The fire raged through our property, fanned by very strong winds. We lost a few of our smaller buildings. But we also lost the bridge that crossed the creek at the entrance to the headquarters property. As a result, we had no easy way to bring vehicles onto the property to restore and reopen the headquarters.

About 10:00 AM the day after the fire, I received a call from Gus Guth, a retired colonel in the U.S. Army Corps of Engineers. At the time, he was in charge of the administrative operations of the International School of Theology, also located on the Arrowhead Springs property.

"I understand you need a new bridge," he said. "You know I used to build bridges for the Army. If you will authorize $10,000 of expenses, I think I can arrange to build a temporary bridge today."

"You've got the money. Go for it!" I said.

At 3:00 PM that day I received a call back from him. I thought there might be some problem. Instead, I heard him say, "The bridge is done!" And by the way, that "temporary" bridge lasted for one year and bore the load of cement trucks and other heavy equipment as we fully restored the headquarters facility. Also it allowed our staff to get back on the job right away.

Gus could have just sat back and allowed a local contractor to take a week or more to build a temporary bridge. Instead he saw the need, knew he could help, and took the initiative. What a wonderful example of what it means to lead!

As I think through the history of the Campus Crusade ministry, I can point to many examples when people owned the task, took the initiative, and got the job done. A lay couple founded our Executive Ministry. They had an idea of having evangelistic dinner parties for leaders to be reached. They tested and refined the idea until it developed into one of the most effective leadership evangelism approaches I have seen.

During the 1960s and 1970s our basic evangelism training spread to hundreds of thousands of people in the U.S. At the center of that growth were a number of key lay people who took the initiative. They cut back on the time they were spending running their companies and put that time, energy, and creativity into training people to share their faith.

About that same time our U.S. Ministries director stepped aside from that position to lead the development of what was eventually called The JESUS Film Project. Some people thought it was not a good idea for him to leave his responsible leadership position as U.S. director. But he saw the opportunity to own the worthy task of giving everyone in the world the opportunity to see a quality presentation of the gospel. There have been over six billion exposures to the gospel as a result. Local churches and denominations have used the film to plant more than one million new churches.

When the tragedy of September 11, 2001, occurred in New York City, Campus Crusade's U.S. Ministries director immediately took steps to respond. Prayer stations were established and a special booklet created to give comfort and share the gospel. That booklet, *Fallen but Not Forgotten,* was developed and printed within ten days after the collapse of the twin towers. Altogether over ten million copies of the booklet were distributed in New York City and beyond. All of that was possible because people were proactive.

My day-to-day responsibilities give me numerous opportunities to take the initiative, make plans, solve problems, and make decisions. Sometimes the din of the shouting needs becomes so loud and incessant that it is tempting to step back, throw up my hands with a sense of futility, and just do the routine details of my job. If I did that, I would not be leading. I would cease to be intentional; cease to own the task and its challenges; and cease to take the necessary initiatives to assign, equip, and encourage people to meet those needs.

You might be thinking, *Being proactive like that will require strength, courage, and persistence.* You are absolutely correct! That is why, I believe, God's exhortation to Joshua (as he took over for Moses) was, "Be strong and courageous. Do not be terrified; do not be discouraged, for the LORD your God will be with you wherever you go" (Joshua 1:9).

On the other hand, sometimes being intentional is as simple as calling people to do what the Word of God clearly tells us to do. A number of years ago, the church I was attending had a church split. Then the pastor left some months later—as did the assistant pastors. The lay leadership group of the church asked me to advise them on what to do next. As I thought and prayed about it, I sensed that there was a lot of bitterness in our church toward those who had left in the split. My impression was that God was not blessing us because of that bitterness. For example, we had not been able to find an interim pastor.

So I met with the leadership group and presented a paper containing nothing but verses from Scripture that portray the importance of forgiving others and the consequences of not doing that. After reading the verses aloud, I simply asked if they thought God's Word was clear on the importance of forgiving others. They agreed it was. I then said, "OK, then the application of that biblical truth today in our church is to extend forgiveness to those who split from us and formed another church."

"Oh, but you don't understand what they did and have been saying about us!" they exclaimed.

I responded, "My problem is, I don't see that factor in Scripture as an acceptable reason not to forgive others."

Finally, they agreed and asked how I would recommend they go about that with so many people involved. I suggested that they start by sending a letter from them, as leaders of our church, to our former members who were attending the other church. I had already written a suggested letter for them to consider. They approved it and sent it out. Now here is the fascinating evidence of God's blessing. The very week that letter arrived in the homes of our former church members, God brought an outstanding interim pastor who led our church until a permanent, new pastor arrived.

So what leadership was exerted in that situation? Simply lifting up the Word of God and saying, "Let's do what God says instead of what we feel like doing." Whatever initiative we take must always be consistent with the Word of God. Leadership is about ownership, initiative, involvement, and being proactive. Your ability and commitment to do those things well are essential foundations to your effectiveness as a leader.

In summary, this chapter has been about keeping it simple. There are many excellent things you can learn about how to be effective in leadership. By all means learn and apply them to your life and ministry. But in doing so do not ignore the basics—the foundational elements of your success as a leader.

My strong advice to you is that throughout your life and in leadership opportunities:

- Live—Live a life worthy of the calling you have received.
- Love—Love your neighbor as yourself.
- Lead—Own the task and take the initiative.

MY LEADERSHIP BOOKSHELF

Lead Like Jesus: Lessons from the Greatest Leadership Role Model of All Time by Ken Blanchard and Phil Hodges (Thomas Nelson, 2006) focuses on the one perfect leadership role model you can trust, and his name is Jesus. It helps leaders examine their motivations, perspectives, goals, and habits.

Bringing Out the Best in People: How to Enjoy Helping Others Excel by Alan Loy McGuinnis (Augsburg Publishing House, 1985) is filled with practical ideas on how to help the people around us know that we care and want to see them achieve their God-given potential.

A Sense of Urgency by John P. Kotter (Harvard Business Press, 2008) is about some of the most critical ingredients in leading change—creating a sense of urgency to overcome complacency.

His Intimate Presence: Experiencing the Transforming Power of the Holy Spirit by Bill Bright (New Life Publications, 2003). At the center of leaders' lives and ministries is their relationship with God. This book focuses on having an intimate, dependent, and powerful walk with him.

////// PERSONAL REFLECTIONS AND APPLICATIONS //////

1. Consider each of the three concepts: Live, Love, Lead. With regard to each, ask yourself the following three questions: What am I doing well? Where do I need to improve? How can I take a first step toward that improvement?

2. Is there an Achilles' heel (a spiritual or personal vulnerability or a secret stronghold) in your leadership armor that you have failed to address fully? Review the three headings in the "Live" section (p. 55) to ensure that you remain close enough to hear God speak to you about what could compromise your high calling.

To broaden your application beyond just the content of this chapter:

3. Can you describe yourself as a learning leader? Or are you on a plateau in your understanding of and approaches to leading—because of past practices and successes and current demands?

4. What are the primary sources for, authorities in, and influences of your thinking about effective leadership? It is not uncommon for many in Christian leadership to be fascinated with, and thus quick to appropriate, the newest secular leadership ideas or techniques. While much can be gleaned by such reading, we must test ideas and techniques against the eternal principles of God's kingdom as revealed in his Word. Not to do so is to unwittingly become infected by secular gods—particularly, core assumptions about things like the value of people, the place of ego, and the evidences of success.

5. Who is the leader you now most admire? Summarize in one paragraph why you have selected this individual, and assess what makes you so responsive to this individual's leadership model.

6. Choose three or four action words that you believe summarize your approach to leadership. Ask those who know your leadership best to also provide three or four words. How do they match up? What do they say about how you and how others perceive your leadership?

///////// **TEAM REFLECTIONS AND APPLICATIONS** /////////

1. Again, consider each of the three concepts: Live, Love, Lead. With regard to each, ask your team/organization the following three questions: What are we doing well? Where do we need to improve? How can we take a first step toward that improvement?

2. How do you encourage and recognize living, loving, and leading like Jesus in your organization? How are those who strive toward this ideal promoted, encouraged, and appropriately recognized? How are they challenged and resourced to mentor others?

3. How knowledgeable, compassionate, and caring is your organization about the needs of your employees? Too often we are so busy ministering to those whom our organization serves that we fail to effectively minister to the ministry. What first step could you, as the leadership team, take this next week to better understand and serve the needs of those who deliver your ministry to others?

4. Some powerful case studies illustrated how the principles and practices work out in personal life, in the ministries of Campus Crusade, and in the lives of others. Develop your own organization's collection of case studies, the stories about how practicing the fundamental principles of live, love, and lead are unfolding to advance God's work in your midst.

To broaden your application beyond just the content of this chapter:

5. Ask for and discuss three words your team would use to describe the leadership culture of your organization. What three words would your employees use to describe the leadership attitudes, practices, and priorities of your executive team? Survey them and see!

6. Does your organization have a well-defined and publicized set of core values that succinctly summarizes what you value and aspire to model? What are your core values, and what do they imply and promise about the approaches, attitudes, and commitments of your leadership team?

7. An in-depth study of Nehemiah can be a rich resource for understanding biblical principles of leadership. Choose one of the recent books written about Nehemiah's leadership mode (such as Cyril Barber's *Nehemiah and the Dynamics of Effective Leadership*). Study it together as a team over the next ninety days. Encourage each team member to present a chapter and share what aspects and insights most challenged his or her leadership thinking and why.

STEVE DOUGLASS
PRESIDENT, CAMPUS CRUSADE FOR CHRIST
///

Steve Douglass leads Campus Crusade for Christ (www.ccci.org) with a passion for ministry built over nearly four decades of service.

Campus Crusade for Christ is a worldwide, interdenominational Christian evangelism and discipleship organization, founded by Bill and Vonette Bright in 1951. Since its founding, Campus Crusade for Christ has become one of the largest Christian organizations in the world.

Douglass came to Campus Crusade with a résumé that included a bachelor of science degree from M.I.T. and a master's degree in business administration from Harvard. During the next thirty-two years, he held a variety of positions with Campus Crusade for Christ, including executive vice president and director of U.S. Ministries. In June 2000, founder Bill Bright personally recommended to CCC's board that Douglass be his successor.

Steve Douglass is the author or coauthor of several books, including *Managing Yourself, How to Achieve Your Potential and Enjoy Life,* and *Enjoying Your Walk with God.*

Along with his wife, Judy, he resides in Orlando, Florida. They have three married children and four grandchildren.

LEADING AND SERVING IN HIS STRENGTH

ISRAEL L. GAITHER

In this chapter, we get to see inside the heart of one of the world's great Christian leaders—a "father" to millions who give themselves daily to serve the least, the left, and the lost through the exemplary worldwide work of The Salvation Army. Israel understands, in the depths of his own leadership journey, what it means to live with "heart to God and hand to man" and be daily committed to "doing the most good" for those most in need. He knows that those Salvation Army slogans are more than slick advertising hooks.

As you read, position yourself one-on-one and listen to the heart cry of a senior, seasoned soldier who has served King Jesus with dedication, purpose, passion, and sacrifice. His poignant personal reflections and professional appropriations of what it means to be a *doulos* (Greek for "bond slave")[1] of Christ will move you to new levels of self-assessment. His call for leadership demonstrates the commitment to character and integrity above all else so that the gospel is not preached or demonstrated in vain. This will cause you to examine carefully your own motivations. And his love for all that his homeland once was and could become again—if our leaders "seek first [God's] kingdom and his righteousness" (Matthew 6:33)—will reignite an understanding of what happens when those who lead commit to be one nation, under God, with liberty and justice for all. This may be an Elijah-to-Elisha passing of the mantle of leadership for you as you listen with your heart to God and with hands extended to serve his purposes in your generation.

// A LEGACY OF AND FOR THE LORD //

I am blessed to have been raised by godly parents. I grew up in the home of a pastor father and a great mother—along with four beautiful (female) siblings. We knew from an early age what it meant to live with an understanding that we were brought into the world for something that is bigger and better than any plan we could ever devise for ourselves. As I watched the impact of my father's leadership on his growing ministry, I gradually became convinced that leaders are not born but emerge through the influence of circumstances that are injected into the disciple's journey. While a person might be born with fine natural leadership qualities, something else must happen to give cause to the emergence of the leader within. Cooperating with God, one can be transformed from an ordinary believer into a leader capable of doing the extraordinary. The consecrated leader who makes himself available for the purposes of God will be surprised at where, when, and how God uses him.

I also have learned that leaders are shaped through the influence of others. Seven men had a strong role in influencing who I am and the way I lead. Prominent among them was my father, who left a deep impression on me, not only as a father but also as a pastor-leader. My wife at times declares that I remind her of him—a tribute that I do not take lightly. My father was an influence on what I would become. I will never forget telling him that I felt God was calling me to be an officer (minister) in The Salvation Army. I was shocked to hear him respond: "I already know." It was not until years later that Dad told me that he had closely watched my growing interest in the various activities conducted in the local Salvation Army building. And apparently, God had told him what I would become—before he called me to do it!

Until that point in time, I had a different plan in mind for my life. However, God used my father's influence to prepare me for *his* call on my life. I never could have imagined receiving a "call to serve" through The Salvation Army. Had it not been for my father's support and influence, I literally would have missed my calling.

The six other men of influence were introduced to me in my journey as I, with my wife Eva, served in various leadership roles for more than forty-seven years of officership. Those six, each unique in their gifts and abilities, are all successful leaders. My guess is that they did not realize how deeply they were contributing to my transformation. As they engaged with me in my professional journey, I felt privileged to learn from them—although they did not serve their responsibilities to impress me. They simply lived and led with the intention to be faithful to that which God had entrusted to them.

// ALL IN GOD'S GOOD TIME //

Reflecting back on my calling, I find it intriguing what God asks the committed to do. Sometimes it might seem odd, but when you are faithful to his summons, in time you will be able to look back over your spiritual shoulder and it will all make sense. You will be amazed at how he has brought you to a moment in time that has proven to be perfect. When God has placed his hand on people, he always has them in the right place, at the right time, for the right purpose.

At the outset, I was not sure why God would have me, an African-American exposed primarily to the black experience, serve in leadership roles in what was then an overwhelmingly white-populated organization. Though content with the fact that I had been called specifically to be an officer, nevertheless I felt I was a curious choice for The Salvation Army. The organization was challenged as well. Where could a black officer serve in a white Salvation Army in the '60s in America?

Then matters became more complicated. God brought a special woman into my life, and a second calling was heard—the call to share ministry together as officers. But where could the first ever, married, interracial Salvation Army officer couple in America serve? There were more than a few who believed that there would come a point in time when the locations in which we could be accepted to serve would be exhausted. And after all, we were young with many years to go before retiring. The natural conclusion of some was that we would eventually be left to "do something else" with our lives.

Ah, but never underestimate what God is doing. Eva and I are proof that when he calls, you can be certain that he has already taken care of every eventual issue that others might see as problems. When God asks you to do something, just say yes; be faithful and watch him work. Everything will be all right!

These many years later, with retirement on the horizon, Eva and I have been given the privilege of serving the second highest roles within the organization internationally, as well as being appointed to key national responsibilities. None of it resulted from personal ambition. Our only desire has been, and still is, to be available for the working out of the will of God for our lives.

Read this carefully: If you are called to serve God, *serve* him . . . faithfully! And expect amazing things to enter your life!

By the way, I have been blessed to learn—and quite by surprise—that just as I have watched seven other men, there are those who have been watching me as I lead. Shame on me for not realizing it all along! I should have known. When discovering that I have served as someone's silent mentor, I felt not only overwhelming humility, but frankly, it scared me!

It reminds me of the question John the Baptist suggested that his disciples ask Jesus. Those whom John mentored probably had never laid eyes on Jesus. Likely, they were only given a physical description, so I can imagine John saying to them, "Now when you see a man who looks like this, and does this sort of thing, don't be timid. Just go up to him and ask: 'Are you the one who was to come, or should we expect someone else?'" (see Matthew 11:2, 3). It really sounds like the disciples asked Jesus: "Are you who you say you are?"

That is a powerful reminder that authenticity is indispensable for Christian leaders. There must never be any confusion in the minds of those who observe us. We must not be mistaken as being mere political leaders or social activists. Be certain of who you are and the reason you have been called. And never deny it—in any way.

Having had the privilege of serving as a Salvation Army officer for over four decades, I have learned some other compelling lessons from life and leadership. Eva and I are blessed to have served on three continents. We've traveled the world extensively. We visited fascinating places and were exposed to a myriad of cultures that we never would have encountered if we had not made ourselves available for God's purposes. Our lives have been immeasurably enriched. And my belief in the power of one man, or one woman, to impact the course of a nation has been dramatically altered.

While serving as the executive leader (territorial commander) in southern Africa from our headquarters in Johannesburg, we had the privilege of meeting privately with Nelson Mandela. We had to pinch each other to ensure it was not a dream. Several years earlier we had watched, with the world, the emergence of "Madiba" from his isolated cell on Robben Island, never imagining that one day God would give us the privilege of sitting next to him in conversation, listening to him share his dream for the rebuilding of South Africa. As a result of that dialogue, I believe more than ever in the power invested in those who are privileged to receive God's call.

I took away from our meeting with Mr. Mandela a fixed belief that if one man can impact the changing of a nation, surely God's anointed leaders, strategically placed, whether in the secular or spiritual profit or nonprofit sectors of the world, *can* participate in the renewing of America—or any nation—for Christ.

// MINISTERING THE MESSAGE OF HOPE //

My travels, however, often leave me heavyhearted. I feel the need to speak into the lives of those who are called to serve, to encourage a higher level of belief and behavior. America is at a tipping point. If we lose spiritual ground, it will loosen our nation's moral footing.

There is an uncertainty about the times in which we are living, and it is evidenced in the faces and heard in the voices of some thirty million people who come to the doors of The Salvation Army every year from five thousand communities across America. There is a fear about the future that is pushing the already marginalized into a deeper state of doubt about themselves. If individuals cease to believe in themselves, in whom or in what good will they believe? What will it mean for our collective future if we see the rising of future generations who have given up hope? What are the implications for a Christian leader in America?

In the early morning hours of August 6, 2007, tragedy struck the Crandall Canyon (Utah) mining community. It was an event that is forever carved in the minds and hearts of a very special community of friends and family. The coal mine collapsed nearly four miles from its entrance. The impact was so strong that shock waves at a magnitude of 4.0 were reported in seismograph stations.

As a nation we held our collective breath—riveted to television screens and anxiously reading the newspaper accounts of the scenes and stories of the rescuers. They were the hero miners who simply refused to give up the search for their six coworkers trapped some eighteen hundred feet below ground.[2] Throughout the ordeal the families and loved ones, who had never worked a mine, could do nothing but stand helplessly by, completely dependent on those who knew the mines and what it means to be a miner. Families and loved ones, even the whole of America, desperately clung to the hope that the skill and knowledge of seasoned miners would save them all—that these heroes would be the saviors of those trapped in the clutches of the earth.

The same could be said of Christian leaders serving in any capacity. God's anointed and appointed leaders are the rescuers of our time. And thank God for an emerging generation who also is answering the call to the hard, even dangerous, work of rescuing those in the grip of an unforgiving social environment. The times demand a sense of urgency in leading. This is a search-and-rescue operation for the soul of our nation. In fact, leaders in the twenty-first century understand that to engage the difficult work of righteousness and justice places one directly in the line of fire. But why be surprised? After all, we are engaged in spiritual warfare!

Some of the most effective Christian leaders are not only those who stand behind pulpits on Sunday morning. On any day there are godly leaders of great value sitting behind desks in corporate America, managing households, and supervising laborers in the workforce. Leaders are standing among us who do not yet know that they are about to receive *the* call—a call to witness in whatever place they find themselves. I pray it often: "Lord, call more of us. Place more of us in the lives and circumstances of those who are waiting for a word and an action that give evidence that their world has not been abandoned by you."

// YOUR RESPONSE TO GOD'S CLAIMS ON YOUR NATION //

The psalmist spoke the decree of the Lord: "Ask of me, and I will make the nations your inheritance, the ends of the earth your possession" (Psalm 2:8).

This is a critical hour in the life of our nation. I do not need to recite the litany of threats to our individual and collective well-being. The most significant dangers facing America do not come from beyond the boundaries of our country. There is a battle for the mind, heart, and soul underway *within* our borders. And the lasting answer is not found in the ways and means to which we have grown comfortably accustomed. Political maneuverings will not reverse the direction in which our culture is sliding. Money will not satisfy the root cause of social dilemmas.

Through the lens of biblical truth, it is easy to see that the moral compass of our nation is broken.

- What was once unthinkable is demanded, celebrated, and tolerated.
- There is a continuing attempt to redefine right and wrong.
- Godly beliefs are regarded by many as biased, intolerant, and something that can be dismissed.
- The best is being overtaken by the less.

The culture war in America calls for spiritual engagement. Never in my adult life has it been required more urgently that those in leadership roles speak and model authentic, eternal truth with clarity and courage. I sense a hunger, a longing, for something better—something of greatest value and worth. There is the belief that surely there must be something more than what we now see and hear. There is a discontent with the way things are. Sadly, the searching is too often for the wrong thing, in the wrong place, with the wrong intention.

Millions of ordinary citizens give testimony to desperate loneliness as they pursue their daily routines. In major and minor choices, an inner exhaustion is taking its toll. The unforgiving strain of daily life is stealing purpose for too many. It seems we are suffering from a collective spiritual dementia. Although it may be unspoken, there is evidence of a need for someone to listen, to care, to act with compassion and courage.

// EMBRACING THE HIGH CALLING //

I have never been more keenly aware of the enormous responsibility of those who serve in public and private leadership roles. God continues to teach me, through many years of privileged leadership service, both nationally and internationally. I remain a student—and I admit that every day of my life is consumed with striving to achieve the greater purpose God has for me.

If you are a leader who is serious about making a difference in your role, I suggest you consider the *why* of the responsibility you have been privileged to engage in. As a believer, you are gifted with a task that is too noble to describe merely as a profession. You are in place to serve the purposes of God. You are an influence not only for the good of your organization or firm; God has called you to participate in the renewing of your country.

Leaders in the grip of faith, who understand that they possess a sacred trust, are a powerful force in society. They should have a clear understanding of who they are and of the high value in what they do. They are not deterred in spite of subtle—or blatant!—efforts to push the presence and voice of Christian belief to the margins of our culture.

In the face of it all, there are three fundamental principles to which, with God's help, I try to remain faithful. They serve as anchors in my private life as well as in my public leadership. I really want to live the link between those two demanding arenas in which I exist.

1. I MUST "BE"

I want my life to honor God. I have been given life in order to discharge a God-intended purpose. I want the principle of "being," as a man of faith with all that it means, to be evident in the way I live and lead. I want to be authentic at home and in public. I understand that I must *be* before I attempt to *do* the work to which I have been called. "True north" for me is leading from a God-centered and ordered life.

2. I MUST LIVE IN COMMUNITY

This is a never-to-be-forgotten principle. No matter what I do or where I arrive in my profession, life is never just about me. That is a nonconventional view of life. In this postmodern period of "me" and "my rights," serving for the sake of others seems absurd. It is dismissed as an antiquated notion from another time. But this moment in America (and for that matter, other countries of the world) calls for leaders who are intent on making their lives count for a higher purpose. We serve from a conviction that every sector of a community can and must change.

It is time for a new model of leadership to emerge that gives flesh to biblical truth. You and I must prove that faith in God does not fracture, but embraces; that such faith does not create confusion, but cares and demonstrates compassion. We serve to prove that there is such a thing as a leader who can be trusted precisely because of his faith.

3. I MUST REMEMBER THAT I AM CALLED TO LEAD FOR HIGHER PURPOSES

We do what we do for an outcome that is larger than we could ever imagine. It is for more than personal or organizational profit. We are invested in something that holds more value than a product. There is a bottom line that is more critical than landing on the surplus side of the ledger. I do not live for material success, although I do not belittle those who achieve it and who understand the stewardship responsibility it bears. As a leader under God, I am called to help others believe they too can achieve. There is a deeper intention for the one who lives and leads for God.

// LIFE'S LEADERSHIP LESSONS //

I link those reflections on life to lessons on leading. Here are a few things I have learned about integrity, character, and serving that I hope make sense to you. Perhaps you will be able to relate to them where you are in your own leadership journey.

LET US FIRST CONSIDER INTEGRITY AND CHARACTER

I am convinced that one of the essentials to leading with a difference is rooted in the understanding of the critical need for personal integrity. How sad it is to be disappointed by men and women we once believed in. We ascribed high value to those who appeared to have their lives in order, but then suddenly the hidden life of shame became public, shattering that image.

It is curious that despite the public and painful lessons arising out of the heartbreaking tragedy of some, there remain others who do not seem to learn from their mistakes. They continue on their perilous course, endangering not only their own lives and reputations; but they also seem unconcerned about the impact their risk taking will have on others who believe in them. Remember, the moral collapse of a Christian leader affects not only him or her but also those who follow. Our great need is for leaders with integrity. And I believe there is a link between the value of an organization and the character of its leader.

Many of the texts on leadership and management that occupy space on my personal library shelves are by authors who focus on ideas to improve performance and product. Few of those books look deeply into what it means to a home, a neighborhood, a city, and a nation to have the influence of an unsoiled leader. Men and women of character—with clean hands and a burning heart fully committed to God—can be trusted, no matter how low the moral temperature in the social environment dips. However, leaders whose actions betray their speech are dangerous to the cause of the kingdom of our Lord.

It is appropriate for leaders to undergo regular self-examination. And a good question to ask ourselves would be: *If those who follow me knew what I know about myself, would they or should they trust me?*

We must never fail to raise character and integrity as the highest virtues of leading. There must be no disconnection between who we are and what we do. The ignoring of this essential is at the core of much colossal personal failure. We must insist that the moral and ethical high ground no longer be accepted as less important than amassing money, power, and privilege. You and I can bridge the yawning gap of trust and mixed messages emerging from Wall Street and spreading down Main Street to the back streets and alleys of America's neighborhoods. There must be a rising up of men and women who courageously demonstrate what it means to be a steward of human capital and fiscal assets. We insist that godly character matters!

AND WHAT ABOUT THE MATTER OF SERVING?

Another lesson that I appreciate seems to be missing in many leadership styles. You do not hear it very much beyond the concept of leadership in the world of religion. It is about servant leadership—or as I prefer to call it, *serving* leadership. It is a formidable task to be in leadership in our time, in any sector of our society. Yet we also lead in a time of unparalleled opportunity. There is mounting dissatisfaction with and distrust of those in charge. Followers are pleading for leaders who will serve their constituencies.

Read the apostle Paul's letter to the believers in Rome, and you might find his call to serving leadership depressing! In the opening line of his correspondence, he described himself as "a servant of Christ Jesus" (Romans 1:1). But it's more than a servant. The original Greek for the serving he demands is the word *doulos,* meaning "bond slave." Paul was painting a vivid picture of the mind of a Roman slave who answered only to one person—his slave master. So by introducing himself as a *doulos,* Paul made it clear to whom he was indentured—and why. Most of us do not think that being a servant of Christ means becoming his slave. Serving as a "slave" does not sit well, whatever your ethnic origins.

Several years ago Eva and I returned to Mocksville, North Carolina. It is a bedroom community for bustling Winston-Salem, which my family would visit approximately every other year. Those visits were good times of fun and laughter with numerous relatives living in the community. It was my dad's hometown. In fact, Gaither Street is presumably named after an ancestor, suggesting that my forefathers must have had a significant impact in the community. So Eva and I took a few days to reconnect with family while in nearby Winston for a speaking engagement. A colleague arranged a marvelous reunion, and we found ourselves in the midst of about fifty Gaithers. Imagine being in a room with so many people whom you resemble! It was a beautiful experience.

During the visit, a first cousin took us to an old, untended cemetery where the remains of several Gaithers rest. We spent significant time reading headstones, some of which had long been abandoned and needed care. My heart raced a bit when I saw the small, abused marker with the name Elijah Gaither inscribed. He was buried a slave. I must admit to having a mixture of sadness, and even a bit of anger, as I stood at the gravesite of my great-grandfather who served in bondage to another human being.

With our understanding of slavery—whether in the age of my great-grandparents who were involuntarily taken into servitude by those who possessed social wealth and status, or whether it is trafficked women or teenage girls today who are exploited for the sexual enjoyment of men of means—no matter the form of the enslavement, one does not normally volunteer for that status in life. We think that to be a slave is an injustice. But the apostle Paul gladly, and proudly with purpose, declared himself to be a *doulos,* a bond slave of Christ.

May I suggest that, like Paul, we too have been called to voluntarily submit to the authority of our Lord. You and I have accepted, gladly, the identity of being his servant when, in fact, we are his slaves, bound to him by chains of love. The twenty-first century Christian leader is a willing *doulos*. I would be a slave of Jesus.

By the way, to be a server is not reserved for the clergy. No matter the form, serving is an equal opportunity vocation. It is an inclusive, not exclusive, activity. The best leaders I know are some of the greatest servers. If one would be a serving leader, it demands new thinking and new behaviors. To serve actually puts the server at risk.

Before the first light of dawn of each new day, I need to submit myself to God. I require the indwelling of his Holy Spirit. I seek fresh cleansing at the start of each day. I am in need of wisdom and courage as I undertake tasks and decisions. On any given day, the requirements of serving leadership demand more of me than I shall realize. I have learned that there is power for serving when one takes the time to commune with the God we serve.

// IT IS YOUR TIME TO LEAD WITH *DOULOS* GREATNESS //

The French statesman Alexis de Tocqueville left us with a word about the greatness of America when in 1831 he wrote that he did not find it "in her commodious harbors, her ample rivers, her fertile fields, . . . her vast world commerce." He "looked for it in her democratic Congress and her matchless Constitution—and it was not there." Rather, de Tocqueville penned, "America is great because America is good, and if America ever ceases to be good, America will cease to be great!"[3]

I know it is true. The blessing of God rests on the endeavors of those who lead good causes. By his blessing they achieve kingdom greatness. It is time to restore greatness to our leading.

But great leadership is hard. So when leading becomes difficult—when you are dry, discouraged, and debilitated—remember this word of the Lord to Moses, that great Old Testament leader: "There is a place near me where you may stand on a rock. . . . I will put you in a cleft in the rock and cover you with my hand" (Exodus 33:21, 22).

You are a leader—unlike the secular world will ever appreciate. However, the results of your impact have eternal consequences. So let your confidence rest in the one who has called you to serve others through serving him.

Stand strong—and lead on!

MY LEADERSHIP BOOKSHELF

Good to Great: Why Some Companies Make the Leap . . . and Others Don't by Jim Collins (HarperBusiness, 2001). The big lesson from this book is simply: shame on us if we lose the passion for greatness in serving the kingdom! Faith institutions and their leadership seek excellence, and this text holds valuable lessons about what it takes, and what it can mean, to take the leap from the ordinary to the extraordinary.

Deep Change: Discovering the Leader Within by Robert E. Quinn (Jossey-Bass, 1996). This engaging book has dramatically altered my view of what it really means to lead effectively through personal transformation. *Deep Change* is one of the most important texts on the shelves of my personal library.

Jesus on Leadership: Timeless Wisdom on Servant Leadership by C. Gene Wilkes (Tyndale House Publishers, Inc., 1998). It is very simple: the most effective twenty-first century leaders are servers. The writer of this book brings new meaning to the power that lies within a servant by examining the impact of Jesus, the model servant leader.

////// PERSONAL REFLECTIONS AND APPLICATIONS //////

1. What is your personal leadership narrative—the story you sense God is writing in and through your life? Take some time over the next week and write a "treatment"—a summary of the major story lines of your leadership journey. Take special note of those leadership moments and crossroads when your greatest lessons were learned.

2. Who has shaped your understanding and practice of leadership? How? If able, take time in these next few days to contact those individuals and share with them their impact—giving thanks to them and to God for a faithful witness.

3. Whose leadership journey are you influencing? Remember, there are many who are watching and learning; you may never know about it until much later in life or in eternity. Also remember that you live and serve in community.

4. Samuel set up a stone memorial and named it Ebenezer (which means "stone of help"). He said, "Thus far has the LORD helped us" (1 Samuel 7:12). We encourage you to create an Ebenezer File into which you can record those significant events, experiences, and people's names through which/whom the Lord has helped you. This will serve you well, particularly in times of difficulty and self-doubt. Create and visit regularly your Ebenezer File to remind yourself that the Lord will never leave you or forsake you and will be with you always.

5. Review the challenge to being a leader of integrity and character in the context of community. Reflect particularly on the calling to a *doulos* (bond slave) attitude. Ask the Holy Spirit to reveal anything in your heart that may war against this sacred calling to becoming a serving leader.

6. Do you still have your sense of urgency about the need to fulfill your specific leadership calling, or have the routines and perhaps the unrelenting demands, pressures, and periodic disappointments (particularly in others) dampened your enthusiasm and energy for your high calling in Christ Jesus? You have been called to a great work that must not be diminished or deflected by distractions, disappointments, or delusions. Reignite your sense of passion and urgency so you can finish your race strong and victoriously. Reflect on verse 1 of the old hymn "Work for the Night is Coming" (based on John 9:4 and written by Anna Coghill in 1854 when she was only eighteen years old):

> Work, for the night is coming, work thro' the morning hours;
> Work while the dew is sparkling; work 'mid springing flow'rs.
> Work when the day grows brighter, work in the glowing sun;
> Work, for the night is coming, when man's work is done.

///////// TEAM REFLECTIONS AND APPLICATIONS /////////

1. What are some specific ways your organization could live out the Salvation Army slogan of having a "heart to God and hand to man"? In what ways will you encourage team members to serve God's purposes in this generation by extending their hands in service to others? How has your team demonstrated that they are a "serving leadership"?

2. How has your organization recently dealt with issues of prejudice? Are there any action steps that you, as the leadership team, need to take in this area? What are they, and how will you proceed?

3. If America is at a moral tipping point, as stated in this chapter, in what ways can your organization set a positive example of moral uprightness? How should this play out in day-to-day decisions in your organization? What kind of "search-and-rescue operations" should you be about?

4. What would happen if your team regularly asked the question, "If those who follow us knew what we know about ourselves, would they or should they trust us?" What are some practical ways in which you could raise character and integrity issues in the conscience of all involved?

5. How has your organization been guilty of underestimating what God might be doing through you? What kinds of things enter the work culture that can cause you to doubt and lose hope at times? How can you overcome these issues and move forward with confidence and "*doulos* greatness"?

ISRAEL L. GAITHER
RETIRED NATIONAL COMMANDER, THE SALVATION ARMY USA
//

Israel L. Gaither was born and raised in New Castle, Pennsylvania. In 1964 he and his wife, Eva, were ordained and commissioned as officers (clergy) in The Salvation Army (www.salvationarmyusa.org). His more than four decades of ministry have impacted The Salvation Army's work in 121 countries—and significantly so in Africa, England, and the United States.

In 2002, Gaither was appointed to serve as The Salvation Army's chief of the staff, the first African-American to hold the position since the founding of the organization in 1865. In 2006, the Gaithers assumed the key executive leadership assignments as national leaders of The Salvation Army.

Israel L. Gaither is the first African-American to serve in the distinguished assignment as national commander.

An efficient administrator and gifted speaker, Gaither is a much sought-after preacher and has addressed thousands of Salvationists and other Christians worldwide.

Among his varied leadership accomplishments, he has obtained many other "firsts" in Salvation Army history. He was the first African-American divisional commander, having served with his wife in southern New England and western Pennsylvania. Those appointments were followed by key territorial assignments for the Army's USA Eastern Territory encompassing eleven northeastern states, Puerto Rico, and the Virgin Islands.

The Gaithers also served as territorial leaders of the Army's work in southern Africa, which marked the first appointment of an African-American Salvation Army officer outside the United States. The work under their charge included the countries of South Africa and Mozambique, the kingdoms of Lesotho and Swaziland, and the Army's ministry on the island of St. Helena.

Honors received by Gaither for his global leadership and ministry include honorary doctorates from Asbury University and Taylor University, being named in the *San Francisco Examiner* as one of the "Top Ten Communicators in 2006," and recognition in 2008 by Dominion and the Dominion Foundation as one of nine African-American leaders to receive the Excellence in Leadership Award.

The Gaithers' marriage in 1967, during the turbulence of the African-American civil rights era, marked the first racially integrated marriage of Salvation Army officers in the United States. They have two children and four grandchildren.

///

NURTURING YOUR ORGANIZATION'S CULTURE

STEVE HAYNER

Research shows that no single force has greater impact on the character and quality (in essence, the culture) of an organization than the person who assumes the primary leadership role of that organization. Two popular witticisms pointedly illustrate this influence: "No stream rises higher than its source" and "Fish rot from the head first." As you read Steve's insights, do some soul searching about the tone and culture of your organization and where it is influenced by the ways in which you exercise your leadership roles. Do people in your spheres of influence blossom or wither—do they flourish or flounder? As a Christ-centered leader, you are as responsible for nurtured relationships and healthy organizational environments as you are for tangible, measurable results.

I asked an experienced woman who had worked in several nonprofit organizations over the years: "What's it like to work here?"

"Oh, this is the best place I've ever worked!" she replied. "It's actually fun to come to work. People work hard here, but they enjoy being together. They laugh a lot. Personally, I feel valued and listened to. And I love that we take time as a whole office to pray every day."

That was quite a contrast from an employee in another organization who described his experience this way: "I don't know how much longer I can work here. It's not only the pressure, but I'm just feeling personally used up. It seems like there are a lot of hidden rules around here, and I feel scared a lot that I'm going to do something stupid that I didn't even know about. I don't like being yelled at."

These starkly contrasting descriptions describe very distinctive "cultures." There are many different work cultures because there are so many variables in what comprises culture. Culture includes all the characteristics of a human environment:

- *!* from what people wear to how they treat one another.
- *!* from how people communicate to what is valued in the workplace.
- *!* from how people view their work to what attitudes they display day by day.
- *!* from how supervision is handled to whether people feel connected.

// THREE TRUTHS ABOUT ORGANIZATIONAL CULTURE //

Every work environment has a culture. As a young leader, I did not pay much attention to the cultures around me. I just tried to fit in and do what I was supposed to do as well as I could wherever I was. However, over time I began to be aware that every organization—every family, every church, and every nonprofit or multinational corporation—has a culture. And I realized three very important truths about culture.

1. CULTURE MATTERS

Culture matters . . . a lot, because culture is like soil. The nutrients and pollutants in that soil deeply affect whether the people who are a part of the organization can flourish and be effective in accomplishing their mission or whether they will be starved and stressed.

2. LEADERS CAN CHANGE CULTURE

While everyone in an organization contributes to the culture, leaders who are attentive can, over time, use their power to help the culture change and become more deeply nourishing to those who live or work in it.

When I look back at the family I grew up in, I am able to describe many characteristics of that family culture. My family lived in a small, mostly farming community. My parents were both lawyers who worked very hard in their careers—hard work and competency were big values. Since political matters were important, so was the ability of each member of the family to learn to argue a point of view. Religion, which was more about right behavior than about faith in a personal God, was assumed. And there was an expectation that all of us were responsible to help the world be a better place. My parents, as leaders in the family, set the tone for these and so many other elements of the family culture that shaped me.

When I was old enough to become more aware of how other peoples' families worked, I realized that not all family cultures were the same. One of my friends had alcoholic parents. In that home the alcohol brought inconsistency and sometimes the fear of abusive outbursts. My friend learned to read the environment of his chaotic home and behave accordingly. After his father, and later his mother, became a Christian the whole culture of his home began to change. Life was different for everyone in the household.

With larger communities or organizations, the people and environments that shape the culture become more varied. However, even in a vast mosaic of cultural inputs, discernible patterns become evident. It is still possible to describe "American culture," even though the United States is composed of significant cultural diversity. Indeed, that diversity in itself becomes a describable cultural element. Culture can be influenced by leaders, over time, in significant ways.

3. THE MORE SIGNIFICANT THE POSITION, THE GREATER THE RESPONSIBILITY

Jesus told his disciples in a parable about managers and servants that "from everyone who has been given much, much will be demanded; and from the one who has been entrusted with much, much more will be asked" (Luke 12:48). Organizational culture requires attention. All the participants in the culture contribute, but organizations are not merely destined to default to whatever they become. Leaders can shape cultures. When organizational culture is deeply nourishing, it's likely because the key leaders have done something right. And conversely, when culture is toxic, it is the leader's responsibility to help it to change.

I love what the psalmist Asaph said about David in Psalm 78:70-72: "[God] chose David his servant and took him from the sheep pens; from tending the sheep he brought him to be the shepherd of his people. . . . And David shepherded them with integrity of heart; with skillful hands he led them." God chose David because he had the right heart and the right skills. He moved him from taking care of sheep to taking care of a whole nation. And David continued to do the work of a good shepherd—guiding, nourishing, protecting, and setting the right example and tone for the people. When we read the details of David's story, we quickly discover that he did not do everything perfectly. No leader does. However, David shepherded the nation and guided them with a skillful hand. That summary statement is all about the effect that David had on the whole culture of Israel, not just about how he handled a particular task or crisis.

Read the Gospels, and there too we discover Jesus' attentiveness to the culture among his followers (such as in his rabbinic-style teaching and illustrations drawn from everyday life). He also promoted a broad, culture-changing agenda for his disciples (with the idea of servant leadership and missional lifestyle, among other things). He set a tone by his character and behavior, and he helped them to grow in how they came to treat one another. He promoted attentiveness to the Spirit (see his upper room discourse in John 13–17) and to the Scriptures. He encouraged teachability and affirmed personal transformation. He guarded and guided them, establishing rituals (like the Lord's Supper observance) to sustain their community and to remind them of truth. Jesus constantly spoke about and demonstrated a whole culture that he called the kingdom of God.

// WHY ORGANIZATIONAL CULTURES GO WRONG //

If creating, nourishing, and shaping culture is such an important part of what leaders do, why do organizational cultures go wrong? It seems to me that two reasons are central.

LEADERS CAN BE INATTENTIVE TO THEIR OWN LIVES

The culture of an organization is a mirror of the character of the leader, but leaders can fail to give attention to their own lives. There are numerous illustrations of this dynamic in the Bible. You only have to look at the impact of dysfunctional parenting among Abraham and Sarah's descendants in Genesis to see the character flaws of parents being played out in the lives of children—sometimes over generations. Or look at the impact of disobedient kings (actually the majority of kings in the books of Kings and Chronicles) on the cultures of Israel and Judah. The history of God's people after the time of King David was frequently marked by long periods of decadent and disobedient culture that destroyed the character of God's people and kept them from fulfilling his mission in the world. The Scriptures make it clear that this was due to the failure of leadership (see Isaiah 3:4-12; 56:9-12; Hosea 5:10; Zechariah 10:1-3, for example).

LEADERS CAN BE INATTENTIVE TO THE CULTURE

Over time, leaders get busier and busier. It just happens. Leaders have gifts. They have vision. And if they also have a servant's heart, they see what is needed and begin to meet those needs. Leaders easily can become distracted by really good and urgent tasks, to the neglect of the more important responsibilities of giving attention to the people and the culture.

When I was president of InterVarsity Christian Fellowship, there was a time when I became so busy with speaking, attending meetings, and traveling that I neglected the people in our National Service Center. As a consequence, the culture in the office began to drift in some unhelpful directions. I simply was not there when the pressures of a large project began to create a culture of fear and anxiety—and the misuse of power and some bad decisions on the part of other leaders began to erode the work environment.

At some point it becomes obvious to every leader that he or she cannot do everything. And so the gift of discernment must kick in. Servant leaders should ask better questions than "What needs to be done?" and "What could I do?" in order to shape their calendars. "What am I *called* to do?" may be a better question to ask to begin this discernment process.

One of my close associates at InterVarsity during this time challenged me to take another look at the priorities of my leadership tasks. One question that he asked has stuck with me ever since: "What is it that *only* you can do as the primary leader of this community?" Asked a different way: "There are many things that you as our leader can do, and many things that need to be done, but what are the things that you are uniquely positioned to do—and that no one else can do quite as effectively as you?" He did not want me to waste my time, energy, or opportunity, but rather to give myself to those things that were really important for pursuing the organization's mission and sustaining the community's health.

The question haunted me, so I began to formulate a list of things that only I could do most effectively in the organization that I was called to lead. At the top of my list was this: *Only I can be the primary steward of the community's culture.* This has come to be one of the more important lessons that I have learned over the years about leading organizations.

// THE QUALITIES OF CULTURES THAT REALLY WORK //

So what are the characteristics of a good organizational culture, and how can leaders nurture such a culture? These are critical questions.

Cultures that work, and that ultimately help people to accomplish a community's mission, are ones in which people flourish. In healthy cultures, people become more of what God intended for them to be. They grow in being more like Jesus in character. And their gifts and abilities are intentionally developed, mobilized, and honored.

One of the best ways to discover what healthy cultures look and feel like is to ask people about their own experiences. Almost anyone who has thought about what helps him or her to flourish as one of God's beloved is able to point to characteristics of the community or organization that have helped. And I would encourage every leader to make such a list.

Here are a few characteristics that I deeply appreciate in a community culture.

EVERYTHING IS CENTERED IN CHRIST AND HIS AGENDA

All our labor, all our relationships, and all our institutional activities are under the lordship of Christ. This is actually true whether we are working within a context that is intentional about these commitments or whether we are working in a so-called secular environment. Jesus is still Lord, and kingdom principles are still operable. As disciples of Jesus Christ, we are called to follow him in *what* we do and *how* we do it. In a healthy culture, it is clear where the ultimate foundation and final authority reside. This is demonstrated consistently:

- in how servant leadership is exercised.
- in how decisions are made with an attentiveness to biblical wisdom.
- in the patterns of a community's life of worship and prayer.
- in other corporate values that intentionally put Jesus and his ways first.

PEOPLE FEEL CALLED TO THE MISSION AND LOVE WHAT THEY DO

There is a big difference in organizational life when people feel called by God to be a part of a team and when they have a personal commitment to the mission. When the majority of people in an organization feel this way, there is a constant anticipation in the air about what God will do. People view even mundane tasks as contributing to something bigger than themselves and don't mind work, even when it is hard or stressful.

There is an old story told about a traveler in Europe who happened upon a town square that was dominated by a huge cathedral. While admiring the building, she heard the sound of hammer against stone emanating from a large tent nearby. Drawn by the sound, she went closer to see what was happening and found a small group of workmen chipping away at a large pile of stones. When she asked one of the workmen what they were doing, he scowled and gruffly answered that he was cutting stones, as if to rebuke her for asking such a stupid question about the obvious. However, when she asked another workman in another part of the tent, he peered up lovingly at the towering edifice before him and, with a big smile, said, "I'm building a cathedral!"

There is a big difference in a culture made up of cathedral builders rather than stonecutters. Cathedral builders live a vision that keeps them going even when the day-to-day tasks could easily wear them down. Cathedral builders love their jobs, no matter how routine, because they see their part fitting into a larger whole.

COMMUNICATION IS OPEN AND OPINIONS ARE VALUED

How information is handled has a deep impact on a corporate culture. If information is used as a token of power or rank, and frequently withheld even from those who may need to know in order to do their work well, a culture of stratification (where people feel excluded from the "in" group) can quickly grow. Obviously, it is not appropriate that everyone knows everything; however, cultures that are more transparent and open generally have less fear and more trust. Cultures with open communication have members who are more engaged with the mission because they feel more ownership. They have a greater feeling of being insiders.

RESPECT, EXCELLENCE, GRACE, AND TRUTH RESULT IN TRUST

Trust is a key factor in corporate cultures that really work. The interesting thing about trust is that it has to be earned rather than demanded. Two good questions about trust are:

◊ What encourages people to trust more?
◊ What destroys trust?

The answers to those questions most often include issues of integrity. Organizations in which people know that mutual respect is encouraged, that excellence is expected, that grace is available, and that leaders tell the truth—in other words, organizations with strong corporate values—are generally places where trust is also high.

Consider, for example, the situation in which a team is working on a very difficult and stressful task. If they come to the assignment with a mutual respect for the contributions that each member can bring, and with a focus on what people do well rather than on where they struggle, the team often will move from tolerating one another to real synergy. An expectation that the task should be done with excellence gives the team a deep sense that what they are doing matters. Appropriate grace along the way helps to alleviate the fear of failure, replacing the fear with an open and teachable spirit. And if the team knows that leaders will tell them the truth about how things are going, and will be consistent with the stories they tell others, much of the negative politics of stressful organizational life is eliminated. This is a culture of trust.

GRATITUDE, AFFIRMATION, AND CELEBRATION ABOUND

Very few cultures are truly nourishing if people are not thanked, affirmed (encouraged), and celebrated. Cultures that are fruitful are also genuinely fun communities. People laugh. People appreciate one another—and express that appreciation. People get excited about the successes of one another and recognize that where one is honored, all share in that honor. And when cultures include people from many backgrounds, the honoring of the various contributions that people bring, and the celebration of their cultural diversity, can make a huge difference in whether diversity is seen as an asset or a problem.

Those are a few of the qualities seen in organizational cultures that work. What would you add to this list of characteristics of great organizations—whether a family, a church, a nonprofit, a volunteer association, or a for-profit business? What are the environments in which you tend to grow and flourish?

// CULTIVATING CULTURES THAT HELP PEOPLE TO FLOURISH //

How does a leader shape a culture? Is the "stewardship of culture," the nurturing of it, even possible? Doesn't culture just happen as a result of the individual attitudes and activities that each person brings into the community?

My strong observation and premise is that leaders can—and do—shape culture. I say that from my experience in various organizations over the years, as well as from the Scriptures. For instance, Joshua's example of unswerving faith moved the people to stand with him on the day he issued his "choose for yourselves this day whom you will serve" challenge—and they maintained that "culture" for a long time after Joshua died (Joshua 24:15, 31).

Shaping culture may be one of the most essential responsibilities of leadership. If we are not intentional about it, the shaping will still happen by default—for better or worse.

So what does it take? How can we as leaders continue to grow in our effectiveness in the shaping of culture? Two distinct categories are important here.

1. A LEADER'S "WAY OF BEING"—PERSONAL CHARACTERISTICS

Paul is clear in Romans 12:3 that none of us should think of ourselves as more important than we ought. However, as people created in God's image, gifted by the Holy Spirit, and invited to partner with God in his work in the world, we also should not underplay the impact that we can have. The call to leading is a call to thoughtful action.

I have tried to think about characteristics that seem most important to me now concerning what it takes to be a good steward of culture. I see these as vital to a leader's way of being within a community. They are not only qualities that I believe to be essential if we are to wisely shape the cultures of the communities in which we are planted, but they are also characteristics that I hope people can use to describe my life.

SELF-AWARENESS

One of the first prerequisites for leadership is self-awareness. If we do not know ourselves, in all our giftedness and brokenness, we constantly will battle with a disparity between our motivations and the results of our behaviors. We will not understand why it is that when we aim to do good things, the results often are not what we intended.

Self-awareness can be thought of as an assessment of our own internal culture with all its elements of temperament, experience, physical and personality attributes, desires, ambitions, relational strengths and deficiencies, persistent struggles and temptations. It all matters. And it all comes into play, one way or another, as we lead. The promise of God is that we who are followers of Jesus are in the process of "being transformed into his likeness" (2 Corinthians 3:18). And who we are today has an impact on the people and processes of life around us. The cultures we are in will pick up the flavor of our lives. So it is a good thing to know what some of those flavors are.

One of the more positive characteristics of my life, for example, is my genuine appreciation of the gifts and visions of others. When I first became president of InterVarsity, the culture included an atmosphere of suspicion regarding anyone who did not share a common institutional heritage. But over time, my willingness to affirm those with whom I did not share a history began to rub off on others, and a greater appreciation for God's diverse work in others' lives and for their gifts began to grow.

PERSONAL DISCIPLESHIP

This is a priority. A leader cannot take an organization beyond where he or she has gone—or at least is intending to go. "Do as I say, not as I do" is only a nice slogan that protects our sense of integrity in the midst of the awareness that we too frequently fail. Leaders who are not growing in Christlike character will never be able to generate organizations that are. Our words must match our actions. So every leader must give priority to personal growth. Bill Thrall, Bruce McNicol, and Ken McElrath, in their book *The Ascent of a Leader,* rightly make the distinction between growing in our capacity for leadership and growing in our character as leaders. Leaders who are growing in character are best able to shape a culture that also exhibits a positive character.

For me this means, among other things, that I need a small group of friends who will help me be completely myself with God and others.

LOVE

This characteristic scarcely needs explanation. No organizational community will flourish without someone attending to the members with deep love—the kind of love that longs for God's very best for others. Love is a gift. Love is a grace. Love is a commitment. Love is embedded in the biblical descriptions of leaders who tend, nourish, care for, feed, guide, protect, and call each member of the flock by name. Note, for instance, how Paul's letter to the church at Rome ends with a list of fond greetings and thanks to specific Christians there (Romans 16:1-16). Leaders who love understand that people are always more important than programs, and that a mission will only be accomplished by people who experience the biblical pattern we might define as "blessed to be a blessing." This is seen in Abram's call in Genesis 12:1-3, when God told him: "I will bless you . . . and you will be a blessing."

A SERVANT SPIRIT

A key component in a fruitful leader's "way of being" is a servant spirit. Leaders always have power. Some people view power as inherently evil. Power, however, is simply the realization of being given agency by God in the world. The question, then, is how that power is used. Jesus, who was the most powerful person who ever lived, always used his power in service to others.

Paul says it this way:

> Do nothing out of selfish ambition or vain conceit, but in humility consider others better than yourselves. Each of you should look not only to your own interests, but also to the interests of others.
>
> Your attitude should be the same as that of Christ Jesus: Who, being in very nature God, did not consider equality with God something to be grasped, but made himself nothing, taking the very nature of a servant, being made in human likeness. And being found in appearance as a man, he humbled himself and became obedient to death—even death on a cross! (Philippians 2:3-8).

That is a challenging command to those of us in leadership who can be tempted to use position and authority to serve ourselves rather than serve the organization's mission and its people. Cultivating a servant spirit within an organization is a key to building trust and ultimately shaping culture.

INTEGRITY OF BEHAVIOR

Max De Pree, in *Leadership Jazz,* says, "At the core of becoming a leader is the need always to connect one's voice and one's touch."[1] His point is that a leader's behavior within a community must always bring together the content and tone of our words with our actions. It is what I imagine is contained in those words about David's tending and guiding the people with skillful hands. Or in Isaiah 40:11, which describes the sovereign and powerful God's actions: "He tends his flock like a shepherd: He gathers the lambs in his arms and carries them close to his heart; he gently leads those that have young."

Change is difficult under the best of circumstances. Being a change agent requires patience, persistence, and focus. However, even the best strategy will not be fruitful if the community does not trust its shepherd. The example of the Good Shepherd, the model of the servant Lord—particularly as contrasted with the leaders of Israel in Ezekiel 34:1-10—should provide strong instruction for those who want to bring positive nourishment and change to a culture. The shepherd who does not tend, feed, and bind up wounds but, rather, uses people and power badly, will never leave an organization better than he found it. Sadly, there are times when (as with ancient Israel) God himself must rescue a community that has been preyed upon by a leader.

IMAGINATION

Caring for culture is always creative work. Therefore, imagination, or what some would call vision, becomes an important asset. Leaders need to be able to see the possibilities. They need to envision the life of the community in terms of what it might look like if the will of God were fully realized on earth as it is in Heaven. They need to listen to the imaginative dreams of those throughout the organization too, because God's ideas often surface from a multitude of sources.

PATIENCE AND PERSISTENCE

Patience and persistence need to be tucked in as well, because the bottom line is that culture generally changes very slowly. So much of culture is rooted in the very DNA of an organization's life and history. It takes careful, consistent attention over time for significant change to occur.

COURAGE

Leadership is never for the faint of heart. There are always difficult decisions to be made and actions to be taken. Leaders are responsible and have to live with and be accountable for their actions. Leadership can be very costly. Christian leaders are always called to follow in the way of Jesus, who courageously did his Father's will even when it cost him the praise of some of his followers, the respect of the watching world, and ultimately his life. Christ-centered leaders play life to an audience of one—and that takes courage.

2. A LEADER'S TO-DO LIST

Let me suggest a few specific activities that will help leaders to guide organizational culture with a skillful hand.

BE ATTENTIVE AND ASSESS

Leaders need to be aware of what is happening within their organizations at all levels. They need to have an ear to the ground. They need to notice the details of life around them as it is being lived. They need to ask questions and then listen carefully to the answers.

I am amazed at how oblivious I can be. I get distracted by the vision before me, or by the immediate tasks at hand, and neglect to notice what is happening to the health of my colleagues—or even my own family. Busyness is an enemy of effectiveness, and that is particularly true when it comes to culture shaping. While it certainly is possible to be attentive on the fly to such areas as relational dynamics, levels of stress, topics of conversation, and the spiritual tone, it often takes time and particular attention to dig into the meaning of what we see happening. Culture is made up of so many parts that assessment requires intentionality.

PLAN THE STEPS

As the reality of what is happening within community culture becomes clearer, it is time for planning the steps that we want to take in moving the culture forward. For example, if a culture includes a great deal of built-in, unproductive stress, leadership needs to be intentional about discerning the causes and then be specific in developing plans and strategies for reducing or transforming those elements. The old saying "If you aim at nothing, you'll hit it every time" is true when it comes to nurturing culture. Ignoring the issues will not help them improve. Being unfocused in planning will not help hit the target. We need to make plans and then execute them with care and persistence—evaluating along the way to determine whether we are moving in the right direction.

When it comes to cultural change, planning should always include an awareness of the past as well as an eye toward future goals. Whenever well-established values and behaviors can be utilized in moving into new directions, the resistance can be diminished. People are comfortable with the way things are, even if they know those current ways are not working so well. Utilizing familiar elements of the culture, and transforming them in positive ways, can help minimize the discomfort with the newer patterns.

COMMUNICATE OPENLY

One of the main components of healthy organizational culture is honest, transparent communication. Therefore, it should be no surprise that one of the key activities of leaders who want to nourish community culture is that they communicate generously. This means both speaking and listening. The communication we model will likely be imitated. Larry Smeltzer, in a 1991 study of forty-three organizations, discovered that the most commonly cited reason for the failure of a change effort within an organization was the presence of inaccurate and negative rumors, often caused by the leader's neglecting to provide timely and accurate information.[2] However, communication is more than just relaying facts. It also is about communicating values, aspirations, and when necessary, apologies.

CREATE RITUALS

One of the most powerful ways of introducing enduring change is to create rituals that illustrate or embody the values and attitudes that we seek to nourish. Rituals are patterned, repeated, often symbolic actions that can strengthen relational bonds, teach values, and provide ongoing opportunities to remember and reaffirm who (and whose) we are. Rituals are a form of communication that helps us remember what is important.

At our seminary, nearly every class begins with the salutation "The Lord be with you," followed by the class response "And also with you." Then the professor prays—sometimes in adoration, sometimes in thanksgiving, sometimes for the needs of specific students, sometimes for those who are struggling in our broken world. Over the years I have observed the effect that this simple, sometimes hourly ritual has on our community. It reminds us every class period that all learning is done under the lordship and grace of God. It nourishes our respect for each other in this journey of discipleship. And it helps us to center our attention once again on God's call to be faithful as teachers and students.

PRAY

An element that should be prominent in any list of practical ways to nourish and shape an organizational culture is prayer. God cares far more about how we function together than we do. God cares about how we treat one another. And God longs for us to be fruitful in our participation in the work of Christ's kingdom. The conversation about our corporate culture should begin—and continue—with the triune God. It is in dialogue with God and with the guidance from the Holy Spirit that we can grow in this vital leadership task. Prayer, both as an individual and as a community, brings deeper understanding, openness, attentiveness, and sometimes insight beyond our natural abilities to figure these things out.

// CULTURE SHAPING—MORE ART THAN SCIENCE //

Corporate culture is complex. We all have a notion about what it is, but where we often flounder is in trying to define it. Understanding what is happening in a culture, and how we can more wisely tend it, is more of an art than a science. It requires wisdom and discernment. There is much more that could be said about what leaders can do to cultivate a culture where people flourish and mission can be achieved. I suggest that you pause and ask yourself where it is that you have seen strong, positive cultures. What do you think contributed to helping those cultures become good soil for missional communities to thrive? And where do you need to take steps in what you are becoming and what you are doing to more positively encourage and nurture the communities in which God has given you leadership?

While I certainly long to be viewed as successful in the fulfillment of the responsibilities entrusted to me by others—those things, for example, that are defined in a position description—I want even more to be approved by God as one who has been faithful in contributing to the presence of Christ's kingdom in the world. In organizational life, I am convinced that being faithful to this broader vision includes, at the foundational level, attending to the culture of our communities. It means helping the others in the community, who are likewise called and gifted, to flourish as children of God. And it means helping us all move together in accomplishing the mission we have been given. This is good work, and as a leader, I love it.

MY LEADERSHIP BOOKSHELF

The Ascent of a Leader: How Ordinary Relationships Develop Extraordinary Character and Influence by Bill Thrall, Bruce McNicol, and Ken McElrath (Jossey-Bass, 1999) describes how leaders develop in order to receive the destiny that God has planned for them. It contrasts developing our potential as leaders with developing in our character as leaders. And it suggests that the latter is far more important than the former. Over the years I have discovered that who I am is often more important than what I do as I seek to lead biblically.

Leadership Jazz by Max De Pree (Doubleday, 1992). Max understands that leadership is an art, not merely a set of skills. In this book full of deep wisdom and not merely techniques, the author seeks to help the artist emerge in each person called to leadership.

Leadership on the Line: Staying Alive Through the Dangers of Leading by Ronald A. Heifetz and Marty Linsky (Harvard Business Press, 2002). Leadership in rapidly changing environments is both challenging and exhausting. This book is not merely a survival plan, but a guide to thriving in times of danger through steady, wise work and a quiet, centered spirit.

////// PERSONAL REFLECTIONS AND APPLICATIONS //////

1. What strengths and weaknesses, victories and defeats, in your personal and professional life shape the way you influence culture as you lead your organization? Where do you see your own character reflected in the life of the organization?

2. Do you view your leadership as a calling or as a job? How does that point of view shape your ability to influence your organization's culture?

3. Who or what is having a significant impact on the culture of your organization now? Is this moving in the right direction?

4. How much focus and time do you give to shaping the overall culture of the organization you lead? Is it sufficient and effective? By what measures?

5. What do you believe are the most difficult elements of culture to change? Why?

6. Use the qualities in the section "A Leader's 'Way of Being'" (p. 97) to assess and develop a strategy for shaping the culture of your organization. Which qualities are strongest in your work environment? What qualities (these or others) would you like to see grow?

////////// **TEAM REFLECTIONS AND APPLICATIONS** //////////

1. How do you assess the corporate culture of your organization?

2. How would you describe the core qualities of the culture of your leadership team?

3. What changes can you make in your corporate culture to help the majority of your team feel more like "cathedral builders" than "stonecutters"?

4. What rituals exist in your organization to shape the culture you desire to create? What new rituals could you initiate? Are there any rituals—even unintentional ones—that should be abandoned? If so, why?

5. Make use of existing tools such as the Best Christian Workplaces survey[3] to help you as the leadership team to consistently monitor the nature of your organization's corporate culture and nurture it.

6. What unique characteristics and/or gifts do each of you on the leadership team contribute to your workplace culture? (If you are discussing these questions, it is best that you identify one another's qualities.)

7. How would you describe the "ideal" work culture? You might want to write a compelling paragraph outlining this ideal.

STEVE HAYNER
PRESIDENT, COLUMBIA THEOLOGICAL SEMINARY
///

D r. Steve Hayner is the ninth president of Columbia Theological Seminary (www.ctsnet.edu). Located in Decatur, Georgia, Columbia Theological Seminary is an educational institution of the Presbyterian Church (USA) and a community of theological inquiry and formation for ministry in the service of the church of Jesus Christ.

Since 2003, Hayner has served Columbia as professor of evangelism and church growth, bringing a long history of experience in ministry to the church and to students.

Previously he served as university pastor at University Presbyterian Church in Seattle, as vice president of Seattle Pacific University, as president of InterVarsity Christian Fellowship, and as associate pastor of two multiethnic churches in Madison, Wisconsin.

He holds degrees from Whitman College, Harvard Divinity School, and Gordon-Conwell Theological Seminary. He completed his PhD in 1984 at the University of St. Andrews.

Steve Hayner has served on a number of national and international boards, including World Vision, International Justice Mission, Presbyterian Global Fellowship, ScholarLeaders International, and The Navigators.

He loves students and he loves the church. His passion is to prepare men and women to lead congregations toward the fulfillment of God's call to be missional churches—churches who are biblically faithful and growing steadily in their love for God, their love for each other, and their love for Christ's work in the world.

Steve Hayner has been married to Sharol since 1973. They have three children and three granddaughters.

GOD-CENTERED
SELF-AWARENESS

MARK G. HOLBROOK

Search me, O God, and know my heart; test me and know my anxious thoughts. See if there is any offensive way in me" (Psalm 139:23, 24).

In this chapter Mark provides us with a candid and transparent look at his personal journey into God-centered self-awareness. Part of the challenge of leadership, given the drive and ego strengths of those of us who are attracted to senior positions in organizations and ministries, is to be willing to be objective about our limitations as well as our strengths. In addition, we often have few people around us willing to speak with directness, wisdom, and compassion the hard truths we need to hear. Every leader needs the prophetic, convicting voice of a Nathan and the loving correction and direction of a Barnabas to ensure that we see ourselves accurately. Mark gives us the understanding and models the courage we each need to know ourselves as God knows us and then respond with humility as God corrects, affirms, and directs. Reflect on Mark's questions throughout the chapter, asking the Holy Spirit to search and know your heart and lead you into a deeper understanding of who you can become in Christ as a leader whose self-awareness is centered on him.

By any definition I am a leader, but a few years ago I came close to crashing. As CEO of a growing and successful organization, I felt that everything was going well. Certainly most people who knew me and knew our organization would have concluded all was well, even wildly so. And in many ways that was true.

However, if you have been around awhile, you probably know that even in the strongest organizations, seeds of destruction are always looking for fertile soil. Some seeds are, for the most part, out of our control—external forces like an economic crisis or a natural disaster. Other seeds arise from within—less-than-competent people in the wrong seats on the bus and some who never should have been on the bus in the first place. And still other seeds include strategies built on shaky and ill-conceived assumptions, dysfunctional boards, tolerance for out-of-control egos, and perhaps most often the very issue I was facing. It was sucking energy from me, consuming my thoughts, and eating away at my effectiveness—but I did not realize it.

What was my looming disaster? Imagine my organization racing down the highway at high speed while I, the lead driver, was going blind. Not a total blackout. I actually thought my visual acuity was pretty sharp. However, a crucial part of my vision—the part called self-awareness—was going dark. I was growing less and less aware: less aware of how my emotional reactions were affecting others, less aware of my response to situations that made me unhappy or uncomfortable, and particularly, less aware that my concern about what people thought of me was becoming increasingly unhealthy.

Others were noting my clouded self-perception; as a result, my effectiveness as a leader was diminishing. By God's grace some key people, friends, coaches, and fellow workers gently (mostly) and gradually helped me realize that I need-ed some corrective lenses—a spiritual Lasik procedure, if you will—or I was going to run myself, and perhaps the whole company, off the road.

Of the thousands of books written on leadership, I wonder how many focus on genuine self-knowledge? A few, I am sure, but not nearly as many as emphasize strategy, teamwork, and the like. After examining my own journey and seeing similar issues in other leaders, I realize that self-awareness is one of the most important of all requirements for successful leadership—perhaps *the* most important.

Self-awareness is the filter through which we see and interpret our behaviors and the responses of others toward those behaviors. When the filter is clear, we are the first to recognize unhealthy responses, and we make the necessary adjustments. When the filter is clouded by our egos and self-interest, we become blinded to our own destructive attitudes and actions, sometimes leaving wounded and confused colaborers by the roadside. I recall, with some pain, the times I have gone on the attack—usually not outright aggression, more like a few jabs—to ward off a perceived threat.

As much as we try to give these behaviors more palatable names, the Bible calls them sins—the sin of arrogance and self-importance (see Psalm 119:21; James 3:14-16). And as much as I profess to abhor such behavior—and even coach and teach exactly the opposite—some of this attitude still crept into my life while I was unaware. I began to care too much about what others thought of me. At the core of my insecurity was a slow slide down the slippery slope of self-regard. I do not think any of us ever intends such arrogance; we just fall into it without realizing that it is happening. For me it found a foothold in the self-delusion that I needed to help others honor those in authority over them—in this case, me. I began to think too highly of myself and not highly enough of those who surrounded me. I was blinded to the very leadership quality I needed most: a humble awareness of how my behaviors affect and influence those around me.

In my ongoing recovery from self-importance, I more clearly see how many of my fellow leaders struggle with these same issues. We may be the first to admit we are sinners, but we often fail to pursue a thorough and honest assessment of how our leadership behaviors affect those around us. We settle for a deeper knowledge of business management principles and skills. We devote significant time, resources, and energy to pursuing greater management competencies. We may expend serious effort in finding our innate strengths. These pursuits often give us good insights and help us grow in leadership effectiveness, but we desperately need something more. We need to understand how our self-awareness can either help or hinder our leadership effectiveness.

Daniel Goleman in his book *Working with Emotional Intelligence* describes self-awareness as "knowing one's internal states, preferences, resources, and intuitions," including:

- **❿** Emotional awareness: Recognizing one's emotions and their effects
- **❿** Accurate self-assessment: Knowing one's strengths and limits
- **❿** Self-confidence: A strong sense of one's self-worth and capabilities[1]

Healthy self-awareness is an ongoing battle, particularly unique to those of us in leadership roles. Make no mistake; it is a spiritual battle against forces of darkness determined to render us blind to our need for God's all-sufficient grace and wisdom. It is a battle between Spirit-enlightened self-awareness and self-important myopia. Sometimes self-importance wins, at least for a season. Such failure puts up walls that can hinder the Holy Spirit from making the internal changes he desires in all of us. We prevent him from teaching us what it means to lead. Those same walls often make our peers and fellow leaders reticent to speak the truth *to* us *about* us.

The psalmists were experts at admitting shortcomings before God. For example, David said, "O LORD, you have searched me and you know me. You know when I sit and when I rise; you perceive my thoughts from afar. You discern my going out and my lying down; you are familiar with all my ways. Before a word is on my tongue you know it completely" (Psalm 139:1-4).

God already knows our every thought and action—it is impossible to fool him. He is not surprised by what we do or think. The wonder of God-centered self-awareness is that it informs us of what God already knows. We are generally the only one blinded to our shortcomings, usually by our own pride and arrogance. Or perhaps we *are* aware but find ourselves hamstrung by fear of that acknowledgment, believing that weakness impairs our ability to lead. The comedic reality is that those close to us clearly see the truth—sometimes the emperor has no clothes!

// THE VALUE OF SELF-AWARENESS //

The position of CEO (or president or executive director) is extraordinarily complex. The details required to manage strategy, business planning, talent development, marketing, sales, the economy, clients, and vendors are overwhelming—even when you are blessed with a gifted management team. In many ways a company (or ministry) *is* the CEO. It reflects his values, which have permeated the organization. CEOs are not merely the public faces of the company; they shape the *character* of the company. The values and behaviors of the CEO set the standard for all employees. The sobering reality is that with few exceptions, organizational success—and failure—lands squarely at the feet of the CEO. Leadership is a mantle that should not be accepted lightly.

Leading people is complex, invigorating, and unusually humbling. For this reason it is vital that a leader clearly understand his or her strengths, as well as areas for improvement. Here are five questions that I have found especially helpful in my own development journey:

1. Am I truly committed to lifelong leadership development?
2. Do I regularly seek honest feedback from those around me?
3. Am I aware of how my attitudes and behaviors affect others?
4. Do I insist on regular, formal evaluations of my performance?
5. Do I have an ongoing relationship with a "truth coach" or mentor?

The answers to those questions can be both wonderfully affirming and horribly deflating. There have been times that I have seriously questioned my ability and calling to leadership. Yet if I accept the mantle of leadership, I must accept the kind of truth that allows the Holy Spirit to transform my motives and my behaviors. Let us consider in some depth each of those important questions.

1. AM I TRULY COMMITTED TO LIFELONG LEADERSHIP DEVELOPMENT?

Our answer to the frequently asked question "Are leaders born or made?" probably influences our development more than we realize. If we believe they are "born," we can easily find ourselves relying too much on natural ability—much like the child musical prodigy who does not practice much because she is so talented. If we think that leaders are "made"—that most anyone can be a leader—we could find ourselves pursuing unrealistic goals. This answer, I think, is both but not equally. Natural ability matters, but how we develop our abilities matters more.

The apostle Paul seems to hold this view when he speaks of the spiritual gift of leadership in Romans 12:6-8: "We have different gifts, according to the grace given us. If a man's gift is . . . leadership, let him govern diligently." There is a gift of leadership given by the Holy Spirit to some believers. This clearly is a gift that goes beyond natural ability; it's a Spirit-imbued potential to lead others.

However, notice the rest of the instruction: "let him govern diligently." We all know, or know of, very gifted people who never quite make it. And we are sometimes surprised when the improbable leader arises from seemingly nowhere. Most of the time, when we take a closer look, preparation and diligent practice account for much of the difference. Someone once commented to golf legend Arnold Palmer that he seemed to make more lucky shots than anyone else. Palmer responded, "It's a funny thing, the more I practice the luckier I get."[2]

Malcolm Gladwell, in *Outliers,* writes about the ten-thousand-hour rule. He cites growing evidence that the difference between good violinists (or soccer players, authors . . . you name it) and those who are truly *great* can be found in their commitment to practice. According to one study, those violinists who are good practice about eight thousand hours in their development years, while those who go on to true greatness have practiced ten thousand hours. According to Gladwell, "The people at the very top don't work just harder or even much harder than everyone else. They work much, *much* harder."[3]

Christopher Parkening, one of the world's great classical guitarists, tells about the pain and discipline of practice. When Christopher was twelve years old, his father realized that the boy had a special musical gift. "You want to play the guitar? Then you need to get up every morning at 5 a.m. and start practicing at 5:30. Your mother will have breakfast for you at 7:00. When you get home from school, you will practice another hour and a half."

Parkening continues, "I was stunned. I thought, *Am I joining the army? . . .* All at once I went from being a carefree kid, excited to play the guitar . . . to a very serious student of the instrument. . . . Every day I was up by 5 a.m.—or else—in a house that was totally dark and quiet. At first I set an alarm clock, but the sound of the loud alarm startled me, so I learned to wake up before it went off. . . . At exactly 5:30 I would pick up the guitar, turn on the metronome, and start my musical exercises."[4]

Granted, there is a threshold level of inborn giftedness that must be present in potential leaders. But that is all it is—potential.[5] If we aspire to leadership, we must pursue a lifetime of rigorous leadership development. That rigor is what Paul had in mind when he wrote, "Run in such a way as to get the prize. . . . I beat my body and make it my slave so that after I have preached to others, I myself will not be disqualified for the prize" (1 Corinthians 9:24-27).

We should also ask, "Leadership to what end?" Am I just as committed to the purpose of Christian leadership as I am to my leadership development? Christian leadership transcends the sometimes too simplistic notion that leadership is merely influence. Our ultimate purpose in leadership is to accomplish that which matters to God—things that have value not just on this earth but in Heaven as well. It is what Jesus meant when he charged his followers to store up for themselves treasures in Heaven (Matthew 6:20). That simple perspective has transformed my leadership values over the years. I want to lead in such a way that God may be pleased with the results across the full spectrum of my leadership responsibilities.

Is it really possible to consider others better than myself (Philippians 2:3, 4), even if only sometimes? Can I really honor and encourage those whom I lead? I am always amazed with the impact of even little acts of thoughtfulness in the workplace. Sharyn just retired after twenty-three years of effective, faithful service in our call center. Over the years her fellow workers would often hear her tell someone, 'You are loved.' At her retirement celebration, she told me, "I still have that refrigerator magnet you gave me." I must have responded with a blank look, so she went on: "You and Cindy went on a trip—it was shortly after I started with ECCU—and you brought me back a magnet that says 'You are loved.'" Such a small way of honoring someone—at least to me—but obviously worth more than twenty years in a prominent place on Sharyn's refrigerator.

Whether we aspire to lead in a company or ministry, as Christians we must first be Spirit-led leaders, evidenced by specific character traits. A place to begin is with the character qualifications for church leaders found in 1 Timothy 3 and Titus 1. While these lists are specific to elders and deacons, why would we settle for less in our leadership roles? Would those who know me best say I am self-controlled, respectable, hospitable, able to teach, not given to drunkenness, not violent, not greedy for money? Would they say I am gentle, not quarrelsome, not overbearing, and not pursuing dishonest gain? Would they think of me as one who rules my own house well, whose children are obedient and respectful? (If I cannot manage my own home, why would I think I could effectively manage a ministry or company?) Would they affirm my good reputation among those outside the church?

These are basic character qualities required of every Christian leader. Yet we do not have to look very far to find leaders in churches and Christian organizations who obviously fall short of these threshold leadership qualities. Why? Too often they are enamored by style and external indicators of success, like making lots of money or achieving lofty business goals or merely possessing an affable personality. God asks for a lot from a leader, but we sometimes let our leaders get away with less than God's best. Perhaps of greater concern, we also often settle for less when we're the ones leading.

None of us fully meets the qualifications listed in Paul's letters to Timothy and Titus. However, potential leaders must ask whether their shortcomings are great enough to cause them to earnestly pursue further growth before accepting more responsibility. Or maybe you meet the threshold character requirements of a particular leadership role, while knowing that further on-the-job development is nonetheless needed. Spirit-led character is a lifelong pursuit as we press on toward the high calling of Christ. Every Christian leader must ask often, "Does my character, albeit flawed, bring honor to God and to the ministry or company I lead?"

We must still have the ability to manage well, demonstrating sufficient technical expertise, training, and experience. Obviously, the bar rises and lowers depending on the position. An emerging leader of a smaller team requires less than the president of an organization. If you have been promoted to a position, then in all likelihood someone has determined that you have enough ability to be offered the position. Now it is up to you to continue to grow and improve.

Finally, are other people confirming my gift and competence? Do other Christian leaders affirm my honest and candid self-evaluation? Do secular onlookers confirm this? Do bosses, colleagues, friends, and family affirm me as a leader? Do they see my character and ability to lead? Do they also sense that I am *called* to this role? God raises up those he chooses. Sometimes he chooses people to lead for a season and sometimes for a lifetime. Either way, we remain utterly dependent on the Lord.

2. DO I REGULARLY SEEK HONEST FEEDBACK FROM THOSE AROUND ME?

I embrace an open-door policy and generally welcome feedback and advice from throughout the company. However, I am wary of this well-intended attempt at vulnerability. Few people actually make an appointment with the CEO to express opinions or concerns, but leaders hold out their open invitation as proof of their accessibility. We need to actively and creatively seek out feedback. That is why our organization regularly participates in the Best Christian Workplaces survey, reporting the results to the entire workforce and identifying specific steps we will take to improve our stewardship of the company.

One of the most informative attributes of a good leader is that she or he is not reluctant to ask for help. Good leaders sincerely ask questions like these:

- "How did I do?"
- "What do you think?"
- "That's my idea. Do you have a better one?"

- *"I have no idea how to manage this problem. Can you advise me?"*
- *"Could you lead this project? I think you're the best person to do the job."*

Some time ago I met with a number of our vice presidents and asked them to be thinking about an important new initiative we needed to pursue. Later I heard some concerns about how I went about introducing such an important new business priority, so I asked one of the younger leaders how I might have done it differently. And he proceeded to tell me! His critique, though gracious, was candid and spot-on. In my intensity to get the thing done, I had bypassed important and appropriate feedback loops, and failed to consider the needless ambiguity I was introducing to our strategic plan. As a result of his candid assessment, we ended up with a much better process—and that VP headed up the team.

One more thing: I am thankful that this young leader felt safe enough and had sufficient courage to respectfully challenge the CEO. It made me wonder how many times I may have stifled much-needed feedback and missed some great opportunities to include our younger leaders.

3. AM I AWARE OF HOW MY ATTITUDES AND BEHAVIORS AFFECT OTHERS?

An executive in our company let me know recently that I had caused him some personal discomfort at a recent board meeting. Actually, it was worse than that. He was giving an important report to the board, and I jumped in with a lengthy extemporaneous analysis of my own, essentially hijacking his report. In the moment, I thought I was adding some helpful perspective, but what really happened was a subtle message that I knew more about the subject matter than my fellow executive. This was a failure of leadership on two levels. The first is obvious—I dishonored my fellow worker by seeming to appear more informed than he was. (I wasn't.) The second level was of greater consequence—I had zero awareness of the impact my behavior had on those around me. It is exactly this kind of blindness that leaves wounded friends and coworkers along our pathway and, uncorrected, renders otherwise gifted leaders ineffective.

4. DO I INSIST ON REGULAR, FORMAL EVALUATIONS OF MY PERFORMANCE?

I am blessed with an excellent, godly board of directors. It is a pleasure to work for and with them. They have just one employee—the CEO. I report to them, and they speak as one to me. One of the most important duties of the board is to give their sole employee regular feedback on his job performance. They do this by holding an executive session every time we meet—no staff present, just the CEO and the board. There are only two things on the executive session agenda: the performance of the CEO and the performance of the board. In these meetings I report on key issues I am facing, and they give me candid and informal feedback on how I am doing. This process helps us keep short accounts and be alert to when things are starting to get off track.

Another way they assess my performance is through a formal annual review. It consists of about twenty-five questions with numeric scores plus commentary. Our board chair reviews the results with me privately. I then dialogue with the full board in executive session. It is a rigorous but respectful and fair process. It can also be affirming and sometimes humbling. A few of the questions are:

- Are short-term and long-term strategies appropriately defined?
- Is the CEO addressing the brutal realities that confront us?
- Has the CEO been effective in executing board-driven priorities?
- Does the CEO have the right people on the leadership bus?
- Is the CEO providing sufficient and appropriate information to the board?
- Has the CEO adequately addressed any issues/concerns raised by the board?

The answers to those questions greatly help both the board and me to assess my performance. However, I always check the board's response to the ninth question first, perhaps revealing a touch of insecurity: *Is the CEO the right person for the job?* Actually, it is the most important question in the assessment, both for the board and the CEO. The directors are not allowed a yes or no response option. The scale is 1–7, with a 4 response discouraged. So a positive score could be a stellar 7 or a lukewarm 5, with the responses to the other questions providing context and perspective.

This assessment can be a powerful tool in identifying job performance skills that need attention. The assessment could point to minor adjustments, such as a need to focus more on expense control. Or it could reveal much greater issues, such as weak strategic planning, a disconnect with the board's vision for the organization, or interpersonal tensions between board members or among the senior leadership team.

One Monday morning a CEO friend arrived at his office to find the chairman of the board waiting for him. He was stunned to hear that his services would no longer be required. He told me later that his last review was positive and that his company had hit or exceeded all its financial goals. Months later he still could not figure out why he was summarily dismissed. As I listened to his story, I began to suspect that he had gotten sideways with his board, and especially the chairman, without ever realizing it. Subtle differences in style, priorities, and vision had crept in but were never addressed. The board slowly began to conclude that this talented and otherwise successful leader just "wasn't a fit." They decided it would be easier to start anew.

No CEO should be totally surprised when the board concludes that it is time for him or her to move on. Yet it happens too often. Leaders should insist on regular informal and formal assessments for their own sake and for the sake of the organization. They must value and cultivate open, candid, and ongoing communication with their boards.

5. DO I HAVE AN ONGOING RELATIONSHIP WITH A "TRUTH COACH" OR MENTOR?

I engaged the services of a professional executive coach about ten years ago, at first to work with my executive team.[6] I was a bit skeptical but quickly realized that I should have had a coach years before. A coach will run you through a battery of tests (or assessments) and dialogue with your team, others in the company, and your board. I was particularly wary of the 360-degree assessment he proposed. My experience with these instruments was not positive, often unleashing a flood of painful and hurtful commentary that left recipients devastated. I soon found out that, though painful, such an assessment administered by a skilled coach helps establish a foundation for a truly transformational personal development plan.[7]

Coaching is not a one-time meeting. Effective coaches will meet for months, or even years, with those they coach. Please do not confuse coaching and counseling. Both are helpful, but the distinction is significant. A counselor focuses solely on the individual. A coach's work is *contextual,* and is not limited to what the individual tells him. A coach should have deep understanding of the leadership team and the business plan of the organization. That is why I invite my coach to join our leadership planning sessions, observing and sometimes facilitating our discussion. This gives the coach intimate knowledge of the company and the personal interactions of the leadership team.

Some of the very best feedback and counsel I receive come from sources outside my employ. Some are friends, some are colleagues in other organizations, and some are other professionals who know me well. Since I am not paying these people, they have more freedom to speak candidly with me. Generally, I know they love me and are only concerned about my own well-being (physical, mental, and spiritual) and the well-being of my family and my organization. I meet with one particularly helpful friend and mentor three or four times a year just to talk about new business ideas, my relationship with my team, my personal life, and the challenge of living out my faith in the workplace.

Ask those five questions candidly and consistently, and you will be well on your way to a process of God-centered self-awareness that transforms you and your organization.

// ELUSIVE HUMILITY //

Most leaders embrace their desperate need for true humility, or at least the idea of it. Actually leading with genuine humility is another thing altogether. Most leaders struggle with some measure of God-displacing pride. It was the first sin (at least many commentators believe that the words of Isaiah 14:14—"I will make myself like the Most High"—are Satan's words in an account that describes why he was cast out of Heaven). And even now that deadly pathogen is constantly waiting, ready to pounce the moment our spiritual immune systems weaken. Leaders are prone to a particular strain of the deadly pride virus, this insidious sense of self-sufficiency. We embrace too much the power and prestige of our jobs. We think too highly of our skills and education, especially when things are going well. We gradually begin to esteem ourselves more than others.

We begin to give God's amazing grace and daily guidance mere lip service. Arrogance creeps in. The verb form of that word *arrogance* is *arrogate,* "to claim or seize without justification, to make undue claims to having."[8] Leadership arrogance is assuming for ourselves that which belongs only to God. In our hearts we give him only partial credit for our success, for sustaining us amid the battle, and even for granting us our daily bread. And we begin to act against some of our seemingly strongest convictions, behaving as if our skills and our wisdom are sufficient. As a result, we do not seek help when we need it most. We do not recognize our dependence on the unique giftedness of our colaborers.

A fellow worker in our company once told about a former boss who lost all credibility with her. He talked a lot about the need to respect and serve one another. Then one day she found herself alone in the elevator with him. He did not say or do anything inappropriate. The issue was that he did not say *anything*. He was oblivious to her presence. It was as if she were not there. Yes, the executive could have been preoccupied that day, but this was not an isolated event. Most people in that ministry saw their leader as aloof. Maybe he thought the role of a CEO requires a certain measure of appropriate professional distance from the workforce. I do not think we should try to be friends with everyone. However, we should ponder just how that reconciles with regarding one another as more important than ourselves.

Humility is seeing ourselves not as we think others should see us but as God alone sees us. In his eyes we are broken human beings saved by the supreme sacrifice of his Son. We all are completely dependent on his amazing grace. The truly humble leader understands that he is, in the eyes of God, better than no one else. Humility also means that we understand our dependence on one another. Leadership is a role, a calling, and a gift, but our role as a leader does not in itself make us better than anyone else. We may be at the top of the organizational chart, but in a way, that only means we are the most dependent.

That reality first hit me when I realized that I could no longer do most jobs in our company; indeed, I did not even understand some of the jobs under me. Sometimes at the end of the day, I wander around the building and try to imagine doing some of the work performed in those offices and cubicles. Could I wire funds to countries around the world, perfectly, day in and day out? Could I reconcile our bank account? (And we are the bank!) Could I operate even one of those computer servers? Hey, I still have trouble transferring calls. The truth is that I am completely dependent on all workers doing their jobs well. Yes, I can set the standard; I can cast the vision (to some degree); and I can exhort, encourage, reward, and discipline. However, I'm still dependent on just about everyone in order to be able to declare that I have succeeded in my job. In a very real sense, I am the most dependent person in our company.

So why do so many leaders have such a hard time asking for help? For me, there are still times I worry that seeking help or expressing my dependence on others could somehow reveal my own weakness, perhaps suggesting that I may not be strong enough or smart enough or capable enough to do my job. Thinking in this way actually weakens my leadership character. A humble sense of dependence, on the Lord and our fellow workers, is a great source of strength as we realize that we are most effective when we are most aware of our own weaknesses. It is what the apostle Paul meant in some measure when he said, "That is why, for Christ's sake, I delight in weaknesses, in insults, in hardships, in persecutions, in difficulties. For when I am weak, then I am strong" (2 Corinthians 12:10).

//THE NEED FOR GODLY CONFIDENCE //

All this dependence, critical though it may be, is in stark contrast to a leader's need for confidence. Who wants to follow an insecure, uncertain, and tentative leader? James tells us that "a double-minded man [is] unstable in all he does" (James 1:8). I believe God requires that leaders be confident, but in the right things. We should be confident in our calling, confident in our competencies, but even more confident in our trust in the Lord. Our greatest source of confidence is a simple trust that the Lord will lead and work through circumstances we simply cannot control. Believing this truth has changed my life and my leadership effectiveness.

There are times when a leader questions his or her competence or fit. And we should. Just because we were called and affirmed five or ten years ago does not mean we have somehow earned leadership tenure. That is why we should regularly seek critique, evaluation, and confirmation of our roles from peers, counselors, and boards. Doing so has led me to a little aphorism that frequently reminds me of my own frailty and ongoing need for personal and spiritual growth:

> The Mark Holbrook of five years ago was not equipped to run our company today. In the same way, the Mark Holbrook of today is not equipped to lead our company five years from now.

We should not be surprised to fail miserably at times. We sometimes shock ourselves with bouts of pride, displays of self-sufficiency, and thoughts of superiority. Leadership is a siren song calling us to lift ourselves higher. So we might feel, at least sometimes, that we need to prove our worthiness; and in so doing we unconsciously seek out the praise of others. We struggle with pride. We are human and, therefore, frail.

The only solution is to plead with our heavenly Father for his mercy and grace in order to obey the command to have the same attitude as Jesus, "who, being in very nature God, did not consider equality with God something to be grasped, but made himself nothing, taking the very nature of a servant, being made in human likeness. And being found in appearance as a man, he humbled himself and became obedient to death—even death on a cross!" (Philippians 2:6-8).

Bottom line: Humility and deep, God-centered self-awareness are required to become an effective leadership disciple of Christ—a marvelous, yet fearful calling.

MY LEADERSHIP BOOKSHELF

Leadership Jazz by Max De Pree (Doubleday, 1992) speaks from the heart of a CEO about the sacred responsibility of every leader to draw out the best in others, much like the leader of a jazz band helps band members express beautiful, yet sometimes unpredictable music. I have reflected often on De Pree's insight, "Leadership is . . . a serious meddling in other people's lives."[9]

The Rest of God: Restoring Your Soul by Restoring Sabbath by Mark Buchanan (Thomas Nelson, 2006) beautifully challenges every driven leader: rest, physical and spiritual, is essential soul care that we ignore at our peril. There is a lot more to life balance than taking days off or even making the kids' soccer game. Buchanan helped me understand, finally, how "busyness kills the heart."

The Five Temptations of a CEO: A Leadership Fable by Patrick Lencioni (Jossey-Bass, 1998) has become a must-read for every leader. Leaders are responsible for results, yet we often let our egos and insecurities torpedo our success. Lencioni's leadership fable quickly draws us into the story, forcing us to ask, "Could this be me?"

////// PERSONAL REFLECTIONS AND APPLICATIONS //////

1. To what ends and for whose purposes do you desire to be a leader? The answers to this question can be your first step into a God-centered self-awareness that fits you more fully for his kingdom work. What is the nature of the treasures you are storing up in Heaven?

2. In what specific ways does your leadership behavior impact others and your organization? What does your leadership behavior reveal about your innermost longings, values, and ultimate goals?

3. Spend some prayerful time in Psalm 139, reflecting on how you might make this passage your own benchmark for God-centered self-awareness. What portions affirm your leadership? Which verses bring conviction to your spirit? What changes do you need to make in your self-awareness to be able to sing this psalm in unison with King David?

4. The childhood story of "The Emperor's New Clothes" is a powerful awakening to our own self-delusions. Ask God to reveal to you how others view your leadership persona. Use this chapter's reflections on the qualifications for deacons and elders from 1 Timothy 3 and Titus 1 to craft a self-awareness narrative, and then test it on some trusted friends and colleagues to see if they see what you see.

5. Who in your circle of family, colleagues, and friends have you given permission to "speak the truth in love" about your impact as a leader?

6. Review the responses you had to the questions throughout this chapter. Develop a plan for growing in your God-centered self-awareness. Select

a couple of people to help you be accountable for the implementation of that plan.

///////// TEAM REFLECTIONS AND APPLICATIONS /////////

1. What assessment tools are you using to help your organization become corporately more self-aware—internally as well as how you are perceived externally?

2. In your efforts to project an image of your organization that appears effective and worthy of support, have you become prideful and arrogant? Do others describe your efforts and results as seasoned with humility?

3. As an organization, do you intentionally encourage and support the development of leadership gifts and skills among your colleagues and co-workers? How well do you affirm positive leadership growth? What steps can you take immediately to encourage the maturing of God-centered and self-aware leadership?

4. Recognizing that while there are some employment law limitations impacting your personnel policies, how can you better utilize Paul's descriptions of mature leaders in 1 Timothy 3 and Titus 1 to set the expectations for leadership development and performance?

MARK G. HOLBROOK
PRESIDENT/CEO, EVANGELICAL CHRISTIAN CREDIT UNION
///

Mark G. Holbrook is president/CEO of the Evangelical Christian Credit Union (www.eccu.org) headquartered in Brea, California.

ECCU is the leading banking resource for evangelical Christian ministries nationwide. A member-owned financial institution, ECCU provides banking, finance, and cash management services to U.S.–based ministries. Its members include churches, schools, parachurch ministries, plus missionaries in over one hundred countries. ECCU has more than 275 staff members nationwide.

Holbrook began his career with ECCU in 1975, shortly after graduating from Biola College (now University), and was named to ECCU's top management position in 1979. He has earned a reputation as an aggressive but focused innovator. Assets have grown under his management from $4 million to nearly $3 billion through a variety of lending and cash management services designed to meet unique ministry needs.

Holbrook's passion is integration of biblical principles into the workplace. Under his leadership, ECCU was named one of the top ten Christian places to work by *Christianity Today* magazine and the Best Christian Workplaces Institute in both 2003 and 2006. He also won the 2010 Ethical Edge Leaders of Integrity Award presented by Passkeys Foundation.

Holbrook has served as board chairman for the Christian Leadership Alliance and on the board for the Evangelical Council for Financial Accountability (ECFA).

He and his wife, Cindy, have served in ministry at Grace Church in Orange, California, for forty years. They have five children and fourteen grandchildren.

7

///

WINNING THE BATTLE FOR YOUR ORGANIZATION'S SOUL

JOSEPH KRIVICKAS

J oseph, who served as one of the editors for this book, shares some key insights from both his professional and personal journey as an intentional Christ-centered leader. His belief in and passion for the next generation of leaders as men and women uniquely equipped for the opportunities and challenges of the digital age of leadership is evident as he challenges them to lead with courage, conviction, hope, and sacrifice.

Detailing his conviction that character-based leadership must be the focus for this emerging generation, he emphasizes that being a great leader is much more than just achieving great results. Character-based leaders are empowered to win the battle for the soul of their organizations. They win by effectively communicating their organization's core values, remaining focused on mission, serving as "the eyes that no one sees," and diligently building a sense of meaningful community and interpersonal connections. Joseph believes that, with God's help, this next generation of leaders can achieve lasting results by using these concepts to measure and mold both their own character and their organization's character, one day at a time.

Would you believe me if I told you that some of the most successful CEOs of nonprofit and for-profit organizations are more concerned about the character of their companies than their financial results? They believe that the daily tests of their organization's character—what their team does when no one is looking—are battles for the very soul of their company. For character-based leaders, an organization with a healthy moral core is the ultimate competitive advantage. CEOs of for-profit organizations who practice character-based leadership usually have a lot in common with leaders of nonprofit organizations. Let's consider how you can win the battle for the soul of your organization—whether it is a ministry, a Little League baseball team, or a business—by being a character-based leader.

// IT'S ALL ABOUT YOU—THE EMERGING GENERATION //

It's all about you—the emerging generation who is already beginning to fill the leadership roles within Christ's kingdom. As a society, we need you. You are well armed to serve Christ. You inspire most of the philanthropic and for-profit CEOs I know. You have a remarkable sense of service and a sense of being part of a much larger world. We cannot wait for you to take on the leadership reins to run our organizations!

One reason you are poised to lead is that our culture is in transition. The previous generation of leaders was among the first to have spent their entire lives with nuclear missiles pointed at them, while you, the emerging generation, are the first to grow up in a global culture defined by media technologies.

People think and make decisions based on a set of rules that they learned growing up. These rules are applicable to the age and environment in which they were raised. Sometimes that age changes, as it did when we shifted from the agricultural age to the industrial age and then, more recently, from the industrial age to the information age. Organizations caught in the middle of these transitions have to change the very foundations on which they were built. When these transitions happen, most individuals, and society as a whole, undergo enormous stress as they adapt to their new environment.

In 1991, I began writing about how we are living in a hyper-information age. Some researchers have hypothesized that an individual living in Western society today receives thousands and thousands more bits of stimulation a day than did a person living in the same society a few hundred years ago. For instance, it is said that a single copy of the *Wall Street Journal* has the same amount of information that someone would have digested during his or her entire lifetime in the 1700s.[1] Having sat on the front line of the information technology business for the last twenty years, I believe it. I have watched individuals who have not adapted to the new requirements of the hyper-information age develop anxiety—expressed through knotted stomachs, pounding hearts, and nervous gestures. I will never forget sitting in a meeting with a well-known executive, who said that the best advice he could give for succeeding today was for everyone to keep a package of Rolaids in their pockets. What really frightened me was the number of people at the meeting who agreed with him!

The stress that technology is placing on organizations can be as severe as two plates of the earth shifting, like an earthquake causing devastation of net worth and regional economies. Facing those stresses requires more than an antacid; it requires a leader who is prepared. Unlike other generations, the emerging generation does not have to adapt to the hyper-information age, because you have grown up in it. You are prepared for the present age both culturally and technologically. The challenge for you is to grow the character needed to lead others in this age. By Christ's grace, you will be the character-based leaders we long for.

// THE SOUL OF AN ORGANIZATION IS ALWAYS UNDER ATTACK //

When I was in U.S. Army officer reconnaissance training, we went through periods when we were deprived of sleep and food for days. And just when we were completely at the weakest point of our mental and physical abilities, they would put us into some of the most stressful and intense portions of our training. We used to huddle together and wonder, *Why in the world are they doing this to us?* I think they did this to see if each of us was capable of being molded to share the soul—the moral core—of an army that had been in existence for over a hundred years. The moral core of the U.S. Army is communicated in its values of loyalty, duty, respect, selfless service, honor, integrity, and personal courage. When we were pushed to our limits of physical, mental, and emotional exhaustion, we couldn't fake what was inside our individual souls. Our true values surfaced.

Such times are also when we get to know the soul of an organization.

Around 1450 BC, Moses dispatched twelve reconnaissance soldiers—one from each tribe of Israel—to scout the land of Israel and report back specifically on the agriculture and the lay of the land. God had promised Israel that they would conquer the Canaanites who were occupying the land. The twelve scouts returned, and ten gave negative reports that the land was inhabited by giants and fortified cities that they would never be able to conquer.

In contrast, two scouts, Joshua and Caleb, gave positive reports that the land was good and ready to be conquered. For their truthfulness, Joshua and Caleb were about to be stoned, but God intervened and punished the Israelites, forcing them to wander in the desert for forty years, one year for each of the forty days that they had had to wait for the scouts to return from their mission (Numbers 13, 14).

Why did Joshua and Caleb respond so differently than the others? All twelve scouts had had a front row seat and witnessed God's hand in the ten plagues against Egypt, the parting of the Red Sea, and many other miracles. Yet the ten—a leader from each tribe—backed down when faced with this opposition. What happened? The soul of the ten tribes, as portrayed by their scouts, came under attack right at the critical hour; and their moral core surfaced, a moral core that did not reflect God's values. On the other hand, Joshua and Caleb's moral core surfaced true to God's values.

Character-based leaders need to understand that the soul of their organization is under constant attack, even in the eleventh hour of a journey. The moral core that has been built into an organization beforehand is what will come to the surface when the attack comes. Therefore, a leader always has to be concerned about building the moral core of his or her organization.

// BUILDING THE MORAL CORE OF YOUR ORGANIZATION //

How do you build the moral core of an organization? There is no simple process, but here are some key points.

COMMUNICATE YOUR ORGANIZATION'S VALUES

Communicate your organization's values all the time. On paper most organizations have good values, such as honesty, excellence, diligence, and serving people. The problem often is how leaders communicate those values throughout their organization.

Many leaders write their organizational values in a list like this:

❶ People first
❶ Customers
❶ Quality
❶ Make money

The problem with such a list is that it is hierarchical—it implies a ranking in which some things are always more important than others. While this may look good on paper, in reality it is difficult to find balance in lists. Rather than a list, your organizational values should look like a wheel with each value as a spoke. A smoothly functioning wheel has balanced spokes.

Every day your team will encounter situations that will test your group's values. Some days the terrain for these tests will be smooth; some days the terrain will be rugged. You want your team to be able to adjust and adapt quickly—to find balance—so they can apply your group's values in a way that is appropriate for changing situations. For example, Jesus represented the values of God at all times. However, he followed a path during his life on earth that emphasized different values for different situations. Character-based leaders can learn from Jesus' example:

❶ His value of love showed him weeping for Lazarus.

- His value of hatred of evil was seen in how he threw the moneychangers out of God's temple.
- His value of trust was demonstrated in Gethsemane when he asked that God's will, not his, be done.

A character-based leader learns how to apply the appropriate value to each situation. For example, sometimes the value of excellence may take precedence over the value of giving followers autonomy to carry out a task the way that seems best to them. A leader needs to see the organization's values as an array that he can apply as best fits a given situation, rather than as a hierarchical list in which any particular value trumps the values lower on the list. Viewing your organization's values as a wheel rather than a list will help you do this.

FOCUS ON MISSION

If your organization's values are the spokes of the wheel, then your mission is the wheel's hub. Your group exists for a purpose—a mission. One of the biggest fears your team members have is that they might be part of something that is meaningless. To lead effectively, you will need to specifically identify your group's meaning, its mission, and then teach them to think of this mission as the central focus, or hub, of all that they do. Of course, to do this you need to have a clear mission statement as the hub of your wheel. An ideal mission statement conforms to the following simple guidelines:

- It is not more than one sentence long.
- An eighth grader can understand it.
- Under pressure, everyone will be able to recite it.

Does that sound simple? It is if you get it right. The Salvation Army has a membership that includes more than 17,000 active and more than 8,700 retired officers. There are more than a million "soldiers," around 100,000 other employees, and more than 4.5 million volunteers. That number of people provides the potential for complexity. But what is The Salvation Army's mission statement? *"Its mission is to preach the gospel of Jesus Christ and to meet human needs in His name without discrimination."*[2] This is an example of a clear and simple mission statement that is highly effective.

Your organization will encounter daily battles that, when added together, test its ability to survive. To grow and thrive, it will need to have endurance. Endurance will develop when your group believes their work is contributing to something meaningful. Character-based leaders give their team a strong sense of meaning in their work by forming an easily understood, memorable mission and making it the hub of all their organization's actions.

STAY ON STRATEGY

Once you define and communicate your organization's values and mission, you then need to clarify and communicate where you are headed. As the spokes of the organization wheel are values and the hub is its mission, strategic vision is the direction in which you want your wheel to be heading. Your team members have a lot of fires to put out each day. So you will be the one who needs to spend as much time as necessary to make sure your organization is heading in the right direction.

Strategic vision is all about *what*:

❦ What is your organization today?
❦ What do you want your organization to become?

The answers to those two questions help form your strategic objectives.

Once you have clarified and communicated your organizational wheel, you then need to step back and *watch*.

BE THE EYES THAT NO ONE SEES

Character-based leaders take an honest look at what their organization is doing when no one is watching. On a daily basis, they check and recheck to make sure their values, mission, and strategic vision are being lived out.

The character of an organization is revealed by what the members do when no one is watching. God instructed Gideon to build an army to fight the Midianites. He started with twenty-two thousand soldiers. But God instructed Gideon to send home those men who were afraid, and he was left with ten thousand. Then God provided a window into the soul of Gideon's army.

> The LORD said to Gideon, "There are still too many men. Take them down to the water, and I will sift them for you there. If I say, 'This one shall go with you,' he shall go; but if I say, 'This one shall not go with you,' he shall not go."
>
> So Gideon took the men down to the water. There the LORD told him, "Separate those who lap the water with their tongues like a dog from those who kneel down to drink." Three hundred men lapped with their hands to their mouths. All the rest got down on their knees to drink.
>
> The LORD said to Gideon, "With the three hundred men that lapped I will save you and give the Midianites into your hands. Let all the other men go, each to his own place" (Judges 7:4-7).

What Gideon's army did when they thought no one was watching was a window into the organization's soul. The Scripture does not tell us exactly why God chose the ones who lapped water from their hands instead of the ones who knelt down. I personally think it may have been because those who knelt down were men who dropped their guard. They took it easy when they were tired and did not stay at the alert. But whatever the specific reason, it is clear that God saw something when these men thought no one was watching—and that something distinguished one group from the other.

What goes on in your organization when no one is watching is also a window into your organization's soul. As a result, leaders need to be the eyes that no one sees, constantly measuring their organization's actions against its values, mission, and strategic vision. Having spent most of your life under the intrusions of the media and high technology umbrella, you are incredibly well equipped to be on constant watch to see what your organization is doing "when no one is watching." The convergence of media technologies such as YouTube videos, Twitter, and Facebook has baptized the emerging generation into the new reality that there is rarely anytime when no one is watching. So apply that same concept to your leadership—be the eyes that no one sees and teach your followers that someone is always watching.

BUILD COMMUNITY

One final emphasis that helps to build the moral core of an organization is community. I think that this generation defines *organization* much more broadly than previous generations—this generation seems to be more apt to include peripheral communities in its definition of *organization*. Communities form around shared values, but then they also build and reinforce those shared values. As a result, the more a leader can do to build a sense of community in an organization, the more the organization will build its moral core.

Community does not happen by itself. Building community always takes leadership. Typically, a leader will have to make sacrifices on behalf of the community in order for the community to grow.

My wife, Lisa, was the best illustration of this principle I know. Lisa was a leader in a special segment of the medical community. She was an internationally accomplished, Harvard Medical School physician, professor, and researcher serving thousands in the Amyotrophic Lateral Sclerosis (ALS) community.

Lisa took on a different leadership role in the ALS community when she developed ALS herself. As her disease entered its final months, Lisa agreed to be the first subject of a risky medical trial that had never been used on humans. She took the risk because it could provide extremely valuable information on the safety and tolerability of this treatment approach for ALS and other similar disorders. This high-risk trial and accompanying surgery was not about Lisa, because it was too late for her to gain any benefit from the experimental procedure. Instead, it was all about her leadership for an organization comprised of tens of thousands of ALS sufferers, their family members, and health-care professionals—she was charged to help lead an organization that was a community.

On June 26, 2009, Lisa had what was supposed to be a minor surgical procedure to implant a pump that would deliver the experimental medication directly into her spinal fluid. However, things did not go well; and after ten days of immobility in the Neuro Trauma ICU and eight days in a rehabilitation hospital, she returned home in a drastically weaker state.

After four days, although she was fully paralyzed and had only 30 percent breathing capacity, Lisa bravely decided to go back to the hospital Neuro Trauma ICU for three more days so that the implanted pump could be activated and the experimental treatment started. In a very weak voice, Lisa courageously told others, "This is part of my responsibility to the ALS community. I need to offer myself up to help ALS sufferers, family members, and the health-care community." Due to the complications in that procedure, Lisa had to travel a dreadful, tortured road for her remaining days. Yet she communicated that she had done the right thing.

It is written in the book of Romans: "We know that suffering produces perseverance; perseverance, character; and character, hope. And hope does not disappoint us" (5:4, 5). In Lisa, while unfortunately we saw her tortured *suffering,* we also saw the strength of her *perseverance* and *character.* And in some way that only God is aware, he used Lisa in her leadership platform to create *hope* in members of her community. In the physical realm, Lisa created hope because she accelerated a cure for ALS by five years by being the first human subject to participate in this radical new medical treatment. In the emotional realm, through her testimony she encouraged thousands of ALS patients and researchers who are on the front lines of suffering. And in the spiritual realm, God used, and continues to use, Lisa to help people turn toward Christ—in so many ways that we will not fully see until God reveals her impact in the life to come.

Lisa sacrificed her comfort and endured increased pain in her final days for the benefit of the ALS community. That is what leaders do. Most leaders will not be asked to make sacrifices of such magnitude to build their communities, but they will have to sacrifice something. May this be a word of encouragement as you take on your demanding leadership role.

God has commanded us to pray for our leaders, for "all those in authority" (1 Timothy 2:2). Now why would he ask us to do this? I think one reason is because the leader's soul is often under attack; and if the leader's soul is weakened, then his organization is too. One area in which you will face attack is in your heart-to-heart connection to your community. Therefore, in your commitment to one another, stay devoted to prayer. As the apostle Paul wrote to the Romans: "Be devoted to one another in brotherly love. Honor one another above yourselves. Never be lacking in zeal, but keep your spiritual fervor, serving the Lord. Be joyful in hope, patient in affliction, faithful in prayer" (Romans 12:10-12).

Keep praying, and also recruit others to pray for you.

// MEASURE CHARACTER ONE DAY AT A TIME //

Being a great leader is far more than just focusing on achieving great results. Character-based leaders are winning the battle for the soul of their organizations. With daily vigilance, you can communicate your organization's values, focus on mission, stay on strategy, be the eyes that no one sees, and build community.

With God's help you can lead your team toward the achievement of great results by using these concepts to measure and mold its character, one day at a time. Our generation is praying that God will equip you for this task.

MY LEADERSHIP BOOKSHELF

The Practice of the Presence of God by Brother Lawrence (Merchant Books, 2009) is one of the must-read Christian classics for every intentional Christian who desires to experience the depths of God's abiding presence. The simple but profound insights will shape and enrich your relationship with the God who is "always present."

Getting to Yes: Negotiating Agreement Without Giving In by Roger Fisher and William Ury (Penguin, 1991) provides a simple and straightforward five-step system for how to behave in negotiations in every area of life—personal, family, business, and social.

Twelve Ordinary Men by John MacArthur (Thomas Nelson, 2006). The author asserts, based on the examples of the twelve disciples, that we do not have to be perfect to be used in doing God's work. Jesus chose and equipped ordinary men—fishermen, tax collectors, political zealots—turning their weaknesses into strengths and producing magnificent vessels from plain clay pots.

////// PERSONAL REFLECTIONS AND APPLICATIONS //////

1. How do you believe God has uniquely prepared you to serve his purposes in your generation? Reflect on your family heritage, natural as well as acquired skill sets, clarity of personal core values (those things that you intend to never compromise), and the providential opportunities for leadership God has placed on your path. Weave these together, praying that God will reveal a distinctive picture of your distinctive calling for just such times as these.

2. All of us are prone to distraction and deflection. Personal core values are a way to keep us both focused and anchored. Think back on some recent experiences and circumstances when you felt you were distracted or deflected. How could your personal core values better equip you to manage these?

3. Are you naturally a people person concerned about and interested in others? That natural orientation can be very helpful as you seek to build a sense of meaningful community among and with those you lead. If you do not have this natural disposition, you will need to work intentionally at developing a heart for the people you lead. One of the best ways is to

regularly pray for those God has privileged you to lead. A second way is to get out of your office and manage by walking around—being present and accessible. A variation that mixes the two might be: praying while walking around. Before or after the work day, stop at each workstation to ask for God's blessings on and provisions for each person you serve.

4. The story of Lisa's spirit of commitment and its impact on her willingness to make significant personal sacrifice is a vivid example of faithfulness. As we seek to lead like Jesus, we too must be prepared for "ultimate sacrifices." What sacrifices have you been willing to make to fulfill your high calling? What sacrifices have you found to be too costly? How might you better prepare yourself to make such sacrifices in the future?

///////// TEAM REFLECTIONS AND APPLICATIONS /////////

1. What are the core values of your organization? How are they communicated, and is that communication effective? If not, how could the communication be improved? What mechanisms do you use to see how well these values are both understood and implemented?

2. What format do you use in presenting your core values? Be alert to the unintended consequences if the core values are displayed in a way that implies a hierarchy of importance. Consider a wheel-and-spokes graphic with each value serving as one of the supporting spokes. Work at ensuring that your followers see the interdependent importance of all your organization's core values.

3. Is the stated mission of your organization compelling enough as the hub of your wheel to truly anchor your core values as well as to motivate followers to serve that mission sacrificially? If not, what can you do to improve on the stated mission?

4. How clearly are you as a team communicating the ultimate destination of your organization's mission? Do your people know where you are headed? Explain. In what ways are you measuring progress? In what ways do you suggest course corrections?

5. Your organization projects character whether you recognize it or not. Ask people in your organization, as well as those you serve, to describe what they believe to be the "character" of your organization. Compare the responses to the core values you established. Is there consistency or inconsistency? What steps can be taken to enhance and preserve the integrity between the actual "walk" and the "values talk" of your organization?

JOSEPH KRIVICKAS
CHAIRMAN, GORDON COLLEGE CENTER FOR NONPROFIT STUDIES AND PHILANTHROPY
///

Joseph Krivickas serves as chairman of the Gordon College Center for Nonprofit Studies and Philanthropy (www.gordon.edu/nonprofit). His focus of interest is to bring the best practices of character-based leadership to the emerging generation of leaders.

Krivickas is a social entrepreneur with three primary ventures: cofounder of a program that serves economically disadvantaged youth in rural Lithuania; founder and chairman of the Gordon College Center for Nonprofit Studies and Philanthropy; and cofounder of the Massachusetts General Hospital Dr. Lisa Krivickas ALS Research Fund.

He has ten years of experience as a public company president and CEO, building value in for-profit organizations where he has served in the high-technology sector. He has helped create $1.2 billion of value for investors and two thousand jobs in the corporations he has led. His businesses have been acquired by companies such as Hewlett Packard and Microsoft.

Currently he serves as the CEO of SmartBear Software, which is comprised of three recently acquired high-technology businesses that are within the Insight Ventures portfolio of companies.

Krivickas received his bachelor of science in electronics engineering from the University of Scranton and an MBA from the Wharton Business School. He has served as a reconnaissance infantry officer in the United States Army National Guard. His additional leadership roles include serving as a trustee of Gordon College, sitting on the board of directors for the Christian Leadership Alliance, and acting as interim executive director of the Engstrom Institute.

Joseph Krivickas lives in Winchester, Massachusetts, with his two children.

WHAT'S THE BIG IDEA?

DAVID McKENNA

In this chapter David challenges us to seek the one great thing we can give our lives to as the first step in establishing a leadership path of both significance and success. We follow his journey across a vocational lifetime of listening to and obeying God's call to a place of purpose. The implementation and context of our calling changes and adapts across a lifetime of application, but the core of that calling usually remains constant. Note how great individuals and great literature influenced his journey to uncover and implement his "Big Idea" calling. Take a moment before you begin reading and ask God to sharpen your discernment as you allow his Holy Spirit to reveal what he's called you to in your work and witness.

One of God's best and brightest asked me, "How can I make a difference as a Christian leader?"

I stunned her with a ready answer honed from years of experience: "You need the explosive power of the Big Idea."

Skepticism clouded her face as she shot back, "What do you mean?"

At the risk of sounding sanctimonious, I replied, "The Big Idea is that to which you are willing to give your life."

With the ball now back in her court, she challenged, "OK, how will I know when I see it?"

As I learned to do long ago, I offered, "Let me tell you a story."

// SHAPING OUR CALLING //

Contrary to conventional thinking, the Big Idea seldom comes as a burning bush in the Sinai Desert. Long before the Big Idea captured my mind and heart, God was using books to prepare the way. Memory takes me back to junior high school when I first read Lloyd Douglas's classic, *Magnificent Obsession,* and then saw the movie. In the film dialogue, a wise counselor tells a carefree playboy, "Once you find the way, you'll be bound. It will obsess you. But believe me, it will be a magnificent obsession."[1] The words swept over me and set me on a lifelong journey to find the Big Idea outside myself to which I could give my life.

Later on I discovered the power of autobiographies. *Markings* by Dag Hammarskjold, who was secretary-general of the United Nations, profoundly impacted my life when he wrote: "The road to holiness necessarily passes through the world of action."[2] Eric Sevareid added excitement to my quest when he wrote about his journalistic exploits under the title *Not So Wild a Dream.*

Still later, during my graduate studies in psychology, Albert Schweitzer, in his autobiography, *Out of My Life and Thought,* put it all together for me. I read about how he left scholarly esteem for his defense of the sanity of Jesus and left his acclaim as the world's foremost interpreter of Bach on the organ in order to enter medical school with the goal of spending the rest of his life as a medical missionary at Lambarene, Africa. Indelibly fixed in my mind is the image of Schweitzer finding relief from his exhausting hours of medical ministry by plunking on an old upright piano. It was lined in lead to keep jungle termites from eating the wood and was frequently out of tune due to tropical moisture.

All the while, he could have been performing in the grandest concert halls of Europe on organs with towering pipes and matchless beauty. For me, the contrast put the stamp of authenticity on Schweitzer's testimony: "I don't know what your destiny will be, but one thing I do know: the only ones among you who will be really happy are those who have sought and found how to serve."[3]

These beginnings came together as I prayed for God's guidance in my search. The psalmist gave me the promise I needed as he sang, "One thing I ask of the LORD, this is what I seek: that I may dwell in the house of the LORD all the days of my life, to gaze upon the beauty of the LORD and to seek him in his temple" (Psalm 27:4). Like David, for whom I was named, I felt open to ask the Lord for "one thing" to which I could give my life. This would be my Big Idea.

// CENTERING OUR PURPOSE //

God answered my prayer by allowing these thoughts to converge in an insight that changed forever the way that I looked at the world. The moment came when I was on the faculty of The Ohio State University. While teaching a graduate class on the history and philosophy of American higher education, I discovered what I concluded to be, for the classical Christian college, the point on which hinged either the school's integrity to Christian faith or the defection from it. It was not the behavioral standards imposed on the students; nor was it the periodic evidence of revival to set things right. It was the courage of the president to lead the campus in the integration of Christian faith and human learning, along with the commitment of the faculty to the principles of integration. One without the other resulted in a lost cause.

While this idea was still germinating, the dean of the College of Education called me into his office to let me know that my proposal for the establishment of the Center for the Study of Higher Education at OSU had been put on the shelf because the Ohio legislature had imposed a moratorium on all new programs at the university. As he blew smoke rings from his ever-present pipe, the dean said, "David, you will have to be ready to give your life for this new program." I was astounded. An avowed secularist was calling me to a lifetime commitment.

As I walked out of his office, I found myself asking, *Do I want to give my life to an individual field of scholarship in the secular university or to an institution of Christian higher education?* Without further reflection, I knew that God was calling me to lead an institution. Make no mistake. I fully honor my colleagues who are called to carry their witness within the secular academic setting or within a special field of scholarship. For me, however, no doubt remained. God chose me to pursue the Big Idea within the institutional structure of the sector known as Christian higher education.

The opportunity came with the call to the presidency of Spring Arbor Junior College and the assignment to transform a small, struggling, two-year school into a fully accredited and debt-free Christian liberal arts college. Admitting that this venture was over my head and beyond my experience, we called in Tom Jones, president of Earlham College, as our consultant. Tom had led the turnaround of Earlham from a college on the ropes to a respected partner in American higher education. He had done so by formulating the "Earlham Idea," put as simply as "a quality liberal arts college in the Quaker tradition," the vision for his presidential leadership. Rather than coming with a cut-and-print formula for transformation, he met every group of our stakeholders with the pointed question, "What's the Big Idea?"

When we mumbled a vague answer to the question, Tom Jones demanded precision and clarity. He probed for historical, theological, and educational connections that gave Spring Arbor its own special character. Slowly the Big Idea began to take shape. When Tom gave his summary report to the college community, he challenged us to dig for the roots of our holistic beliefs in our Wesleyan theology and our Free Methodist history. In that moment, my call to Christian higher education and the future of Spring Arbor College came clear. The integration of faith and learning was the Big Idea to which I would give my life and the foundation on which Spring Arbor College would be built.

// FUELING OUR PASSION //

Like "the expulsive power of a new affection" (the title of Thomas Chalmers's classic sermon), the Big Idea clears away the debris of complacency and hones ideas to frame a concise statement that becomes the cornerstone on which everything else will stand. Hour upon hour of discussion and debate took place among trustees, administration, and faculty during this time. Together we scoured such volumes as Arthur Holmes's *The Idea of a College*, Harry

Blamires's *The Christian Mind,* H. Richard Niebuhr's *Christ and Culture,* and Bernard Ramm's *The Christian College in the Twentieth Century.* Finally, the Spring Arbor Concept was ready for formal adoption and public presentation in these contemporary words: "Spring Arbor College [now University] is a community of learners distinguished by our lifelong involvement in the study and application of the liberal arts, total commitment to Jesus Christ as *the* perspective for learning, and critical participation in the contemporary world."[4]

I purposely emphasized the word *the* in the Spring Arbor Concept in order to highlight the center of debate among the Spring Arbor faculty. Without rancor, faculty members were divided over the question of whether our personal commitment to Jesus Christ was *a* perspective for learning or *the* perspective for learning. Valid arguments held on each side of the question. Proponents of the *a* perspective for learning expressed concern that alternative viewpoints could not be fully and fairly explored if *the* were chosen. Other faculty members voiced equal concern about the possibility of slipping into relativism if the *a* were adopted.

Finally, the choice was made for Jesus Christ as *the* perspective for learning, because of our obedience to the Scripture to "take captive every thought to make it obedient to Christ" (2 Corinthians 10:5) and our conviction that "in him all things hold together" (Colossians 1:17). Once this commitment was clear, the faculty found new freedom to explore freely and fully the alternative perspectives of theological and philosophical viewpoints.

// DIRECTING OUR DECISIONS //

Statements similar to the Spring Arbor Concept have been written many times, only to end up as vacuous words on a dusty shelf. If so, they fail the test of the Big Idea. Any statement of vision, mission, or cause must have the power to personalize itself in people and produce itself in programs. Concrete symbols are also needed for the idea to stick. At Spring Arbor, "lifelong involvement in the study and application of the liberal arts" was represented by the lighted lamp of learning, "Jesus Christ as the perspective for learning" found its meaning in the cross of Christ, and "critical participation in the contemporary world" could be seen and felt in the arms embracing the globe.[5]

Vision and symbols then came to life in a curriculum called The Christian Perspective in the Liberal Arts. Courses integrating faith and learning in the humanities, natural science, social science, religion, and philosophy were required of freshmen and sophomores. As part of the sophomore year, each student had an exploratory experience with a college alumnus, in a vocational field of choice, not only to assist in career decisions but also to see how Christian faith is integrated with calling. After advancing through the professional requirements of their chosen fields of the upper division and completing their major studies, all students participated in a senior seminar in which they presented a paper that came to grips with the question of integrating faith and learning in their chosen field of study. Moreover, to fulfill the commitment of "critical participation in the contemporary world," a cross-cultural experience was required of every graduate.

Faculty came fully alive with the challenge of the curriculum by asking, "What are the basic ideas in my discipline that invite us to the integration of faith and learning?" Innovative course names like these came to mind as answers to the question:

- Image and Idea in the Creative Arts
- Mind and Motivation in Human Development
- Energy and Matter in the Physical World
- Structure and System in the Living World
- Concepts and Values in Human Behavior
- Thought and Symbol in Human Expression
- Freedom and Order in Human Society

More than curricular reform took place. A spirit of renaissance energized the faculty.

Almost fifty years later, the Spring Arbor Concept still guides the university, its curriculum, and its faculty. Some changes have been made to incorporate expansion into graduate and professional studies, but the essential components have been passed from generation to generation of faculty and students as the defining character of the university. Succeeding presidents reaffirmed the Spring Arbor Concept as they shaped their generation's application of the Big Idea. Visiting teams for regional and professional accreditation invariably note that students can quote the concept verbatim. Better yet, they can explain what it means.

// EXPANDING OUR HORIZONS //

The Big Idea transcends institutions as well as individuals. In 1968, I was elected as president of Seattle Pacific College (now University), a much larger and well-established institution with its own particular philosophy of Christian higher education. Would the Big Idea of integrating faith and learning transfer? In my first chapel series, I chose the subject "A Vision of Wholeness" and stated the principles of integration for the curriculum as well as the climate for the college. For the next five years, however, financial crises required my full attention; but bit by bit we championed the integration of faith and learning in curriculum reform, faculty development, new program initiatives, and relationships between the campus and the city.

New faculty members were asked to give a lecture, as a part of the hiring process, on integration between their faith and their field. Offerings of graduate and enrichment programs for adult learners always included what we called "needle point gospel," a precise statement of our mission in Christian higher education. In building the case for the change of name from *college* to *university*, emphasis was placed on the commitment of our faculty to the integration of faith and reason as a dimension of teaching and learning that set us apart from the University of Washington (our neighboring institution), a national research university.

The Big Idea came clearly into focus in the founding of the School of Business and Economics. At a time when business, economics, and ethics were separated in the curriculum of most business schools, Seattle Pacific declared its Christian faith as the foundation for business ethics and built its faculty, curriculum, and professional relationships around the integrative principle. Today the school is nationally recognized by its breakout claim: "Another Way of Doing Business." The Big Idea cannot be contained within the halls of the academy, but must be about challenging the next generation of leadership with the business of "engaging the culture, changing the world."

The call to the presidency of Asbury Theological Seminary put the Big Idea to the test of graduate theological education. Since seminary scholarship tends to be narrow and deep, the integration of faith and learning became the natural means to open the windows to a wider academic world and let fresh breezes of contemporary issues blow through. Incentive for bringing the Big Idea into theological education came directly from Methodism's Charles Wesley, who penned the words, "Let us unite the two so long divided—knowledge and vital piety."[6] The seminary's Wesleyan heritage with its strong emphasis on the integration of personal and social holiness added its own energy to the Big Idea.

// BRIDGING OUR WORLDS //

The Big Idea may begin small, but it does not stay small. Originally conceived as a rather narrow intellectual construct, the "integration of faith and reason" soon extended to "learning, living, and serving" as it embraced the holistic purpose of the Christian college. Robert Havinghurst, a noted Christian educator at the University of Chicago, opened another frontier for us when he counseled me to see that the Christian college had a responsibility to the larger community in which it found itself.

His wise words prompted us to think again about the separation of "Town and Gown," a term that characterized the tension between the community and the college ever since the earliest days of higher education in England. The same latent suspicion had existed in the village of Spring Arbor, Michigan. To help break the tension, Havinghurst suggested that our mission include being an educational and cultural resource for the people of our town. So we enlarged the Big Idea to say "The Village Is Our Classroom" and started a "Town and Gown" series with speakers, music, and drama that would appeal to both the campus and the community.

When we moved to Seattle Pacific, we were located on the north side of Queen Anne hill just blocks away from the Space Needle, Seattle Opera House, Pacific Science Center, and Key Arena. Knowing that it would be foolish to try and duplicate these rich resources, we stretched the idea of integration to embrace this new relationship to say "The City Is Our Campus." We opened dialogue with the educational leaders in the African-American community to develop together an integrated model school. Responding to the realities of an aging population in our immediate community, we were one of the first in the nation to offer free tuition to senior citizens to attend any class that did not have capacity enrollment.

Asbury Theological Seminary posed the greatest challenge as well as the greatest opportunity to make the Big Idea even bigger. Wilmore, Kentucky, the stopping place for Francis Asbury on his camp-meeting circuit, is located just ten miles from the sophisticated city of Lexington, home of the University of Kentucky, and yet within a stone's throw of the economic and educational poverty of Appalachia. Balanced between these extremes, the seminary and its sister school, Asbury College, are institutions of academic distinction and revival history. Without apology they foster a campus climate in which personal and social holiness are compatible goals. However, the college and seminary also share the vision of John Wesley, who was thinking globally and acting locally when he said, "I look on all the world as my parish."[7] To make his bold declaration our own, we adopted "The World Is Our Parish" as our Big Idea for Asbury Theological Seminary.

Applying this vision we became active members and leaders of Appalachian Ministries, a consortium of graduate schools of theology serving the needs of the region. And as a step toward a global parish, we telecast my presidential inauguration via satellite to downlinks across North America so that our alumni and other pastors could participate in the event. Twelve years later, at my farewell, we used the resources of a major bequest to create the first "smart" seminary campus with two-way interactive conversation on our campus between the delegates of the North American Section of the World Methodist Council and Donald English, WMC International president, from a studio in Leeds, England. Today under new leadership, globalization has come into full view. The Big Idea has never been bigger.

// UNITING OUR MOVEMENT //

As the Big Idea grows from center to circumference, its outer edge is the place where innovative action takes place. I saw the idea come to fruition in the creation of the Christian College Consortium in 1971. At that time, dire predictions forecast the demise of the small Christian college in the 1970s. Rather than succumbing to that future, Lilly Endowment made a grant for a selected number of Christian colleges to explore their options. Presidents of fifteen Christian liberal arts colleges strategically located in each region of the nation were invited to meet in Phoenix, Arizona, to consider the possibility of strength through cooperation. Across the country the prevailing sentiment in higher education was the creation of consortia arrangements as a mechanism for survival and significance.

When the fifteen college presidents met and worked through the gloomy predictions about the future of Christian higher education, they heard the prophetic words from William Jellema, one of our consultants, "Frail reeds must be tightly bound." The message came through loud and clear. Unless Christian colleges and universities came together in common conviction around what Robert Bellah (sociologist and a foremost interpreter of religion and American character) called "a binding address," we were doomed to mediocrity or death one by one.

The presidents at the meeting had to make a decision. On what premise would we stake the future of those colleges? After all the options were on the table, we chose to risk our future on the principle—the Big Idea—of the integration of faith and learning.

Out of this decision came the formation of the Christian College Consortium, not as an elitist group but as a think tank with pilot programs demonstrating the integration of faith and learning as the "binding address" of Christian higher education. The CCC advanced under this banner until the political need for a face in Washington, D.C., became evident. Advocates of political action brought the needs of the evangelical Christian college in the formation of the Christian College Coalition, a combination of the schools in the CCC and those who merited entry into membership for a larger thrust of political leadership. Yet as the Christian College Coalition, and later the Council for Christian Colleges & Universities formed, the common commitment was not political but conceptual, with the integration of faith and learning as the motivating center.

Almost forty years later, the Christian College Consortium and the Council for Christian Colleges & Universities stand together as advocates with complementary roles for advancing the Big Idea. Consequently, Christian higher education is recognized as one of the most significant movements in American higher education leading into the twenty-first century. The growth of the movement is more than matched by its vitality and visibility. No one talks about "frail reeds" anymore. Around the Big Idea of integrating Christian faith and human learning, we are tightly bound together and stronger than ever.

// IMPRINTING OUR IDENTITY //

If this story seems self-serving, it is not intended to be. The tale is told for several reasons. First and foremost, I wanted to tell how the Big Idea had life-changing power. As the story unfolds we see the Big Idea shaping our calling, centering our purpose, fueling our passion, directing our decisions, and expanding our horizons.

Even then, the Big Idea has more to offer. Within this framework we can see how the Big Idea assesses the effectiveness of our leadership. Any sense of bragging is dispelled when I think of the times I have let lesser ideas distract me. Presidents in particular have a hard time keeping their focus under the pressures of the office and temptations to personal pride. I had my moments when the competitive sirens of the educational marketplace (with promises of economic windfalls) diverted my attention. At other times, I personally gloried in accolades that far outstripped the limits of my family background. I also remember buying into the latest academic fads, such as long-range planning models that sacrificed the Big Idea to other models of institutional development. Or big-time fund-raising that called for softening the Big Idea in order to meet the donor's wishes. Even more, I recall the political pressures of government, accreditation, and professional societies, in which we may win the battle and lose the war.

Now that I am in retirement, I see clearly how an unswerving commitment to the integration of faith and learning might have sharpened my identity as a Christian leader. I have thought a lot about the identifiers that we put on our leaders. When I retired from the presidency at Asbury Theological Seminary, a reporter asked me, "What epitaph would you want on your tombstone?"

I answered, "He struck a note of joy." Yes, that speaks of the spirit I have lived to convey. However, I have given my life to supporting a principle, which is where the Big Idea comes in. So I would choose this epitaph: "A life dedicated to uniting knowledge and vital piety."

My story concurs with whoever said, "We each have one good book in us. Everything else is a sequel." My mentor, Fred Smith Sr., reinforced that thought by noting that our greatest leaders are always in role. Wherever they are, their actions are consistent with the identity by which we know them. Think of great leaders in human history—a Big Idea captured each:

- Jesus never wavered from his mission to give his life as a ransom.
- Paul never lost sight of his task of taking the gospel to the Gentiles.
- Martin Luther contended for grace alone.
- John Calvin focused on God's response to our total depravity.
- John Wesley invited people to the heartwarming experience of perfect love.

Leaders who have changed our modern world are obsessed with the power of a Big Idea, whether good or bad. Consider these:

- Lenin's vision for the Communist worker
- Freud's fixation on subconscious behavior
- Gandhi's belief in nonviolence
- Hudson Taylor's passion for the Chinese people
- Martin Luther King Jr.'s "dream" of racial equality
- Billy Graham's unrelenting commitment to evangelism

Human history is written in the names of persons who were so consumed by a Big Idea that everything else was a sequel. So when all is said and done, I write my story of the Big Idea as an inhabitable narrative in which you can see yourself. The script will never be the same for two people, but each of us has a role to play in the grand drama of human redemption. By discovering the Big Idea to which we are willing to give our lives, we join Christian leaders who have made a difference in human history. None of these celebrated names, however, has more impact on me than the story of an unsung friend who lived and died for the biggest idea of all.

// JEANNE'S STORY //

I first met Jeanne Acheson-Munos at the headquarters of the Free Methodist Church in Indianapolis, Indiana. She served as the executive assistant to John Van Valin, director of communications for the church. Her vibrant spirit and sense of humor challenged me at every turn. If I poked fun at her, she poked back and won the day. If I challenged her decisions, she said, "Let's work it out." Our relationship deepened from colleague to friend and then from friend to family. When I wrote the updated history of the Free Methodist Church of North America, Jeanne held sway as managing editor and became my editorial critic, cutting sentences and questioning words. Together, however, we put together a text that symbolized the push and pull of persons who had learned to know, respect, and even love each other.

Each time I met with Jeanne to go over the text for the history, she brought me up to date on the leanings of her own ministry. She and her husband, Jack, had gone to Haiti on a short-term mission. Out of that experience, Jeanne and Jack fell in love with the Haitian people and could talk about nothing else. I remember her words: "We love Haiti. This is where we want to be." Our conversation spun out to the long path of getting a degree at Asbury Theological Seminary in order to qualify as a missionary to Haiti. Jeanne did not hesitate. So with a little boost from a former president and a bigger sacrifice from her husband, Jeanne enrolled for the long haul to qualify as a graduate ready to follow her heartbeat.

She made it. In 2004 she was awarded an MA in biblical studies, as well as an MA in missions and evangelism. After intense language study, she headed to Haiti with Jack. From a distance, we supported them and followed their ministry. At one point they were evacuated from Haiti along with thousands of refugees because of the threat of political revolution. Jeanne would not let her vision lapse. When an urgent call came for support to get them from Indianapolis to Miami so that they could continue their ministry to Haitian refugees, we were able to buy a car that would take them to the people whom they loved. After a fast drive, Jeanne wrote from Miami that they had arrived and, as partners in exile, found an open door for ministry.

A year or so went by. Jack and Jeanne returned to Haiti. Regular communication flowed between us as Jeanne's passion found joy in the impossible demands for preaching, teaching, and counseling, along with the down-and-dirty work of helping impoverished people survive under the superstitions of voodoo. Out of the dregs, however, came her dream for developing a seminary for training Haitian pastors. I urged her to put the dream into the realities of strategic planning and resource development and then seek support for a cooperative venture with other Wesleyan missions. She responded with a masterful preliminary document that is still in my files.

When the earthquake of January 12, 2010, destroyed Port-au-Prince, Jeanne was at her post on the fourth floor of the Free Methodist building that also housed the offices for the mission. On the floor directly beneath were two missionaries who had arrived only two hours before. In an instant, four floors collapsed into one level with Jeanne and her guests crushed in the rubble. A gas fire in the basement added to the holocaust and took away any chance for recovery. As so often happens under such random destruction, only one marriage partner was taken. Jack, equally dedicated to the Haitian people, escaped death by a miraculous recovery operation.

How do we memorialize the life of Jeanne Acheson-Munos? Every letter and e-mail that she wrote ended with the impassioned claim *"Haiti pour Christ!"* Hoping against hope and serving against odds, God gave Jeanne the Big Idea for which she was willing to give her life. In her story we see the meaning of the Big Idea—shaping her calling, centering her purpose, fueling her passion, directing her decisions, expanding her horizons, assessing her ministry, and imprinting her identity.

In answer to the young and emerging Christian leader who asks, "How can I make a difference?" I can hear Jeanne saying, "Find the Big Idea to which you can give your life. *Haiti pour Christ!*"

MY LEADERSHIP BOOKSHELF

Most books on leadership are quick scans or single reads that—even though they may be best sellers—you put on the shelf and seldom, if ever, pick up again. Each of these three classics I return to time and time again for source material.

In the Name of Jesus: Reflections on Christian Leadership by Henri Nouwen (The Crossroad Publishing Company, 1992) penetrates to the soul with the biblical message of incarnational leadership with its cost to Christ and his commission to us. I find myself quivering in Peter's sandals every time I hear Christ's question, "Do you love me?"

Leaders: The Strategies for Taking Charge by Warren Bennis and Bert Nanus (HarperBusiness, 1997) drives us to the core of the relationship between leader and follower: leading others, managing yourself. What is more fundamental than a leader bringing followers to attention through vision, to meaning through communication, to trust through positioning, and to learning through self-deployment? All other leadership books are expansions on those principles.

Leadership Is an Art by Max De Pree (Dell, 1990) lifts us above all the notions, buzz words, and recycled theories about leadership to the ultimate of fatherly wisdom based on actual experience. Even though Max writes for a widespread audience, the spirit between the lines is profoundly Christian.

////// PERSONAL REFLECTIONS AND APPLICATIONS //////

1. What and/or who are the most significant influences in your life to date as you search for the Big Idea of your life's callings? How and why have these been so influential?

2. Is there a defining point in your life's journey when you discovered your central purpose? If you cannot recall a specific point, reflect on the series of experiences and insights that produced your conviction about your central purpose.

3. What resources do you use to fuel your passion and keep you energized for your sense of calling? What seems to sap that energy and deflect from that purpose?

4. What are the nonnegotiables as you pursue your calling to the Big Idea?

5. How has your Big Idea changed and adapted over time?

6. What would you like to see as your epitaph? Is your Big Idea compelling enough to become your epitaph? How does it describe how you want to be remembered? Will it have been worth living for as well as dying for? How so?

///////// TEAM REFLECTIONS AND APPLICATIONS /////////

1. What is the Big Idea that drives your organization and guides the work of your team as they contribute to it?

2. What are the defining moments in your organization's history as the Big Idea grew, changed, and adapted?

3. What would be lost to God's kingdom work if your organization failed to fulfill its central purpose? What would be gained for the kingdom if your organization were to achieve the driving vision?

4. Define and discuss the top three functions, programs, and processes that are most important for your team to achieve the Big Idea to which your organization has been called.

5. What are the current distractions and deflections that keep your team from contributing its full measure to the primary calling of your organization?

6. What activities, resources, and experiences can your team deploy to keep the Big Idea fresh, fueled, and relevant?

DAVID McKENNA
FORMER PRESIDENT, SPRING ARBOR UNIVERSITY, SEATTLE PACIFIC UNIVERSITY, AND ASBURY THEOLOGICAL SEMINARY
///

D r. David McKenna has served for more than fifty years in Christian higher education, including thirty-three years as a college, university, and seminary president.

At Spring Arbor University (www.arbor.edu), he developed a junior college into a four-year Christian liberal arts college. At Seattle Pacific University (www.spu.edu), he led the transition from a four-year college to university status. At Asbury Theological Seminary (www.asburyseminary.edu), he gained and guided the largest grant ever given in American history to a freestanding graduate school of theology. In 1994, McKenna retired as president emeritus of Asbury Theological Seminary to write, speak, and consult on subjects related to leadership in Christian higher education and ministry. In 2003, he retired as chair emeritus, board of trustees, Spring Arbor University.

David McKenna holds a BA degree in history from Western Michigan University, an MDiv from Asbury Theological Seminary, and an MA in counseling psychology and PhD in higher education from the University of Michigan.

He has been awarded ten honorary doctorates, named as a Paul Harris Fellow with Rotary International, and honored by Stanley Kresge's endowment for the David L. McKenna Christian Leaders Scholarship for business students at Seattle Pacific University. As an educational leader, he served as founding chair for the Christian College Consortium (parent organization of the Council for Christian Colleges & Universities) and secretary for the National Association of Independent Colleges and Universities.

In 1980, he was a finalist for Secretary of Education in the Reagan Cabinet. As a religious leader ordained in the Free Methodist Church, McKenna has held positions as vice president of the North American Section of the World Methodist Council, consulting editor for *Christianity Today*, and a national radio commentator.

David McKenna is the author of thirty-two books that range across the fields of psychology, biblical commentary, leadership, history, and theology. He and his wife celebrated their sixtieth wedding anniversary in 2010. They are the parents of four children, twelve grandchildren, and one great-grandchild.

LEAD REAL!

ELISA MORGAN

I f you have ever personally encountered Elisa, your life of leadership has been energized by her passion for truth, commitment to excellence, and willingness to invest everything in the calling of God for her life. Elisa has the unique ability to get to the heart of the matter—directly, quickly, and always inspirationally. In this chapter she focuses her attention on new and emerging leaders, particularly those young in years and experience. As a dynamic and gifted communicator, she is able to make profound truths memorable as well as applicable. Here she uses an acrostic based on the four letters of the word *real* to challenge, encourage, and stretch our thinking about essential issues and attitudes that will transform the motivations for and practices of our leadership callings. We know no one more REAL than Elisa!

When I ask younger leaders what they need from older leaders, I hear the expected, survey-proven answers:

- An opportunity to have a voice at the table of decision making
- Mentoring by those still leading
- Authenticity modeled in everyday relationships

Since this chapter is focused for the younger leader and not the older one, I will not belabor the importance of those qualities. You already know them because you report that you need them. Instead, this chapter will build on the assumption that you are moving in a direction that seeks out those elements around you. But while you can *ask* for them, you cannot *make* them happen. Older leaders have to offer them to you.

What you *can* do is important though—and only you can do it.

Perhaps the greatest asset we bring into the leadership arena is *ourselves*—the people God has uniquely created each of us to be. However, contributing this asset is a challenge. Whether due to our own inadequacies, struggles, or sins, we not only hold back on bringing our gifting forth; we can at times replace our legitimate offering with a masquerade.

Everybody knows that authenticity in leadership is essential for success. But how many of us know what authenticity *really* looks like in the day to day of leadership? (Does a real leader keep an open door policy, eat lunch with the staff every day, wear jeans on Fridays?) Just how authentic should one really be in order to lead well? (Should a real leader confess personal shortcomings in public or admit to having no idea where to take the ministry next?)

An acrostic for the word *real* can help us both understand and apply authenticity in our leadership. Let's take each letter one at a time to discover four elements of authenticity that guide us as we lead in a REAL way.

// R–LEAD IN REALITY //

As leaders, reality is our friend. It is our confidante and our comrade, as well as our mirror of accountability. We lead REAL when we face and embrace reality and navigate others in it and through it.

In my earliest days of leadership with MOPS International, I tended to shrink from reality. Well, not the good realities. I embraced *them.* When our organization grew from 350 to 1,000 groups, I looked intently at why. When a donor responded with a generous gift—the kind with lots of zeroes in it—I rejoiced. When I exited a platform to applause and knew that God had anointed the words he led me to speak, I absorbed his leading and followed happily.

However, the flip side of reality—what I viewed as the bad side—I avoided. In a year when our membership dipped, I pushed harder on our efforts to increase numbers and saw success. In a season when donations decreased, I watered our development efforts with more communication, more visits, and more prayer. My efforts worked, restoring the organization to vibrant growth. But I missed some points of insight—some realities that needed to be recognized.

Our ministry held charters in only one-half of 1 percent of the churches we could have been in. Our average group size had shrunk from forty to thirty-five. For several consecutive quarters, the ministry had not achieved its growth or income goals. While management had addressed our financial shortfall through expense cuts, we had not achieved greater penetration of our audience.

Then there was the makeup of our audience. The demographic of our member audience was white, married, college educated, and (by some standards) wealthy—a demographic that made the mouths of marketers water. While white, educated, married, and somewhat wealthy moms need to know Jesus and how to mother the best they can, our ministry's mission called us to reach *every* mother of preschoolers.

In this season of fact facing, I learned that reality is my friend. It took our executive team's pushback, some poor quarters of financial performance, and a tough couple of board meetings, but I eventually began to welcome what I had seen as the dark side of reality. As I befriended it, I learned that reality—in all its dimensions—offers insights every leader must face.

A series of questions directed my posture *toward* reality rather than away. These questions informed me as I acknowledged reality for myself and then began to guide others toward and then through it:

- ❚ What do the trends say? Are we growing or declining in comparison to what is happening in the country? in the world?
- ❚ What does our performance say? Are we achieving our outcomes and projections, falling below them or surpassing them? What factors are influencing our performance?

- What does our staff say—both about our mission accomplishment and about how we are implementing it in our methodology and our staff culture?
- What does our board say—about our mission accuracy, accomplishment, and where we are headed next?
- And perhaps most important: What does our target audience say—those to whom God has called us? In what ways are they "voting" with their membership, their donations, their purchases, and their testimonies of life change?

Bottom line: When we stand before Jesus and "give an account" of how we have stewarded the mission of the ministry he has entrusted to us, will we in reality be able to answer that we did all we could with what he has given us?

Reality can be rude. But it is our friend and directs us clearly toward the next step in leadership. Instead of dodging reality like a pothole in the road, we are wise to slow down, examine the facts, and adjust our course accordingly. Leading REAL is leading in reality.

// E–LEAD EVERYWHERE //

It is tempting to be one person in public and a different person in private—to put on for the public an I've-got-it-together-and-really-trust-God-in-just-about-everything face, even when that is far from our experience. We expect such a posture from good leaders—even if the good leaders are ourselves. Leading REAL means integrating who we are everywhere we are.

A zillion years ago when I was a young mother of a very young baby, I inadvertently stepped in the messy truth of this lesson. And in the moment, it did not smell so good. It was Christmastime. Any woman reading this knows what that means. Women give birth to Christmas. One woman literally did. But we women continue to give birth to Christmas every year—in addition to our other responsibilities like working or running the home or mothering.

I completed the annual gift purchasing, wrapping, and packaging for the out-of-towners on my list. One snowy morning I bundled up my six-month-old baby and the seven boxes of perfectly prepared gifts—in those days wrapped in brown paper and tied with string—and took them to the local mailing outlet. I parked as close as I could, but I still had to carry in just a box or two at a time, balancing them precariously atop the infant seat in which I towed my daughter back and forth.

By the time I made the fifth trip from car to counter and back again, sweat was trickling down my back beneath my parka.

"Whew!" I announced to the clerk as I completed my haul.

But no sympathy came my way. Instead, she pursed her lips and said, "You know, you can't use string on packages anymore. You have to use tape." I looked at her incredulously, trying to register her words.

"*What?!* You watched me schlep in and out five times, and you're just now telling me?"

"You can buy some tape from us if you like," came her reply.

I was steamed—and not just from the exertion. "This is ridiculous. Your tape is way overpriced, and now that I've trudged all this in here, I am basically your prisoner. Fine. Give me the tape! And some scissors please?" I reassembled my packages, all the while toe-rocking my now awake and not happy baby in her infant seat. I wrote out my check and thrust it at the clerk.

Eyeing my signature, she said, "Hmm. Elisa Morgan . . . I think you were the retreat speaker at my church this fall." She saw my shot-up eyebrows and stunned face and added, "You never know who's watching, do you?"

Ugh. Nope, you don't. And in our day of security cameras, satellite imaging, and instant media, you can be sure that lots of people are watching . . . everywhere you go.

It is tempting to be one person in public and then another person in private—to be one person when we think no one is looking and then to create an exterior personhood like a bubble around us when we know we are on display. We put on our "ministry masks" and out the door we go, sliding the masks off upon our return when we punch down the garage door.

The truth is, you never know who is watching. And it is not just the leader at the top of an organization who lives a life on display. Every one of us represents the cause and character of Christ along with the reputation of the ministry we serve. But just because leaders live an unpredictable life of being unknowingly on display does not mean we have to fake it. People want to see the real us wherever we are—not the pretend perfect us, but the *real* us. Sure, that means exhibiting a humble attitude when we actually handle life well. It also means being honest when we mess up—grabbing on to God in tough moments, crying out for help when falling down, admitting inadequacies and failures—and bravely trying again.

In Hebrews 4:13 we read, "Nothing in all creation is hidden from God's sight. Everything is uncovered and laid bare before the eyes of him to whom we must give account." God invites us to be who we are before him at all times and to lead authentically before others. Over the years I have grown to cherish one compliment more than any other: "Thanks for being real." In response I find myself chuckling, "It's *way* too hard to be anything else."

Leading REAL means reducing the difference between who you are in private and who you are in public and, instead, leading as the same person everywhere.

// A–LEAD ALL THE TIME //

We lead in a REAL way when we steward the mission of the ministry 24/7. We always are leaders and we always are leading.

When you are the leader, all you have to do is walk into the room and the eyes turn to you to start the meeting, approve the agenda, offer or assign the opening prayer, manage the progression of topics, review the action steps, and disband. You may have delegated such responsibilities to others who are present and capable. You may speak often or seldom. You may be a level one or a level five leader in style and personality. Whatever. The reality is that whatever your role or approach, leaders are leaders *all* the time. 24/7. Night and day. On Saturday and Sunday. On Monday when Sunday is a workday. On vacation . . . unfortunately.

You never are not a leader. You never are not leading.

Such a truth is more comfortable in some seasons than in others. For twenty years I served as the CEO of MOPS International, a ministry that helps make better moms who make a better world. Honestly, most of the time I truly enjoyed the reality that I was always leading. I loved the ongoing questions from staff and board about "What's next?" I found it intriguing that moms I had never met were being impacted and transformed by the work we did. And I enjoyed being out on the road speaking, where I could serve as the receptacle for testimonies of God's work. I learned to think before I offered an opinion in staff meetings, because my comment might be perceived as more "right" than another's. I tried to attend to the inner prompting from the Holy Spirit that instructed me to stop and sincerely ask a coworker how she was doing. Gradually I grew less stunned when I was recognized in an airport restroom. I thrilled to the unceasing experience of being needed all the time. It was cool.

However, in other seasons of ministry, we may pull back from the all-the-time element of leading REAL. When we discover we have fallen into the trap of the messiah complex or when we slip into exhaustion under the wearying load of the unending demands around us, leading all the time can be anything but rewarding.

Deep into my tenure came a season of heavy challenges with my family, specifically with our then teenage children. Just name the issue—we pretty much saw it evolving before us. For at least a decade, my husband and I found ourselves mired in the choices and consequences—sometimes troubling and sometimes disastrous—of our not-yet-grown kids. I considered stepping down. He considered moving to the moon. But under the guidance of our pastor and boards (my husband also serves with a ministry), we stayed—and led. We drove from hospitals to boardrooms and from platforms to counseling offices and from schools to home to the office and back again, sometimes together and sometimes taking turns, sometimes allowing our staffs to serve us as we served them—but always leading, leading, leading.

Leading REAL means negotiating the all-the-time element. Several strategies assist us in this process.

SET BOUNDARIES

Even though a leader is never *not* leading, you can lead well when you set the example of having times when you are off duty. On your day off, determine to be "off"—unless there is an emergency that no one else can handle and that cannot wait until the next day. You lead when you set a boundary and then keep the parameters yourself, by not answering e-mails or phone calls or letting stray appointments slip into your days.

ASK FOR HELP

Resist the temptation . . . no, make that resist the *lie* that you can lead alone. Every leader leads best when he or she leads under a "covering" of accountability and authority. Whether in a board or by a supervisor, recognize the help available to you and then take advantage of it with regular check-ins—for work-related issues, of course, but also for personal and spiritual perspective.

INVEST IN YOURSELF

Figure out what both deepens and widens you—spiritually, personally, and professionally—and invest. Stretch your knowledge through a conference or an online course. Expand your skills by leaning into the role of learner rather than expert. Refresh your soul with art, nature, relationships, or physical exertion.

PLAN FOR FAILURE

Rather than leading a life that is stunned by less-than-perfect results, grasp the fact that failure is part of success. It will happen; so when it does, recognize what or who has failed, own it, and process through it. At times your failures will require confession before others. In other moments you will sit with God and his redemptive grace.

KEEP YOUR SPIRITUAL ANTENNAE UP—ALL THE TIME

Even the wisest boundaries, careful accountability, and excellent personal care can never fully protect you. Stay aware. Though it may sound dramatic in the light of day, Peter's words to believers in 1 Peter 5:8 carry great truth: "Your enemy the devil prowls around like a roaring lion looking for someone to devour." Pay attention. Take in the cues of the Holy Spirit's leading. Stay in the Word. Keep your guard up. Don't go on vacation from God.

Leaders are leaders 24/7. The all-the-time element in leadership can leave us feeling like either a sucked-dry juice box or a valued participant in God's kingdom work, depending on how we manage ourselves in the process. Leading REAL means embracing and managing how we lead all the time.

// L—LEAD BY LISTENING //

We lead REAL by opening our ears to God in a vibrant, current relationship with him and to the people with whom we are leading as they confirm God's direction for us.

God cares about two elements in the execution of ministry plans:

1. He cares hugely about the accomplishment of the mission to which he has called us. Feed the hungry. Care for the poor. Heal the sick. Adopt the orphan. Spread the gospel. Make disciples. God cares enormously about the accomplishment of his purposes, and leading REAL means listening to his leading about mission accomplishment.
2. God also cares—and I believe equally as much—about the people who are doing his work. Who they are and what they are becoming and how

they are doing his work. We are called to mission—and equally called to the people with whom we accomplish it.

Strategic plans put feet on the vision of a mission and move it from dream to accomplishment. So it is important to listen "fluidly" as we lead the implementation of plans. In my experience, even the best-laid plan shifts and changes in execution. Usually the changes are about God's specific purposes and his people, toward better accomplishing his mission.

In one season of ministry at MOPS International, our leadership team and I were experiencing an impasse regarding how to move next. The ministry was stable, but our mission was far from completed. A vast number of moms remained unreached and needed to know of the hope and help available to them in Jesus. But as we rose up to plan for the future, we experienced a fog and no leading at all.

Thinking that we needed a retreat time to focus in more specifically on God and his direction, we slipped away for a day in an off-site conference room. The night before, as I prepared the devotional, I sensed God wanting me to read Matthew 14, the story of Peter walking on the water. As I read the passage, I noticed that all the disciples in the boat thought Jesus was a ghost coming toward them. Scary stuff. Then I was pierced by Jesus' word to Peter in verse 29: "Come." The words that followed said, "Then Peter got down out of the boat, walked on the water and came toward Jesus." Peter did not recognize Jesus from where he sat in the boat. "Lord, if it's you . . ." he had said (v. 28). It took the action of getting out of the boat and walking on the water for Peter to be able to identify Jesus on the waves.

The words seemed to be directed straight at me—as if Jesus were asking me to get out of the boat, walk on the water, and come toward him. Peter's truth was becoming mine. I was not able to detect Jesus' leading from where I sat, safe and snug in the boat. In order to discern God's leading, I would have to get out of the boat—whatever that meant—and approach Jesus on the waves.

Wouldn't it be lovely if God wrote out a daily to-do list for us as leaders? Then as we sipped our morning coffee, we could take in his instructions for the hours ahead of us? In reality, such moments of divine inspiration aren't everyday occurrences for most of us as leaders. When they come, I find the need for affirmation. Even in moments when my spiritual antennae direct me that God is working in a unique way that requires my response, I am not big on "pronouncements," as if I alone have the truth. I prefer to lean into the confirmation that comes from the wisdom of many counselors.

The next morning I gathered our team around the table, and we dove into the passage together. Purposefully, I did not share God's words to me from the night before. I needed to know if he was leading us. Two times we entered the passage and listened to it being read. Two times we discussed what we each had heard in the verses. And then on the third time through, one leader announced, "As I listened to the words this time, I felt God was saying that Elisa is out of the boat—will we join her on the waves with Jesus?"

As we prayed, processed, and received broader staff and board input, we determined that God wanted us to stop doing ministry as usual but rather put ourselves in a place of dependency on him, even if it meant risking ourselves on the waves. Going forward meant that we slim down our infrastructure and re-form teams. Vice presidents became directors. Tenured leaders were reassessed and reassigned. Life was different, and segueing through the differences required a lengthy transition process in which listening was essential to both retaining our staff and empowering them to serve in spots better suited to their skills.

Leading REAL means listening intently to God's leading and listening intently to the people he has called us to lead alongside. These two elements of listening braid into one force to accomplish God's purposes.

While veteran leaders may hold the power to invite you into certain leadership capacities, only you can bring forth the gifting and offering you possess. Do not hold back under objections or accusations that you do not have what it takes, that you are too unformed, that you want to lead differently and so, therefore, cannot lead in the here and now. Instead, move forward into leadership with confidence that you are exactly what is needed in a given moment in a given ministry.

Lead REAL by leading in reality, by leading everywhere, by leading all the time, and by listening. Lead on.

MY LEADERSHIP BOOKSHELF

Boundaries by Henry Cloud and John Townsend (Zondervan, 1992). Every leader needs to know where he or she "starts and stops" in interpersonal settings. *Boundaries* is Life 101 for every leader, providing the tools necessary to develop and model healthy relationships.

LeadershipNext: Changing Leaders in a Changing Culture by Eddie Gibbs (IVP Books, 2005) helps multiple leadership generations understand each other and, therefore, connect with each other. An essential read for future effectiveness.

Good to Great: Why Some Companies Make the Leap . . . and Others Don't by Jim Collins (HarperBusiness, 2001) helps every level of leader identify and analyze the essential ingredients of success in their work.

The Five Dysfunctions of a Team by Patrick Lencioni (John Wiley & Sons, 2009) is both a super read and interactive tool for all kinds of teams. It helps diagnose problem spots and suggests steps for effective leading.

Spiritual Leadership: Moving People on to God's Agenda by Henry and Richard Blackaby (B & H Publishing Group, 2005) addresses the spiritual dynamics and challenges of leading from a biblical perspective.

////// PERSONAL REFLECTIONS AND APPLICATIONS //////

1. What do you need most right now from those who are leaders in your life? Why are these things so important to you? Make a list of leaders you believe could be helpful to you in taking the next step in your leadership calling. Make an effort to seek out one of them in the next week and ask for that person's assistance.

2. Do you have an emerging leader who has asked for your mentoring assistance? Every Paul needs a Timothy, just as every Timothy needs a Paul. What one thing in your life of leadership would you like this individual to emulate? to avoid? Why?

3. As you seek to become REAL, make a list of any stumbling blocks the Holy Spirit brings to mind. These might include poor attitudes, extreme fears, excessive self-confidence, being unconvinced of God's love for you, and so on. Ask for forgiveness and then for help to overcome these barriers. Invite someone you trust to hold you accountable for progress.

4. Is there any major difference in your private and public leadership persona? What one thing in your private life would you not want to become well known in your public leadership life? Why? Remember that nothing will remain hidden—particularly those things that war against God's best for your calling. Take steps today to deal with any secret sin or habit that could become the destroyer of your leadership role.

5. How do you respond to the statement: "You never are not a leader. You never are not leading"? What boundaries have you set? When do you ask for help? Who do you ask for help? How do you invest in yourself? How have you planned for failure? What disciplines are you developing to prepare for the inevitability of the spiritual warfare that being a 24/7 leader will produce?

///////// **TEAM REFLECTIONS AND APPLICATIONS** /////////

1. One wise leadership expert said that the first responsibility of leadership is to define reality. What realities about your organization have you as a leadership team been ignoring? Are there any realities that are off limits for discussion and resolution? Why?

2. Take some extended time as a leadership team to discuss the questions on page 165 about listening to your organizational reality.

3. How does your team help those who do the work of your organization set the appropriate limits so that they have time, resources, and energy to invest in themselves and prepare more thoroughly for the spiritual battles that often result from doing God's kingdom work? In what areas can you specifically improve?

ELISA MORGAN
PUBLISHER, *FULLFILL*™ / PRESIDENT EMERITA, MOPS INTERNATIONAL
//

For twenty years Elisa Morgan served as CEO of MOPS (Mothers of Preschoolers) International. Under her leadership MOPS grew from 350 to more than 4,000 groups throughout the United States and in thirty other countries, impacting over one hundred thousand moms every year. She now serves as president emerita.

MOPS International is a nonprofit ministry that creates communities and resources to help "Better Moms Make a Better World." A MOPS group is a place where moms of young children can come to experience an authentic community of friendship, to receive practical mothering support, and to grow personally and spiritually.

MOPS serves moms from all walks of life and exists to encourage, equip, and develop every mother to realize her potential as a woman, mother, and leader in the name of Jesus Christ.

Elisa Morgan received a BS in psychology from the University of Texas and an MDiv from Denver Seminary. She served as the dean of women of Western Bible College (now Colorado Christian University) and on the board of ECFA (Evangelical Council for Financial Accountability).

She is one of today's most sought-after authors, speakers, and leaders. She has authored more than fifteen books. Her latest work is *She Did What She Could (SDWSC): Five Words of Jesus That Will Change Your Life*.

Now as the publisher of *FullFill*™—a leadership development resource for women of all ages, stages, and callings—Morgan's current mission is to mobilize women to invest their influence in God's purposes. *FullFill*™ is a quarterly digital magazine (www.fullfill.org).

Elisa Morgan is married to Evan, vice president of strategic development for RBC Ministries, and they have two grown children and one grandchild who live near them in the Denver, Colorado, area.

10

///

THE THREE Cs OF THE DISCERNING LEADER

JOHN C. REYNOLDS

J ohn has a long and distinguished career in leadership—both as a leader and as one who equips leaders. His cross-cultural and international experiences provide valuable perspectives on the inner calling to leadership. He suggests that effective leadership for the Lord's kingdom is more than giftedness and personality traits; it is that inescapable sense that God has "called" us to lead for just such times as these. This calling has its roots in character formed by a serving heart and a sacrificial will, making us available to pay the price and not just reap the rewards of leading. The proof of discerning leadership will be seen in the kind of character reproduced in our followers. In a day when leaders too often are motivated by the perks rather than the purposes of leadership, John's challenges will help us "live a life worthy of the calling" we have received (Ephesians 4:1).

In my thirty years of working in Christian organizations, primarily World Vision and for the last decade at Azusa Pacific University, I have made a significant part of my career the equipping of emerging leaders. Through professional workshops, mentoring, or executive coaching, the most common but insightful question has been, "What makes a Christian leader different from any other successful organizational leader?"

Leaders in Christian organizations and ministry are different from general leaders. I've spent much time in study and reflection trying to understand whether this distinctive of being Christian can be qualified, quantified, and even replicated. While I have not found the formula, the good news is that as I serve with and coach emerging Christian leaders, there are common, significant attributes evident in the lives of those Christian leaders making a difference for the kingdom.

Many attributes are fundamental to successful leadership—such as being a visionary, a good communicator, optimistic, self-assured, encouraging, and empowering—and these attributes generally are visible in many successful leaders, both Christian and secular.

What fuels this commitment to dependence on God and to a focused mission is that the Christian leader is *called*—called to make a difference. These leaders have discerned who God is calling them to be, and to what end their leadership contribution will serve in the building of the Lord's kingdom here on earth.

In the Christian community, the word *discern* has great scriptural value and depth. *Discernment* communicates maturity, experience, and wisdom. In studying Scripture, we often equate *discernment* with *godly judgment,* so that even in the most humble sense, being discerning positions us as God's earthly proxy in matters of critical decision making. The basic meaning of *to discern* is "to separate," "to make a distinction," or "to differentiate."[1] Thus, discernment is the ability to examine, test, try, judge, or prove something with the result of separating, or distinguishing, the good from the bad. Many times in my experience, however, this means discerning the good from the better or the best!

From a community perspective, discernment communicates a sense of calling. For example, in the health, child welfare, and education sectors, much is written about discernment. Some might see these vocational professions as ones to which they are called—often with personal sacrifice. The discerning Christ-centered leader might be described in this way: a leader who is called, manifesting a character of maturity and wisdom, whose first interest is in the people who follow him or her. Does that describe you? Is that your personal leadership desire?

The discerning leader is called to lead, not necessarily by title or organizational position but by a deep sense of calling from God. Consider, for example, the call of God to Jeremiah: "Before you were born I set you apart; I appointed you" (Jeremiah 1:5). The call of Paul, Peter, and many other biblical leaders could be cited.

This chapter addresses what I believe to be the three essential attributes of a discerning leader. These might help answer a question you may still be wrestling with: How then are Christian leaders different? Or more personally, how are *you* different as a Christian leader?

These distinctive attributes—calling, character, and consequences—are best visualized by real-life examples of exceptional leaders as illustrated in this diagram.

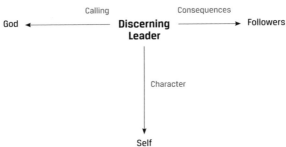

Discerning leaders have a *calling* from God to lead. This calling encourages self-awareness and an intentional evaluation of who they are as individuals— including an understanding of their own strengths, talents, and gifts. The calling molds *character*, influences how they manifest this character, and guides how they behave as discerning leaders.

The calling and character of the discerning leader will result in discerning leadership, which is easily identified by the *consequences*: a growing number of followers. My mother had a saying: "The proof of the good pudding is in the eating." The proof of discerning leadership is that when a leader looks in the "rearview mirror," he sees visible followers.

// CALLING //

I once heard a humorous line regarding successful men: "Behind every successful man is a very surprised mother-in-law." Genuine and discerning leaders are often as surprised as anyone to find themselves described as leaders—especially *discerning* leaders! This is an honest discovery that they have evolved into a role of leadership influence, not by their own design but by a personal response to a clear call from God to do what is right for those they serve. In most cases these leaders often feel out of their comfort zones, because they never intended to seek a leadership role. Discerning leaders respond in obedience and humility to a deep sense of calling, which often positions them in roles and with responsibilities for which they do not feel adequately prepared.

I serve with an amazing leader, Jon Wallace, president of Azusa Pacific University. In the last decade we have worked and traveled together. We have prayed and cried over significant health issues, and laughed like children at changes we have seen in the university. And yet I believe that Jon (who started at APU as a student and then served as a custodian, campus safety officer, dean of students, executive vice president, and now as president) is successful because of his dependence on God and his leading. If for one minute he felt that his current role was not what God wanted for his life, Jon would move on. He is a discerning leader.

God tends to position us in ministry and life where we must rely on his strength to be successful. What better understanding for leaders than to know that we cannot, and should not, lead within just our own human ability. The next time you meet a leader you believe is a discerning Christian leader, check his knees. They are calloused from prayer! Discerning leadership requires a total dependence on the greatest leader in history, Jesus Christ himself.

Leading people is not, to use a systems principle, a closed system. There is no beginning or end to the lives of followers in the organization. Followers are not robots or automated servants. To be a discerning leader, you not only will deliver products or outcomes but also must be an agent for changing lives. The key question asked by today's organizational contributor (employee) is, "How am I significant to the work we are called to do?" The discerning leader strives to ensure that every follower feels significant as a member of the organizational community, valued by recognition and reward, and respected as an individual.

A Christ-centered discerning leader draws on the power of the Holy Spirit within. Scripture reminds us to "keep watch over yourselves and all the flock of which the Holy Spirit has made you overseers. Be shepherds of the church of God, which he bought with his own blood" (Acts 20:28). Though this directive from the apostle Paul was intended for church elders to be overseers, shepherds of a flock, there is a sense in which a leader of a faith-based ministry or organization is called by God to care for his group as he leads and shepherds with discernment.

Even without a calling by the Holy Spirit, it is possible that a Christian leader could lead with some discernment. However, with a clear calling by the Spirit, there is no question that we are in place as overseers of a community. This requires us to be intimately and passionately concerned about the people who follow us. It requires us to put, without question or hesitation, our role as leader in his hands as he leads and guides us to shepherd the flock.

It is not without significance that this verse begins with the phrase "keep watch over yourselves" and *then* "all the flock." Your inner character, strengths, beliefs, values, and experience are the core of your leadership behavior and style. We need to know ourselves completely before we claim the right to lead others.

No person in Scripture underwent a more significant transformational journey of leadership than the disciple Peter. He learned who he was through what happened between the Garden of Gethsemane and the shores of Galilee. This journey changed Peter from a simple fisherman to a leader called by the resurrected Christ to "take care of my sheep" (John 21:16). In 1 and 2 Peter, he records the importance of being a shepherd leader, or a leader of discernment. Remember this passage: "Be shepherds of God's flock that is under your care, serving as overseers—not because you must, but because you are willing, as God wants you to be; not greedy for money, but eager to serve; not lording it over those entrusted to you, but being examples to the flock. And when the Chief Shepherd appears, you will receive the crown of glory that will never fade away" (1 Peter 5:2-4). Again, those words were originally intended for church elders, but I believe that we can apply some of the principles to our discerning leadership today. Walk with me through some of the key terms in that insightful passage.

SHEPHERDING WITH A SERVANT'S HEART

We begin with the description of a shepherd. Being a shepherd is a lonely position (think about King David as a young boy). A shepherd is always on the lookout for the good of his sheep, watching for the earliest signs of disease in the flock, constantly scanning the horizon to search out opportunities for grazing, and assessing potentially dangerous circumstances. Does it sound like a full-time, all-consuming role? I believe it is.

"Serving as overseers" is a powerful phrase that brings together the idea of the role of the overseer with the ideal of being a servant. In modern leadership terms, this might be translated as "servant leader." We, as discerning leaders, serve at the calling of our master, the Lord Jesus Christ. It is a personal act of obedience—a conscious act of submission. The personal reward is that this overseer role comes with the essentials—the rich wisdom and knowledge of a loving and knowing master.

This Scripture again reminds us that leading is a calling, with the phrase "because you are willing." A discerning leader must be willing to serve as an overseer as an act of submissive obedience. This is a sacrificial willingness to respond to the call by saying, as Isaiah did, "Here am I. Send me!" (Isaiah 6:8). We do not lead for recognition and rewards. Few of us in Christian ministry can claim that prize! But we respond with eager willingness when we believe that we can be a small part of extending his kingdom here on earth. For this goal every one of us is called.

MODELING, NOT LORDING IT OVER OTHERS

Peter had learned the hard way that "lording it over" others is really not the best style of leadership. Do you remember in Scripture when Peter was the only disciple to speak, to assert himself into the "first disciple" role?

(for example, John 13:6; Luke 5:8)? But at some point a deep sense of humility and self-awareness become more characteristic—beginning with his conversation with Christ on the shores of Galilee, through his leadership transformation recorded in Acts (note Acts 2:14 where "Peter stood up with the Eleven"), to the mature "Simon Peter, a servant and apostle of Jesus Christ" (2 Peter 1:1). How different Peter is depicted in the foundation of the church (as a strong, discerning, servant leader) in the book of Acts, compared to his earlier days as a new disciple. If a leader feels compelled to lord it over others, then he has lost sight of who his Lord really is.

In two decades of teaching, researching, and consulting in the field of leader development, I have found that the single most visible trait of a leader who will have the greatest impact on his followers is modeling. Leaders live in fishbowls. They are watched constantly for what they do and say, as well as for what they do *not* do and say! Nothing destroys the health of an organization more quickly than leaders who do not "walk the talk." Among the symptoms are a lack of the honesty and integrity necessary to model discerning leadership. Followers demand leaders who are models. In the Acts 20:28 passage, Peter provides a practical framework in which leaders today can operate. Note the following characteristics of discerning leadership:

- You must know who you are and keep careful watch over yourself.
- You are called by the Holy Spirit to oversee as the trustee of your followers.
- You will be challenged constantly to be both a servant and a shepherd.
- You will be watched—you set the example by how you model yourself to your followers.

That Scripture reminds us that discerning leaders are not only called but are distinguished by the character they manifest to their followers and to the world. Knowing who you are as a leader is critical to fulfilling God's call to you to lead in his image.

// CHARACTER //

The second attribute of a discerning leader, after a clear calling, is character. The character of the discerning leader, loosely defined, is the application of the leader's personal call to the execution of his or her leadership. A leader's character begins with a strong awareness of who he is as an individual, and this informs how he manages relationships. While *calling* is the personal relationship between the leader and God, the *character* of a leader is who the leader is as a person and how he relates to his followers.

I have had the privilege of working for, learning from, and serving with many discerning leaders from around the world. So what did I learn? After their calling, these leaders shared several common characteristics that defined them. Their leadership was genuine and disciplined—it was not just the "leadership flavor of the month." Reflect on the following as a checklist. Do you have these seven characteristics, and how do you manifest them for the Lord?

1. PASSIONATE

Discerning leaders have a clear vision and purpose that is defined by their relationship with God. It is evident when we find it hard to see anything they do, or say, that does not come from a deep-rooted passion and urgency to make this vision/purpose/dream a reality. It is easy to follow a passionate leader—you always know where he is going!

Generally, passionate leaders want to leave a legacy. Their calling, passion, and energy are not only for today. God does not call discerning leaders to provide just the proverbial fish. He calls us to a build a foundation for teaching others to fish—this is our legacy.

2. PRINCIPLED

A review of world history creates for us a list of great leaders evidenced by their traits. In leadership theory we would call this the "great man theory" or "trait theory." Such a list might include the names of Nelson Mandela, Martin

Luther King Jr., Winston Churchill, Eleanor Roosevelt, and William Wilberforce. And I believe that we would find a clearly defined set of principles that each leader followed with courage, zeal, and integrity. So if we were to develop this list, it would consist of a subset of nonnegotiable principles.

But principles on their own are not enough. These must be sacrificial and selfless principles that permeate the organization, influencing the followers. For the discerning leader, it is not about who *I* am—it is about who *we* are. Principled leaders leave their egos at the door and, as a result, cultivate acceptance, credibility, and trust among their followers. Principled leaders are respected. We know what their principles are, leaving little doubt about what is important to them. Followers may not necessarily like or agree with the leader, but principled leaders are generally highly respected.

Principled leaders tend to give credit to others rather than take credit for their own leadership. This credit is plentiful, sincere, and genuine. Discerning leaders realize and publicly acknowledge that they do not do anything on their own. They say, "This is all about my team."

Discerning, principled leaders know that they have to do the right thing, that there is no compromise—often making choices between the most popular solution and the right solution (that is, the solution that reflects who they are, and therefore, they have a sense of God's peace in the decision). With principle comes the courage and authenticity of knowing who God has called you to be, to make the *right* decision. Be sure of your principles, pray through them, and communicate clearly with action and word that these are who you are as a leader in the organization.

3. PEOPLE MINDED

Discerning leaders are genuine managers who facilitate real human relationships. The social aspects of the organization are as important to them as the technical structure and systems. Structure needs to happen (the finances, the facilities, etc.), but it should always be oriented, if not biased, toward what it will mean for the people within the organization. Discerning leaders acknowledge that followers choose to be led. Followers must work for whichever manager is over them, but they *choose* which leaders they *follow*.

Discerning leaders create, enable, and empower community by communicating and behaving in ways that demonstrate that they value people. The community then trusts and understands that decisions made by the leader will always be intentional in considering the human factor. This manifests the Lord's command to "love one another" (John 13:34). Will others know you as a disciple by the way you deal with people? This is not easy for many leaders, as there is confusion between the role of professional leader and the personal neighbor.

4. PERCEPTIVE

Discerning leaders are recognized for being perceptive. This is manifested in several ways, but a good sense of judgment is perhaps the most obvious. They listen well, are intuitive, and are able to contextualize situations quickly. Discerning leaders align daily operations with the organization's future. Do you have a big picture of the end game? Think of a jigsaw puzzle for a moment. Most of us find it difficult to build a puzzle without the cover of the box. We need to know what the final picture will be. A good friend of mine, Dr. John Volmink, currently the inspector general for education in South Africa, is a discerning leader with an enormous amount of leadership perspective supporting a personal passion. An academic, administrator, churchman, husband, and dad, he knows that the future of South Africa is dependent on excellent basic education. Every board that John is a member of and every spare moment (not many) are devoted to basic education for the people of South Africa.

5. PREPARED

Nothing shakes people's foundational trust in their leader more than the feeling that he is ill prepared. Discerning leaders are prepared to lead their organizations in pursuit of the big picture.

Joshua is one of my favorite biblical leaders. He lived 110 years and was one of only two adults (along with Caleb) to come out of Egypt and enter the promised land, following the arduous forty-year journey through the wilderness. Joshua trained under Moses to become a leader. We read God's charge in Joshua 1:9: "Be strong and courageous." God had prepared him for many years, and he was clear on the big picture: get God's people to the promised land.

Discerning leaders are amateur historians seeking to understand and learn from the past. They know what the current plans are and what needs to be achieved. They tend to be knowledgeable and well informed. And they are absolutely clear about the future.

6. POLITICAL

Discerning leaders, unfortunately, are not excused from being political. However, they are political in a different sense of this term that has earned so many negative perceptions. There are two aspects to politics for a discerning leader. The first is the ability to have good judgment, be prudent, and wise. The second is the ability to use these gifts from God to govern in organizations where colleagues' opinions, expectations, and beliefs may be different from one another's—and perhaps from yours. This ability is the art of being political! Discerning leaders need to be political in a positive style, with the right God-given motivation, positioning their egos way behind the process of manifesting what they believe God is calling them to implement. The leader who is political for God's kingdom will:

- *❙* exercise influence where it is appropriate and necessary.
- *❙* persuade followers toward a desired future with integrity.
- *❙* create understanding and clarity.
- *❙* change attitudes that distract from the purpose and mission.
- *❙* engage commitment to a path and destination where the vision may not be as clear as it is to the leader.

We sometimes forget that the origins of the word *political* are derived from the word *politic,* which carries the idea of exercising good judgment: "seeming sensible and judicious under the circumstances"; "shrewd or prudent in practical matters; tactful; diplomatic"; "using or marked by prudence, expedience."[2] Being prudent and of good judgment is essential for the leader with discernment.

We do not have to go far in Scripture to discover that many of the great biblical leaders were not only known for their "politics" but in addition served in key political roles. Joseph, Nehemiah, Daniel, David, Solomon, and Paul, to name a few, were discerning leaders who were both kinds of political.

7. PROFESSIONAL

A discerning leader serves with excellence. Much of my leadership development has been with World Vision and, for a large part of that time, was under the mentorship of Dr. Ted W. Engstrom. Both organizationally and personally, this experience instilled in me a core sense of excellence and professionalism. There is no second place for Christian leaders—we are the models. This is both a blessing and a burden. Leaders must model behaviors and a style that reflect God-honoring excellence on a 24/7 basis. As followers follow the example, the norm for expected behavior will evolve, and a ministry or organizational culture known for excellence and professionalism will result.

Each of those seven fundamental characteristics is found in a discerning Christ-centered leader. How did you do as you considered each one? Do you see a foundation of each of those characteristics in your life that you can build on to improve your leadership?

// CONSEQUENCES //

In attempting to differentiate the Christian leader from leaders in the world, we positioned the Christian leader as a discerning leader. Discerning leaders are called, they are identified by certain principles, and they strive to love God daily and show godly characteristics through their leadership behavior. Leadership does not happen in a vacuum—leadership depends on strong relationships with those who have been called to follow. Literature today labels this relationship with a transformational leader as *followership.* There are consequences, or a measure, of being called by God to be a leader: followers. The model of Jesus and his twelve apostles comes to mind.

How do you as a Christian leader relate differently, compared to the successful leader we see and read about in the business world? We know that we are accountable, with excellence, for the purpose for which our organizations were founded. But how is that played out as we relate to and lead, specifically, those who are employed or volunteer in the organization? Discerning leadership is a relationship between those who are *called to lead* and those who *choose to follow.* With the goal of good consequences in mind, the discerning leader:

- develops an effective leadership style that unconditionally includes a deep and personal concern for the soul, heart, and mind of those within his or her span of care.
- looks beyond success—and the necessary outcomes of goals and objectives in the organization—to transformed lives.
- develops followers who are on a journey of personal and professional transformation in the organization and in the constituencies they serve.
- understands and nurtures the relationship between his role as a leader and the followers he is called to shepherd.
- understands the relationship between leader and follower because he is a follower as well—of the Lord Jesus Christ.
- is a person people choose to follow because they believe their leader is following Christ's example.

A discerning leader knows that if followers choose to follow, there is significant effort needed to support that relationship. After a few decades of observation and experience within this relationship, I have found the following formula to be a trustworthy tool:

Finding the voice of the follower =
unique + personal + significant

Every follower is unique, and a discerning leader knows the danger in believing that one voice speaks for all. Good judgment and a discerning spirit are keys to recognizing that there are unique voices that each should be valued.

It is difficult to ensure a personal and unique relationship with all followers in the organization, especially one that is large and geographically distributed. However, identifying and nurturing followers who are directly influenced and guided by the leader (direct reports) is nonnegotiable. These relationships should be well balanced between professional management and personal interest—in their families as well as their spiritual and professional journeys. Followers are committed to the leader and the cause. They search for and desire to be recognized and valued for their significant contribution to the mission. In a sense, followers are really "professional volunteers"; and although material rewards are important, there is a greater need for value and contribution to the mission. There is no greater legacy for a discerning leader than to mentor and coach the emerging generation of leaders.

So how might this relationship between discerning leaders and followers be implemented and nurtured? Several excellent frameworks evolve out of transformational leadership theory and best practices. Choose one that supports your style and behavior. For those who are keen to begin right now, a popular model that is well researched and practiced is the "Five Fundamental Practices of Exemplary Leadership" model developed by James Kouzes and Barry Posner.[3]

Several books develop this model in the context of nonprofit leadership. To this thinking I add some thoughts on the five practices as they relate to the discerning leader.

1. MODEL THE WAY
Discerning leaders know that to build and develop the leader-follower

relationship, they will need to display and be an example to the organization. This modeling visibly demonstrates the behavior and norms, or the desired culture, of the organization.

2. INSPIRE A SHARED VISION

Two concepts are critical in this particular leader-follower practice. First is the ability to develop and articulate a shared vision. Discerning leaders effectively communicate with their followers—motivating them with a vision that is collaborative, as well as igniting and energizing followers to be significant members in the journey toward the vision. Second, the ability to inspire a group of followers is important for both the leader and the follower. As a leader, do you feel the passion and energy? Do you feel inspired to be on this journey to a new future? Followers are so intuitive that if there is any sense that the leader does not feel that the vision is both inspired and rooted in a relationship with Christ, they will regard the leader as disingenuous.

3. CHALLENGE THE PROCESS

Discerning leaders are committed to excellence and to executing strategy both effectively and efficiently. This demands a continual challenging of the status quo. This is not an ongoing pursuit of change for change's sake, but a desire to implement a structure that is supportive of the pursuit of the mission and purpose for which they were called. Continual reflection, learning, and appropriate change—if done with the right purpose—will enable followers and build trust and respect.

4. ENABLE OTHERS TO ACT

Discerning leaders create and maintain organizational environments that empower and enable followers to be significant and valued contributors to the mission and purpose of the organization. Followers expect that the leader is not going to achieve the goals of the organization alone. Discerning leaders know that this is a community effort. Some important enabling strategies include the reduction or removal of obstacles, delegation with accountability, and unconditional support of followers.

5. ENCOURAGE THE HEART

Without encouragement and celebration, leaders would be missing the critical relationship with their followers. An encouraging word, a visit, or notes of support or recognition are all tools of a leader who desires a transformational relationship with his followers. Celebrations are important and an essential ingredient to organizational health. However, there is no substitute for the personal encouragement that causes followers to feel within their hearts that their membership in the organizational community is valued and significant.

It is relatively simple to outline, as I have done here, the fundamentals of what I believe characterizes a discerning leader, but the obvious question is "Do I walk the talk?" The several hundred followers I now have under my sphere of influence would answer the question better than I, but let me share a little of my testimony. I am a first-generation Christian, born and raised in a developing country to a working-class family. Church was a foreign concept; only through the divine intervention of a believing schoolmaster did I come to know the Lord. Through a series of bizarre circumstances (humanly speaking; miracles from a Christian view), I was educated in the field of computer science.

How, in the early 1970s, on the continent of Africa, would computer science make me available to be a servant for the Lord and bring the gospel to the world? It seemed like the wrong choice at the time for a new believer, but even with a prayer of confusion, I felt and heard God's call to enter the field of computers. This leading from God put me in a position to place the first personal computers in the field for both World Vision and the United Nations Development agency in the early 1980s, and ultimately to finish an almost twenty-year career with World Vision International as the organization's partnership chief information officer (CIO). It opened the door to join Azusa Pacific University as their first CIO in 2000, and today I lead as a senior administrator on two continents and am privileged to be involved in Christian leadership around the world.

However, I am a reluctant leader, an introvert, a geek. God has called me to this service for him, and he will call me to another in the future. Until that time my passion is to develop who I am as a discerning leader, spread this passion, and trust through his grace that followers will see his kingdom being extended through what we accomplish together (good consequences, I pray). I pray that we model a dependence on God, a faithful prayer life, a personal and professional walk that honors God, a common belief that we are called for an outcome far greater than any of us can imagine.

We are *all* called to lead; every one of us is a leader and has followers. Do you see yourself as different from the leaders we read about in the press? Let's lead with discernment and honor God!

MY LEADERSHIP BOOKSHELF

Spiritual Leadership: Moving People on to God's Agenda by Henry and Richard Blackaby (B & H Publishing Group, 2005) is a must for every discerning leader's desk. It reminds us that we are leading in God's plans as they are revealed to us—and need guidance from and dependence on him to see these plans realized.

Deep Change: Discovering the Leader Within by Robert E. Quinn (Jossey-Bass, 1996) provides inspirational thought on personal change, motivations of the leader, vision, and excellence. Discerning leaders are agents of change.

The Leadership Challenge by James Kouzes and Barry Posner (Jossey-Bass, 2007) is a classic that provides five practical practices of how leaders can engage with their followers. This is a model for exploring the consequences of being a discerning leader.

Basic Christian Leadership: Biblical Models of Church, Gospel and Ministry by John Stott (InterVarsity Press, 2002) is a reminder that a biblical approach to leadership should be as important as the secular models we readily adopt in organizations and ministries today. Discerning leaders are servant leaders.

Certain Trumpets: The Nature of Leadership by Garry Wills (Simon & Schuster, 1995) examines leaders of history and highlights the simple but effective combination of leaders, followers, and a common goal or purpose. It is an excellent resource for developing the discerning leader's principles and how they might be put into practice.

////// PERSONAL REFLECTIONS AND APPLICATIONS //////

1. How do you lead differently as a Christian leader compared to successful leaders who do not claim a relationship with Christ?

2. If you were being rated on a scale of 1 to 5 on the seven characteristics of a discerning leader (p. 186), how would you score on each characteristic? What might you consider doing differently to move these personal scores higher?

3. Would your employees/subordinates follow you if they had a choice? Or do you have followers by virtue of your organizational title? Explain.

4. Do the leaders in your ministry/organization have a sense of what it means to be a "difference maker" through their leadership? How do they hold each other accountable?

5. What systems exist to measure your team's leadership effectiveness with the organizational community? How do you know that the way your team leads is transformational?

////////// TEAM REFLECTIONS AND APPLICATIONS //////////

1. As a team/group, consider sharing your individual stories of how you felt God was calling you to be a leader. Reflect on the differences of your callings. Then celebrate the wonder of how God has called you to be a team or small group, noting the unique contribution each brings to the organization's leadership calling. Consider how you might hold each other accountable for this calling.

2. In what ways might you manifest the principles of discerning leadership in your team or group? How do you believe this will make a difference to the effectiveness of your team or group?

3. When your team/group evaluates their effectiveness in leading the ministry or organization in its mission, how important are the followers in the evaluation? Are they employed to achieve the goals only, or are you as a team/group considering how they might be personally transformed in this process? How are you measuring this?

4. As your team has reflected on the five leadership practices of Kouzes and Posner (p. 192), where do you see your team positioned in terms of strengths and gaps in these practices? How might you intentionally work on the strengths and reduce the gaps?

5. In a team exercise, let each member reflect and write a short overview of your team's leadership style as each of you understands it. Share and compare, identifying whether you as a team have a common view; or if there are differences, why that may be. Pray, reflect, and act on how you as a team might exhibit more clearly your calling, character, and expression of these attributes in the future, so you will reap the consequences of being defined as discerning leaders people are excited about following.

JOHN C. REYNOLDS
EXECUTIVE VICE PRESIDENT, AZUSA PACIFIC UNIVERSITY
///

John C. Reynolds is executive vice president and adjunct professor in organizational leadership at Azusa Pacific University (www.apu.edu). APU, located in Southern California, is a private, faith-based university of ten thousand students, delivering undergraduate, graduate, and doctoral programs in seven schools.

Reynolds, a native of South Africa, holds undergraduate and graduate degrees in computer science and information systems. He currently is completing his PhD in leadership and organizational effectiveness at APU.

He has been employed in higher education, the mining industry, and for ten years as the global CIO for World Vision International, a large, private, international relief organization. This experience has given Reynolds the privilege of visiting more than seventy countries for the purpose of teaching and consulting.

John C. Reynolds serves on several boards, including Christian Leadership Alliance, African Enterprise (USA), Open Doors (USA), LCC International University (Lithuania), and AP Educational Foundation (South Africa).

He and his wife, Carole, have two sons and reside in Southern California, where he serves as an elder at Glenkirk Presbyterian Church in Glendora.

11

///

LEADING BEST BY FOLLOWING FIRST

RICHARD STEARNS

E merging leaders often wonder if it is possible, or even appropriate, to utilize the best practices of business and industry when leading faith-based organizations. Often there is the assumption that since most secular organizations are driven primarily by the profit margins of the balance sheet's bottom line and the need to produce ROI (return on investment) to stockholders and stakeholders, leadership practices in those settings must be tainted or limited.

Richard demonstrates in this chapter that many of the best practices he developed while leading profitable corporations are fundamental to leading with excellence and accountability. However, these practices can only be effective when the leader embraces unconditional surrender to the purposes of God, casts and embodies a vision that God can bless, and builds a team he or she can coach as Jesus did his founding twelve. Fully conscious of who we are and who we are becoming in Christ, we follow in the footsteps of the one who taught us in word and action that you lead best when you follow first.

I did not grow up in a family that produces Ivy League–educated CEOs. Neither my mother nor my father finished high school. I grew up in relative poverty. Yet amazingly, I was able to attend Cornell University and the Wharton School of Business. And I went on to become the CEO of three large organizations. The religion of my youth was survival and self-reliance, but God eventually got hold of me, and in his grace today, I am in full-time Christian service as the president of World Vision U.S.

My journey from a poor kid in a broken home to the leader of an organization that *fights* global poverty is unquestionably atypical. God used all of it to shape who I am today and teach me lessons about leadership that I now know to be true. The wisdom I am about to pass along is gleaned from diverse leadership experiences over decades in wide-ranging industries—from shaving cream to video games, from fine china and crystal to humanitarian aid.

// SURRENDER UNCONDITIONALLY //

The first lesson is the most important, and for many—including me—it's the most difficult. To be a Christian leader, you must submit to God's will and be ready to serve him completely—not your boss, not your investors or donors, and certainly not yourself. That didn't happen so easily for me. God has been patient as I struggled to understand just what he expected of me in my life and career. And finally I have come to understand this: God asks us for *everything*—a total life commitment.

As proof of God's amazing grace, I am probably one of only a handful of people who became a Christian while pursuing an MBA at the Wharton School. The day I knelt in my dorm room and accepted Christ, I understood that I was making a total commitment, was "betting the farm" on Christ and agreeing to follow him no matter where and no matter what. The old catechism I learned as a boy rang true—God made me to love, serve, and obey him. I was going to do that with every decision, in every aspect of my life.

Some of that was easy. The woman I married, Reneé, helped lead me to Christ and was a strong spiritual partner. We went on to have five children. I was a church elder, we tithed our income faithfully, and we were involved in Bible studies and fellowship groups. My career was defined by success. At Parker Brothers Games, the well-known toy company, I was promoted nearly every year and became president at age thirty-three.

But then the unthinkable happened: Parker Brothers Games went through a change of ownership, and I was let go. I found a new position at a higher salary with The Franklin Mint—and then got fired again after just nine months. In total, I was unemployed for fourteen months. For someone who had enjoyed so much success at such a young age, it was devastating and a major crisis of faith. What was I doing wrong?

My greatest discovery from that period was that God had sidelined me to learn something. My life had become more about the American Dream than about following him. I was too busy pursuing my career rather than my calling. As John Ortberg wrote, "For many people a career becomes the altar on which they sacrifice their lives. . . . A calling, which is something I do *for* God, is replaced by a *career*, which threatens to *become* my god."[1]

I made a renewed commitment to love, serve, and obey God. Eventually I was offered a job at Lenox, the fine china company, and good things began to happen again. The division I led tripled in size over the next three years. Senior management noticed, and I got promotion after promotion, eventually becoming president and CEO.

And yet God was not done with me. Back in graduate school I had committed my life to Christ and "bet the farm"; then in 1998, God came to "collect the deed." It came in the form of a phone call from a headhunter, inviting me to apply for the job as president of World Vision U.S.

"Are you willing to be open to God's will for your life?" he asked.

My wife and I had been donors to World Vision for fifteen years, and I believed in the ministry. But I did not think I was the man for the job. Quit my high-powered job at Lenox for a 75 percent pay cut? Sell the home my wife loved, move my five kids across the country to a city where we knew no one? Leave friends, family, and a great church? All this to walk alongside children and families living in horrible conditions of poverty?

At the root of any calling is a choice—to follow God's call or to turn away. This was the dilemma for the rich young ruler in Mark 10:17-22.

"What must I do to inherit eternal life?" he asked.

Jesus gave him a fairly conventional answer: "You know the commandments."

"All these I have kept," he said.

Whew. That was easy.

This was my attitude as CEO of Lenox. And "poster boy'" for the successful Christian life. Wasn't I doing all God wanted me to do?

The Bible tells us that Jesus looked at the rich young ruler and loved him, but then said, "One thing you lack. . . . Go, sell everything you have and give to the poor, and you will have treasure in heaven. Then come, follow me."

This wasn't the answer the young man was looking for. "He went away sad, because he had great wealth."

I read this story during my "dark night of the soul" while I agonized over the World Vision job. I realized I had confused my success with God's approval. The time had come to submit.

Before we can lead, we must first offer our service to God—unconditionally and on his terms. We must be sold out totally to his calling in our lives. And it requires careful monitoring of our motives. Am I in this for my own sake, or for God's? If we are in it for ourselves, we will be hobbled as leaders.

Consider what your "farm" is—your career, income, comfortable home, community, or even the little things that pull you away from your commitment to the Lord. Take the same challenge Jesus gave the young man, to give up everything and follow him. If you cannot answer that challenge with an unconditional yes, then you probably have some work to do with God.

// CAST A VISION—AND EMBODY IT //

Once you have surrendered to God's call on your life, your most crucial role as a leader is to cast a vision for the organization—and embrace that vision. You have to believe in the importance of what you are doing, and you can't fake that. When your words and actions embody organizational values, you shape the internal culture and the external impact of the organization. Effective corporations have leaders who embody their organization's vision and values. Where would Apple be without Steve Jobs, or Microsoft without Bill Gates?

It is easy to embrace a vision like World Vision's: "Our vision for every child, life in all its fullness. Our prayer for every heart, the will to make it so." Serving at a for-profit company may not be as inspiring as that, but certain values—honoring people, striving for excellence, working with integrity—were just as crucial for me when I was selling shaving cream at Gillette, games at Parker Brothers Games, and fine china at Lenox.

On the other hand, there's a key difference in leading a Christian nonprofit. The stakes are even higher for a leader trying to cast a new vision, because people are so deeply invested. The employees are not there only for their careers and salaries, and donors want more than a basic return on their investment.

Just sixty days after I started at World Vision U.S., I sat in a thatch hut in Rakai, Uganda, listening to Richard, a boy with the same name as mine, whose parents had died of AIDS. At thirteen, he was trying to raise his two younger brothers by himself with no running water, no steady food supply, nor even beds to sleep in. He said he loved to read the book of John in the Bible "because it says God loves the children."

I returned from Uganda heartbroken and angry. Where was the church in the midst of this crisis? When I tried to marshal support from World Vision staff to tackle AIDS, many were extremely uncomfortable with the issue. As one person said, "We're a G-rated ministry focused on children and families. AIDS is an R-rated issue." The external challenges were even greater. A Barna Research Group poll of evangelicals in 2001 showed that they were "significantly less likely than are non-Christians to give money for AIDS education and prevention programs worldwide. Only 3 percent of evangelicals say they plan to help with AIDS internationally."[2] To me, this seemed to indicate that American Christians felt OK about not caring for people affected by AIDS. And in Africa those most affected were children like Richard, children left behind.

I had to paint a picture that changed the way people looked at HIV and AIDS. So we focused on James 1:27, "to look after orphans and widows in their distress." Once Christians began to see AIDS from a completely different vantage point, we were able to challenge them directly: "What is our responsibility before God in the face of this global humanitarian crisis?" I went around the country speaking to audiences that moved from skeptical to repentant.

World Vision launched its AIDS Hope Initiative in 2001. It changed our hearts and the hearts of our donors. It changed our model of community development. And it ultimately changed the lives of millions of children and families affected by AIDS around the world.

The story of Nehemiah applies here. Nehemiah was a brilliant leader who cast a motivating vision for the exiles who had returned to Jerusalem. The temple had been rebuilt, but the great walls needed to protect the city still lay in ruins nearly a century and a half after they were destroyed. He must have wondered, *Why didn't anyone else care about this?*

Nehemiah sat down and wept, then mourned and fasted and prayed (Nehemiah 1:4). He traveled to Jerusalem and challenged the Jews there to action. He called them to a higher vision, to lift up the holy God of Israel by rebuilding the walls. He divided up the tasks and inspired each family—despite repeated opposition from hostile neighbors—to do their part. The result was amazing. The great wall was rebuilt in fifty-two days! (6:15).

Our world, like Nehemiah's, also lies in ruins. We too need a fresh vision. That is our task as leaders.

// BE A COACH //

The success of any organization will depend in large part on whether the leader has chosen the right people for the right jobs—just like a coach forming a team. Once the right people are on the team, a coach helps them succeed by allowing them the freedom to use their gifts.

I feel so strongly about this that I believe that the right people will succeed even if they are given the wrong strategy—they will adjust and figure out the flaws. But the wrong people, even with the right strategy, will probably fail. It may surprise less experienced leaders that the right *people* are more important than the right *strategy*.

A good CEO realizes that unless we have people with the right gifts around us, we will fail. Hopefully, we recognize this earlier in our careers. Inexperienced leaders can be particularly tempted to make the mistake of thinking, *I got here because I'm smart and I'm capable, and since there's nobody more capable than I am, I'll just do all this work myself.* Making the transition to leadership means moving from being a doer to being a coach of those who do.

We all have had bosses who thought they knew how to do our jobs better than we did. I worked with a brilliant leader who had a tendency to frustrate his staff by micromanaging, but he didn't believe it was a problem. He was so smart that he probably could have done any of his direct reports' jobs better than they could. But that was not his job anymore. It became a lose-lose situation for both him and his staff—he did not get the best out of their creativity and ideas, he slowed down decision making, and he de-motivated them.

As leaders we need to choose staff we can trust and then judge their work based on whether it accomplishes the goal, not on whether they produce it exactly as we would have. A coach empowers his team to do what God equipped them to do but resists the temptation to do it for them. He does not compete on the field with the players but creates the plan and works with the players so that they can carry it out. A coach creates a team environment with clear goals and a strong culture of teamwork in which they can succeed.

Jesus is the model of a great coach. Talk about an important job—selecting people who were going to bring the good news to the ends of the earth. He chose just twelve. And his selections were unlikely. He saw past the résumé and into the heart. Of course, we could say that not all of his hiring decisions were good (Judas), but even that was a part of his plan.

Jesus spent three years casting the vision, investing in his disciples, and teaching them. He allowed them to question him and make mistakes. Peter denied him three times. Jesus let Thomas touch his wounds to quell the doubts.

Then he said, "Go and make disciples of all nations" (Matthew 28:19). In other words, "I'm leaving now, and you need to do it." They had the guidance and encouragement of the Holy Spirit, but Jesus didn't come back every month to adjust what they were doing. The results speak for themselves—from twelve disciples there are now two billion Christians.

// DEVELOP SELF-AWARENESS //

The coach metaphor of getting the right people on the team and empowering them to succeed is only half of the "people" equation. We can cast the right vision and have the right people, but we also have to *be* the right kind of leader. We must realize our own strengths and weaknesses, how we are perceived, and how we—intentionally or unintentionally—impact those around us.

Leaders who lack self-awareness are blind, constantly bumping into things because they do not see them. They have a terrible time navigating their jobs because they do not realize the impact they are having on others.

We might believe ourselves to be approachable; however, we often underestimate the chilling effect of title and status in large organizations. As leaders, we must acknowledge that the higher we are elevated in leadership, the louder our voice is. That can be a great benefit when we want something accomplished; we can use our position to influence people in positive ways. However, a CEO's whisper can sound deafening and have unintended consequences. I am always amazed that I can make a comment in a meeting about something that should be done—input, not direction—and find out later that whole task forces were formed just because I made an offhand mention.

When a CEO of a large organization walks into a meeting, everything changes. Some people who might have spoken up with a great idea in front of their peers will not take that risk in front of the CEO. It is important for a leader to understand this negative dynamic and diffuse it. If we can get people past our title, it creates more freedom to communicate.

A few years ago we held a daylong meeting at World Vision with top management staff to brainstorm a major reorganization. I needed their creativity and honest feedback. But it could have been a threatening exercise for people who had insights that might conflict with those of their bosses, who were also in the room.

So I stated up front that there was no rank in the room, that all opinions were equal, and that I needed their best thinking to do the right thing for the ministry. This honesty cut through the tension. We had an incredible meeting and discovered innovative ways to structure our ministry.

If you are not sure how you are perceived as a leader, there are two things you can do to develop self-awareness. First, do an anonymous, objective, 360-degree review on yourself. Ask some board members or your boss, a few direct reports, and a few colleagues for feedback on you, and be sure to include people who love you and people who might not. Do this every one or two years—and heed the results.

Second, identify one or two trusted, well-placed people who will tell you the truth. A lot of leaders fail to give permission to people to talk honestly with them. But you need that. There is someone on my team I rely on to tell me the truth. We have the kind of relationship that allows her to come to me after a staff meeting and say, "That didn't go well. Here's what I'm hearing. You need to consider changing that delivery or direction." But I also appreciate how she will affirm me for things I do well, without letting me fall into the trap of believing my own press clippings.

The body of Christ is structured so that the gifts are distributed. I do not have them all. No one does. It is God's plan that we rely on one another to help navigate through decisions. As Paul said, "The eye cannot say to the hand, 'I don't need you!' And the head cannot say to the feet, 'I don't need you!'" (1 Corinthians 12:21).

To be a gifted leader, you need to know your own strengths and weaknesses, as well as what is needed to complement them. When I worked at Parker Brothers Games, I was tasked with coming up with a strategy to help us enter the then emerging consumer electronics business. I knew I needed someone on my team who could think completely differently. I chose a man named Bill whom no one else seemed to want. In fact, when I asked for him to join our team, both his current manager and Bill himself wondered why.

Bill was an outlier in that culture, a man who had pursued a PhD at Harvard in Germanic literature and subsequently got an MBA. I chose him because I needed a brilliant person with a totally different perspective. We ended up making the bold recommendation that Parker Brothers Games, the one-hundred-year-old board game company, should go aggressively into video games, something they had never done (remember, this was thirty years ago). Bill and I then built a team that doubled revenues in eighteen months.

That's the power of self-awareness and harnessing our different gifts.

// PURSUE EXCELLENCE //

Once the vision is cast and the right people are on the team, we are ready to make the bold decisions only leaders can make. Of course, we do not create dramatic turns in the road just for the sake of creating them, but there come times when the only person in the room with the ability to really make the crucial change of direction is the leader.

One of the boldest decisions a leader can make is to hold the staff, the organization, and himself accountable to the principle of excellence. To whom are we accountable? Certainly to God. But that can be an excuse for those who would rather not be accountable to anyone else. Our job as leaders is to establish a culture in our organizations where people feel accountable to excellence.

I spent twenty-three years in the corporate world, where the bottom line is always financial and the means to that end is some product or service. One of the first challenges I faced at World Vision was how to mix performance, goal setting, and excellence with prayer, devotions, and strong Christian relationships. Excellence is a tricky issue for nonprofits and ministries. It is even more complex in the Christian community. When I first came to World Vision, I found well-meaning people doing good things—often with a great deal of passion. And I found overheads that were too high and growth that was too slow. The attitude was, "We are good people doing good things, and that's good enough." But the Lord does not call us to be "good enough." The Lord calls us to be excellent people doing excellent things.

Success is defined very differently for a ministry than for a corporation. It is more than dollars and cents. The bottom line is changed lives, impact—and finances are only a means to that end.

At World Vision, we can measure dozens of metrics that speak to impact: fund-raising costs as a percentage of funds raised, overhead as a percentage of revenue, growth in average giving per donor over time, as well as the increase in the percentage of children attending school and the decrease in child mortality in the communities where we work. If we define what is important and measure it with diligence, we become accountable for excellent results.

Some in the Christian community can be suspicious of excellence. They see it as a worldly concept tainted by profit motives—a concept that might conflict with Christian community. At World Vision my push for excellence was met with murmurs among staff that I wanted to turn World Vision from a ministry into a corporation. I addressed this head-on at an employee meeting by reminding staff that World Vision is not a ministry *to* us but rather a ministry *by* us *to* others. Results matter, and we are accountable for excellence. If we shun the pursuit of excellence, what do we get? Mediocrity. And mediocrity weakens the impact of our ministry.

I would love to see World Vision featured in the media alongside global corporations for its effectiveness and impact because, for us, lives are at stake. It is not about delivering increased earnings per share so stockholders can get wealthy. It's about the twenty-two thousand children who die every day[3]—and we have the power to change that. It's about donors who sacrifice in the hope of bringing life in all its fullness to these children and their families.

Those of us at Christian nonprofits have good reason to be accountable to the principle of excellence, because God deserves no less than our best. "Always give yourselves fully to the work of the Lord, because you know that your labor in the Lord is not in vain" (1 Corinthians 15:58).

Again and again in the Bible, we see God sending leaders to call his people to choose excellence and faithfulness in serving him. At the end of his life, Joshua gathered the people of Israel together in the promised land. He recounted to them how God "brought your fathers out of Egypt" (Joshua 24:6) and "gave you a land on which you did not toil and cities you did not build" (v. 13). Recalling God's faithfulness, Joshua challenged the people to be faithful in return.

Joshua called for a choice and a covenant: "Choose for yourselves this day whom you will serve," he said and added that "as for me and my household, we will serve the Lord" (v. 15).

Like Joshua's standard for excellence, ours too extends even to our personal lives. I remember when Reneé and I told our five children years ago that whatever we had left at the end of our lives was going to World Vision instead of to them. One of my sons gasped, "You can't do that, Dad. It's illegal!" I explained that I wanted them to strive for excellence in their own lives. Now that son has embarked on a successful career, and he and his wife sponsor fourteen children through World Vision.

// LEAD WITH INTEGRITY AND HUMILITY //

Being accountable to the principle of excellence, however, should not be interpreted as a defense of workaholism or achievement regardless of the cost. How we do our work is just as important to God as what we do. God calls us to excellence, but this does not justify engaging in behavior in his name that is destructive to our relationships, our families, and the lives of our employees.

Ministry can be to a workaholic like heroin to the drug addict. Faith-based nonprofits like World Vision offer an extreme temptation to the workaholic because lives *do* hang in the balance. Children *are* dying. And they just might be saved if I do one more thing.

Our work is important. But it is dangerous to conclude that *I* am essential to this important work. The root of workaholism is pride and arrogance. It implies that God cannot accomplish his purposes unless I connect with that donor, attend that meeting, or manage that extra project.

God can and does use others to accomplish his purposes. He has gifted others in special ways. And he can sideline us if we are no longer useful to him because we are burned out, we have become bitter, our family has disintegrated, or we have been led into sin.

The only way to approach leadership responsibilities is in the presence of the Lord with humility. I have worked for leaders who only think of themselves and could care less about the staff or the organization except as a means to their own fulfillment. It was de-motivating and frustrating.

The root of humility is integrity. One of the standards we apply at World Vision for decision making is how our decisions will affect our witness. "We are taking pains to do what is right, not only in the eyes of the Lord but also in the eyes of men" (2 Corinthians 8:21). Our strategies to raise more funds, and thereby help more children, must reflect the integrity of our faith.

It is an easy temptation for a young leader's passion and energy to justify compromises in the name of achieving great things for God. We have all seen Christian leaders who start to believe they are irreplaceable because God has blessed them. They lose their focus and end up making poor decisions for themselves and their organizations.

I value humility even above ability. That may seem counterintuitive to inexperienced leaders, but I would rather follow a capable leader who is full of integrity and selflessness than a high-performing leader who has no integrity.

Throughout the Bible, I see God making the same choice. Take Moses, for example. God did not tap Moses for the miraculous assignment of setting the Israelites free from slavery while Moses was a prince in the house of Pharaoh. God waited until late in Moses' life—after he had been humbled.

Moses' response upon hearing that God was sending him to Pharaoh "to bring my people the Israelites out of Egypt" was to say, "Who am I?" God addressed Moses' doubts not by affirming his great abilities but by reminding him of who *God* was. Moses was to tell the people, "I AM has sent me to you" (Exodus 3:10-14). God used the simple tool in Moses' hand—a staff—as his instrument of miracles. And when Moses was still afraid of not knowing what to say, God sent Moses' brother Aaron to help.

It seems that what God saw in Moses was not great ability or even willingness to do whatever it took, but humility. God wanted to show his own power, not Moses'. And Moses was the perfect person for that.

// IN CONCLUSION //

God has a plan for each of us as leaders. He has gifted us as well as the people around us. Eric Liddell was an Olympic gold medalist portrayed in the Academy Award–winning movie *Chariots of Fire*. Before he went into full-time missionary work, he was criticized by some for participating in the Olympics. His response was, "I believe God made me for a purpose, but he also made me fast. And when I run I feel his pleasure."[4]

We serve *at* God's pleasure and *for* his pleasure. And when we focus on Christ, God is glorified, not us. Like Moses, I have been guilty as a leader questioning God's call, hiding in my own comfort zone. But each time I have trusted God and surrendered to his plan, I have been amazed.

There is a freedom in being released from my career ambitions to pursue God's calling. I am released from my selfish ambitions and the worldly demands for more success because my life becomes about God's glory, not my own. As William Sloane Coffin wrote, "I love the recklessness of faith. First you leap, and then you grow wings."[5]

Once you realize that God has invited you to be part of his incredible plan for the world, it becomes a thrill and privilege to be part of something bigger than yourself. And when we surrender, when we help carry out God's vision, when we work with excellence and integrity with others of like mind, then we get to see the Lord's prayer become a reality—"Your will be done on earth as it is in heaven" (Matthew 6:10).[6]

MY LEADERSHIP BOOKSHELF

The Wisdom of Crowds: Why the Many Are Smarter Than the Few and How Collective Wisdom Shapes Business, Economies, Societies and Nations by James Surowiecki (Doubleday, 2004) reminds us to trust our advisers and to create environments that foster good decision making. Never stop listening.

Jesus, CEO: Using Ancient Wisdom for Visionary Leadership by Laurie Beth Jones (Hyperion, 1996) explores how Jesus mastered the art of coaching.

Hot, Flat, and Crowded: Why We Need a Green Revolution—And How It Can Renew America by Thomas L. Friedman (Farrar, Straus and Giroux, 2008). Faith-based leaders should always be open to expanding their worldview. Friedman will challenge yours.

Good to Great: Why Some Companies Make the Leap . . . and Others Don't by Jim Collins (HarperBusiness, 2001). Don't let the good you are doing keep you from doing what's great.

Team of Rivals: The Political Genius of Abraham Lincoln by Doris Kearns Goodwin (Simon & Schuster, 2005) will challenge you to surround yourself with the best people—whether they agree with you or not.

////// PERSONAL REFLECTIONS AND APPLICATIONS //////

1. The powerful colloquialism "bet the farm" was used to challenge us as leaders to make a full and complete sacrifice to follow the Lord's calling on our lives. It means to take everything that represents our dreams as well as security and commit it to God for whatever purposes he reveals. Have you "bet the farm" on God's plan and promise for your life? What are you keeping "in reserve" in case God does not do what you desire? Why?

2. Have you ever been sidelined on your leadership journey—lost your job, been passed over for promotion, been off-line due to illness or injury, or felt underutilized? What important lessons did God teach during those times? Are those lessons still important or do they need to be taught again? Why?

3. Is your style of managing more that of a coach or a player? This chapter asserts that in leadership our primary role is to find the right people for the work to be done and then enable them to do that work rather than do it for them. How can you be a more effective coach and less of a player?

4. What strategies, tools, and relationships are you utilizing to become more fully self-aware? Knowing yourself as others know you is important so you do not just assume your "press clippings" are accurate representations. Be sure you have at least one person in your organization whom you have given permission to help you see yourself as your followers do.

5. Prayerfully reflect on the statement "The only way to approach leadership responsibilities is in the presence of the Lord with humility." Also spend some time in Philippians 2:1-11, noting the ways that Jesus, knowing he was God, was able to spend himself for the sake of those who followed. In this passage it is clear that leadership is more about the led than the leader. How can your leadership better reflect this attitude of Jesus?

///////// TEAM REFLECTIONS AND APPLICATIONS /////////

1. We live in difficult and demanding times that require organizations to take great risks to achieve their highest visions and missions. This chapter spoke of an "R-rated" challenge to call World Vision (supported primarily by a "G-rated" constituency) to the urgent task of addressing Africa's AIDS crisis. Have an open discussion with your leadership team about any major calling you are unwilling to consider or address because of its risk to your organization's reputation, future, or supporting constituency. What specific leap of faith is God calling your organization or ministry to? What steps do you need to take to be obedient to what you know is God's leap of faith for your organization?

2. Ponder the statement that "the right *people* are more important than the right *strategy*" and the idea that the right people with the wrong strategy can succeed as often as the right strategy with the wrong people fails. Is this a core leadership idea your organization should consider carefully? Why or why not?

3. How clear and compelling is your organization's vision and its stated mission? Note the simplicity and impact of World Vision's mission statement (p. 203). How is your vision statement embodied and lived out by your leadership team? How does it call you and your stakeholders within and outside the organization to God's highest calling for your work?

4. What management practices and attitudes slow down decision making and de-motivate staff in your organization? Make finding and resolving these a high priority in your efforts to understand your organization's ethos and culture.

5. What are the "good enough" barriers to excellence in your organization? Do not let the priority of relationships and the commitment to careful stewardship become the excuses for presenting less than the best possible offering for God's kingdom work. Lives are at stake—requiring us to do our work with diligence, accountability, and eternal results in mind.

RICHARD STEARNS
PRESIDENT, WORLD VISION U.S.
///

After a quarter-century business career, including roles as CEO of Parker Brothers Games and Lenox, Richard Stearns joined World Vision U.S. (www.worldvision.org) in 1998 as president. He has led this Christian relief and development organization to unprecedented growth, calling on the American church to respond to the global AIDS pandemic.

One of the largest nonprofit organizations in the country, World Vision U.S. has more than twelve hundred staff in the United States, and partners with U.S. corporations, government agencies, foundations, churches, and more than a million individual donors to help children and their communities reach their full potential by tackling the causes of poverty. It is the largest member of the global World Vision Partnership, which touched the lives of an estimated one hundred million people internationally in 2009.

Since joining World Vision U.S., Stearns has built a strong leadership team focused on bringing corporate best practices to the nonprofit sector and inspiring a culture of outcome-focused management at all levels of the organization. Donations tripled from $358 million in 1998 to over $1.2 billion in 2009, and overhead has been reduced by almost one-third.

One of his first initiatives was to empower senior leadership to increase awareness and funding for AIDS programs. Stearns chronicles his journey from corporate CEO to advocate for those affected by poverty and injustice in his 2009 release, *The Hole in Our Gospel*. The book challenges readers in the faith community to rise out of apathy to meet the challenges of global poverty and injustice.

Stearns serves on the boards of InterAction, the Evangelical Council for Financial Accountability, the Center for Interfaith Action on Global Poverty, and Seattle Pacific University. In 2010, he completed a term on President Obama's Advisory Council on Faith-Based and Neighborhood Partnerships. Stearns earned a BS degree from Cornell University and an MBA from the Wharton School at the University of Pennsylvania. He has received honorary doctorates from Eastern University and Azusa Pacific University.

Richard Stearns and his wife, Reneé, live in Bellevue, Washington, and have five children.

12

INDISPENSABLE ATTRIBUTES OF LEADERSHIP

MICHAEL T. TIMMIS

I n developing these chapters for emerging leaders, we felt it was important for you to hear from significant lay, non-employee leaders who serve on the boards of faith-based nonprofits. Our Christian missions require the work, wisdom, witness, and wallop of these dedicated volunteers. These board members are more than the oversight body required by the IRS for 510c3 organizations; they serve as the elders of our work—helping us sharpen the vision. Additionally, they provide expertise beyond staff experience, guide and support the CEOs, and hold us accountable to the highest standards of excellence, innovation, integrity, and humility.

Michael has a distinguished record of service to a number of nonprofit organizations, being deeply invested in terms of time and resources in their visions and missions. Those who work with and for him bear testimony to his clear, unwavering commitment to ensure that our service achieves the highest standards of performance while never compromising Christ-centered redemptive work for individuals, cultures, and societies.

Leadership is a calling. In my own case, I became a leader as a lawyer and a businessman—in both Christian and non-Christian nonprofit settings. I never set out to be a leader. It was only when in my mid-thirties that I realized I had become one. The realization of leadership comes when people begin to follow you, look up to you, count on you, and have great expectations of you. I became a leader because I worked as hard or harder than anyone I was ever associated with, and I was willing to pay a price that very few men wanted to pay. Because I both practiced law and purchased and owned companies along with a partner, I worked six to seven days every week.

As my leadership responsibilities grew, I became harder on myself and on those around me. Consequently, my marriage suffered, my parenting suffered, and I suffered. It was not until I asked Jesus to take control of my life, making him my number one priority, that I began to understand what true leadership entails. The more I studied the life of Jesus and the leaders that are lifted up in Scripture, the more I understood that a true leader has his or her priorities in perspective.

My goal in this chapter is to help young leaders avoid the pitfalls I didn't avoid. Many leaders forget that we are all sinners who have fallen short of the glory of God (Romans 3:23). Certainly I did—notwithstanding that I was very religious. As I grew more successful, I felt that I didn't sin because I didn't commit adultery or cheat in business. The fact that I lost my temper frequently and used harsh and vulgar words . . . well, that was only a way of expressing myself. Obviously, leaders who act this way have a very short tenure because, ultimately, they begin to fall apart in their own emptiness and arrogance.

I have met very few leaders who really stay the course as far as growing inwardly throughout their lives. As I have embraced Jesus more and more in my life, I've grown inwardly. And because of this inward transformation, he has been able to use me outwardly for his purposes. We see the failure of leaders every day in the newspapers—the politicians who let us down, the religious leaders who fall into sin, the business leaders who take advantage of others.

What follows is a discussion of those attributes that I believe a leader must develop in order to stay the course.

// ACCOUNTABILITY //

Scripture teaches us the principle that to whom much has been given, much is expected (Luke 12:48). Even though I was not in the Word in my thirties, I realized the truth and responsibility of that principle. When people disappointed me, I was critical of them. Over thirty years later, I still believe that a leader has to critique the people he is depending on. However, there is a way of being critical without denigrating so that the end result is helping the person who has failed, or been mistaken, to grow rather than be beaten down by the experience.

As I read the Gospels, I see that Jesus expected a lot from the disciples. When they failed to understand their responsibility, he did not hesitate to point it out, and in some passages, with great exasperation. The difference is that we know, based on Jesus' character, that he never attacked the person but, rather, addressed the behavior.

To be a successful leader means that one has to be accountable. It is important for a leader to have two or three trusted friends with whom he can be totally frank and honest. Normally, these are people outside your own organization. These would be individuals who know you and who are not afraid to speak truth into your life. These people have to be like-minded in their pursuit of holiness as well as love you enough to tell you the truth, even if it risks the friendship. Not only does this bring accountability; it also brings perspective. Often as leaders we are so caught up in a problem that we don't see the alternatives that exist. A wise, godly friend can help us think through a problem to an appropriate resolution, because God speaks into our lives through other people.

// APPROACHABILITY //

A leader who is not approachable substantially increases the possibility of failure, because he does not hear the truth about the organization. Many people are naturally reluctant to approach leadership about a problem, primarily for fear of the consequences. Some people have welcoming personalities, and some do not. So how does one become approachable? The leader has to make it clear that he or she *is* approachable. This is done both verbally and in writing. In the many businesses that my partner and I owned, I would tell our executives that it was extremely important that they bring problems to our attention immediately, because mistakes can or will be forgiven but failure to disclose a problem can be fatal. Since failure can be so damaging to the organization, an individual must understand that if he fails to bring the problems to the leader's attention, it is a form of dishonesty and cannot be tolerated.

I recognize there is a fine line between being approachable and maintaining the responsibilities of leadership. This was brought home to me recently when a friend told me how he had started off in his father's business. The father had him work in almost every position. Even though my friend was the boss's son, the fellows called him by his first name. However, his father died suddenly in his fifties, and my friend was cast into the role of the leader of that company. He remembered that after the funeral, as he took over the position of leadership, men who had called him by his first name were now referring to him with the title "Mr." He said that bothered him because he wanted them to continue to look on him as a friend. However, one of his employees said, "You are now our leader, and we want you to assume that leadership. We want to pay you respect as our leader."

That company grew to well over $1 billion in sales because the individual accepted the mantle of leadership.

// RESPONSIBILITY TO COMMUNICATE //

One of the major problems in organizations is lack of communication, which breeds fear and anxiety. Conversely, morale is improved by proper communication. It is critically important to have a presence among the people you lead. One of the ways of fostering approachability is through humor and light conversation when times are good. It can be as simple as walking around an office, caring enough to ask people about their families, their holidays, or something that is personal to them. But times are not always good. An effective leader takes nothing for granted but, rather, explains and listens to the anxieties of the organization too.

My wife and I had the privilege of being in the White House for a small reception with President Reagan. I had met him a number of times and, consequently, saw one of his Secret Service men frequently. On this occasion I engaged the man in conversation while we were waiting for the president to come downstairs. I asked about his role as a Secret Service officer and the responsibilities of protecting the president. I will never forget how he looked at me with tears in his eyes and said, "This president I would gladly die for. He never forgets my name and remembers the names of my children. He remembers each grade that they are in and asks about my wife. I can't tell you how that makes me feel."

President Reagan demonstrated that one of the cardinal virtues of a great leader is caring personally and sincerely for other people—and communicating that care.

// FAITHFULNESS //

One of my favorite passages in Scripture says that when the boy Jesus returned to Nazareth, he "grew in wisdom and stature, and in favor with God and men" (Luke 2:52). What a tremendous formula for a young leader! When one becomes a leader, his or her quest is just beginning. If you do not continue to grow as a person and seek wisdom from others and, above all, deepen your relationship with Jesus, you will never mature into the leader that you could become. Once an individual accepts a leadership role in a Christian ministry, he is held to the highest standard of faithfulness. If he fails, scandal has the potential to result in leading people away from the Lord.

In my early days, after asking Jesus to become the center of my life, I started giving my testimony and proclaiming the gospel. An older and wiser friend came to me and pointed out that I was a business leader and that many people were watching me to see if I would remain faithful. He said words that have remained with me ever since: "Mike, if you fall you will take many with you." I believe that is true, because the nonbeliever looks at the leader who is a Christian and wonders if what he is professing is true. When we fail to follow the teachings of Jesus and we fall into sin, the nonbeliever uses that as an excuse not to accept the truth, concluding that we are hypocrites.

One of the key aspects of being a leader is faithfulness. Faithfulness means always living what you preach and always keeping your word. One remains faithful through a continuing and deepening relationship with Jesus.

For many years my wife has admonished me, saying that if the devil couldn't make me bad, he would make me busy. Some years ago a well-known pastor of a megachurch spent two days with me. His church was in a state of crisis, as was as his marriage and relationship with his children. He blamed everyone from the elders of his church to his wife and family for being judgmental and not understanding how hard he was working. I listened as he poured out his anger and frustration. After a period of time, I asked him how much time he spent praying each day.

His answer: "Not as much as you do."

I asked, "How do you know how much I pray?"

He said, "I don't know—I just know you do."

He had become so engrossed in the work of Christ that he had lost his personal relationship with him. He had fallen into the trap that *doing* is more important than *being*. Do you know anyone like that?

Unless we go to the Father daily as Jesus did, and be refilled with the Spirit of God, we will end up operating on our own. The most common thing that Jesus did in the Gospels was pray to the Father. Jesus recognized that in his human capacity, he was powerless to accomplish the role of leadership the Father had given him. He constantly returned to the Father for the power and the grace to continue what he was doing. The hallmark of a great leader is recognizing that leadership begins each day on your knees—seeking God's will, direction, and protection.

Over twenty years ago, one of my spiritual mentors challenged me that whatever else I was studying or reading, I should never spend a day without reading something in the Gospels. This revolutionized my life, because the greatest leader who ever existed is Jesus Christ. Despite the fact that the past two thousand years of history have given us many great men and women leaders, Jesus is the one we consistently talk about today. Many books have been written about Jesus' leadership style; however, the bottom line of Jesus' "secret" is the daily process of seeking God's will in his life through prayer. That is the condition, the prerequisite, to being a true leader.

I remember hearing a Christian CEO of a major *Fortune* 500 company being asked, "When you make a critical decision, do you ask yourself 'What would Jesus do?'"

He replied, "No, I do not, because every day in my morning prayers, I set the course for the day, and I ask Jesus to be with me throughout that day to direct my attitude toward his will. Consequently, I feel his presence, and when I exercise my God-given abilities, I know that he is with me."

I think that is an excellent approach for every leader—to set his course in the morning to accomplish the will of Jesus that day.

I had the opportunity to go to India twice and meet Mother Teresa. Certainly most people recognize that she was one of the great leaders of our time. One day I asked her how much she prayed, and she told me two hours in the morning and two hours at night. A little bit later, as we were walking in the slums of Calcutta, she said, "I told you how I prayed, but really, to be honest with you, I feel like I'm praying all the time. That when I'm helping a leper or changing a baby, these are acts of prayer." I have never forgotten that. I believe that as we go about our day, if we have truly set our course with Jesus in the morning, he is present with us. And we will feel his presence and acknowledge his being with us throughout our day.

// GENEROSITY //

Many years ago an evangelical brother who served on many boards told me that a true leader is always generous—with his time, his kindness, his money, and always putting other people before himself. I have never forgotten that and attempted to live my life in that way. It does take personal sacrifice, but a leader who is not willing to sacrifice is not a true leader. Jesus was the epitome of leadership as he sacrificed himself for others. He was constantly surrounded by crowds but didn't complain. He sought solitude from the crowds; and yet when they found him, he always directly met their needs. In other words, Jesus always puts others first.

// PROBLEM SOLVING //

One of the most important aspects of leadership is learning how to deal with serious problems—people problems and crisis problems. Most organizations of any size have a human resource person to deal with people problems. Regardless, the failure to act can certainly jeopardize an organization.

Leaders in business tend to understand the urgency of dealing with people problems more clearly than Christian leaders do. My experience is that Christian leaders are slow to react even when they realize a person cannot do the job for which he was employed. In many years of dealing with this problem, I have found that when it was necessary to terminate a person, almost always that person realized he was not meeting expectations—often working and living with the fear of being terminated. Usually the decision brought great relief because it enabled the person to be who God intended him or her to be.

Allowing a person to continue in a position where he is not suited is really dishonest and lowers the morale of the entire organization. There are compassionate ways of terminating an employee, and as Christian leaders we are called to compassion. However, the problem must still be dealt with. This can be very painful; but by submitting ourselves to prayer and guidance by the Holy Spirit, we can move forward.

The other problem is dealing with crisis. Very few crises occur suddenly. Most are born out of the inaction of leadership or failure to address problems as they were growing. Ultimately, problems ripen into a crisis. In all my years of leadership, I would say my biggest failures were when I failed to act in a timely manner. On the other hand, we were successful in our businesses when we sought to resolve a serious problem as soon as we learned about it. Problems that aren't dealt with never go away—they only increase. Some Christians have a tendency not to act because to do so may be deemed un-Christian, as in a case of needing to terminate someone. I don't believe that attitude is biblical, and I don't believe it is Christ-centered. Jesus never asked us to leave our brains at the door; rather, he expects us to perform to the best of our ability. There is no reason why you cannot confront a problem in a godly way.

One point I have learned in the crises that I have faced is that I must remain calm and confident. If I am not confident, it will become contagious and people will become immobilized and uncertain.

Confidence is born of hope, and hope comes from knowing that, as a believer, I am part of God's plan. As I study Scripture I see that I am part of God's plan—a plan to represent him in every facet of my life. Of course, there will be problems in life. In many translations of 1 Corinthians 10:13 the word *temptation* is used, but the better translation is *test*. God tells us that "no [test] has seized you except what is common to man," and God keeps his promise to "not let you be [tested] beyond what you can bear" (also see Philippians 4:13).

// SUCCESSION PLANNING //

An effective leader is one who recognizes that his leadership is only for a season and that he has the responsibility to help raise up his successor. In my own case, I pray daily that God would reveal who should succeed me in my roles as chairman of the board of Prison Fellowship International and Prison Fellowship Ministries (USA).

The Old Testament gives us many examples of leaders who failed to pass it on, such as Samuel. He did not raise up his sons to follow him, and therefore, the Jews demanded that a king be appointed over them (1 Samuel 8:1-9), which frustrated God's purpose for the Israelites.

Another way to facilitate succession is for an older leader to mentor a younger leader. This is something that I have done for the last twenty years. There is no substitute for experience.

One of the problems I have seen in ministry is that people tend to serve in leadership capacities (such as being members of boards of directors) for too long. I believe that having term limits is extremely important. For example, if you are elected to the board of The Navigators, you serve a three-year term; and before you can be reelected to another term, you take a year off. This allows both The Navigators and the individual a period of time to determine whether continuing to serve is appropriate.

Transition Plan by Bob Russell and Bryan Bucher (Ministers Label Publishing, 2010) details how Russell, the longtime minister of the Southeast Christian Church megachurch in Louisville, Kentucky, successfully passed the baton to Dave Stone.

// GREAT PASSION //

In my study of history, as well as in my personal experiences, the greatest leaders I have read about or met are men and women of tremendous passion. The greater the passion, the greater the leader. The greater the passion, the more people will follow the leader who is making extraordinary effort and sacrifice in the exercise of his responsibilities. Passion is an attribute that should only increase. This can be accomplished only if an individual never stops growing. Jesus talks about the thirty-, sixty-, and hundred-times person (Mark 4:1-8). In my judgment, the hundred-times person is the person whose passion increases as he knows Jesus better and better and, consequently, becomes more like him.

One of my most precious memories is when Chuck Colson, my son Michael, and I went to see Bill Bright about a year before his death. Bill was on oxygen and obviously deteriorating. However, despite being sick and eighty years of age, he told us he was more excited by Jesus than at any other time in his life. It was like meeting someone who was twenty-one and had just met Jesus. His enthusiasm was so contagious. He had so many ideas for us as leaders of Prison Fellowship. He expressed great excitement over the work we were doing. In my opinion, Bill Bright was a hundred-times man. He never stopped growing. He never stopped changing as he embraced Jesus in his life in a deeper and deeper way.

Another great example of a man whose passion to serve Jesus has never stopped growing is my friend Chuck Colson. He is just as active at age seventy-nine as he was thirty years ago. Today his radio program, *BreakPoint,* airs on more than a thousand stations. And he travels constantly around the country, sharing Jesus and speaking on the issues of the day in a Christ-centered context.

In this chapter I have shared what I feel are some of the most important attributes of leadership. However, the *most* important point is that our leadership begins and ends with our relationship with Jesus. Unless we meet with him daily in worship, prayer, and the Word, we can never grow into the leader that God wishes us to be. The greatest joy a leader can receive is in knowing that he is serving and pleasing Jesus.

MY LEADERSHIP BOOKSHELF

Heroic Leadership by Chris Lowney (Loyola Press, 2005) examines organizational principles derived from the history and teachings of the Jesuits and applies them to modern corporate culture. Based on the four core values of self-awareness, ingenuity, love, and heroism, this book identifies practices that sixteenth-century priests developed to foster strong leaders and achieve longevity.

The Longview: Lasting Strategies for Rising Leaders by Roger Parrott (David C. Cook, 2009). Become a leader who values transformation over turnaround, one who measures eternal outcomes as well as immediate effectiveness. Consider this book your personal guide to a leadership lifestyle of lasting significance. *The Longview* will revolutionize the way you lead.

Honesty, Morality & Conscience: Making Wise Choices in the Gray Areas of Life by Jerry White (NavPress, 2007). Examining the origin and depth of our conscience, our moral compass, and truthful living, the author explains how God has given us everything we need to face the ethical questions of today in all areas of our lives.

////// **PERSONAL REFLECTIONS AND APPLICATIONS** //////

1. Take some time to reflect on your personal relationship with Jesus Christ. Is it as vibrant and intimate today as it was earlier in your Christian walk? If not, why not? How diligent and disciplined are you at cultivating a daily relationship with Christ in order to focus on and resource your leadership calling?

2. In your daily work and service as a leader, do you have a continuing sense of Jesus' presence and direction throughout your day? If not, how can you cultivate that in a greater way?

3. How do you demonstrate your interest in both the personal and professional lives of your employees and fellow workers? A wonderful place to begin is to pray through your employee roster over the period of the year, asking for God's blessing and provision for each. Send them a note saying you prayed for them that day, and invite them to share with you a special prayer need. If you have a large organization, pray for those who are your direct reports and encourage them to do this throughout the organization.

4. What keeps you from quickly and decisively addressing the problems you face as a leader? Note which types of issues you seem slowest to address (for many these are often personnel related). Why do you postpone resolving such problems? Seek counsel from another leader who is effective in addressing these types of challenges. Ask him or her to mentor you.

5. Where do you demonstrate true sacrifice for the vision and mission God has entrusted to you? Is it a joyful sacrifice or one that is given out of duty and obligation? Jesus went to the cross willingly, knowing that his temporary suffering would produce eternal joy for his Father and for all who would follow him.

///////// TEAM REFLECTIONS AND APPLICATIONS /////////

1. How well do you and your leadership team know the hearts, as well as the heads, of those who supervise your organization as overseers, trustees, and directors? What can you do to help your board embrace their God-appointed calling as stewards of the vision and mission of your ministry? The Engstrom Institute of the Christian Leadership Alliance has many helpful resources to increase the effectiveness of your board. Go to www.christianleadershipalliance.org/ei/ for additional information.

2. How does your corporate culture encourage people to point out (and pass up to those who need to know) any challenges or issues that could hamper your organization's mission? What mechanisms could be employed to encourage more open communication about issues, challenges, and problems so that these can be addressed before they become major crises? It might be helpful to provide a suggestion box or recognize (and perhaps reward) people who alert you to issues.

3. Take some time to do a case study of how your leadership team has managed recent crises. Is your first response to pray or to lay blame? It is better to focus energies on fixing the problem rather than fixing the blame. How could these crises have been anticipated? Do you have a crisis management plan in place? Most organizations are required by state laws to have a working emergency plan. Use it as a pattern for developing a crisis management plan. Having a framework in place allows clear thinking to emerge and gives time to make prayer your first response. How could you go about doing this over the next month?

4. Can your senior leadership team be more accessible to employees, supporters, and the people your organization serves? Advisory boards, town meetings, and task forces that work across existing organizational structure to advise on critical issues can be helpful. A tried and true practice is

to encourage your leadership team to walk among the employees where they work. What other practical ideas could be implemented?

MICHAEL T. TIMMIS
CHAIRMAN OF THE BOARD, PRISON FELLOWSHIP INTERNATIONAL AND PRISON FELLOWSHIP MINISTRIES (USA)

//

Michael T. Timmis serves as chairman of Prison Fellowship International (www.pfi.org), a trans-denominational Christian organization comprising 118 chartered countries. In 2006, Timmis succeeded Chuck Colson as chairman of Prison Fellowship Ministries (USA) and now chairs both Prison Fellowship entities.

The world's largest and most extensive criminal justice ministry, Prison Fellowship International (PFI) is a global association of over one hundred national Prison Fellowship organizations. PFI is active in every region of the world with a network of more than one hundred thousand volunteers working for the spiritual, moral, social, and physical well-being of prisoners, ex-prisoners, their families, and victims of crime.

Timmis has a distinguished career as both an attorney and businessman. He was senior partner of the law firm of Timmis & Inman L.L.P. and cofounder and vice chairman of Talon LLC, a privately owned company.

He earned his undergraduate degree from Wayne State University and graduated with highest honors from the Wayne State Law School. While in law school, he received the school's Distinguished Law Alumni Award and served as a governor of Wayne State University.

Michael T. Timmis holds memberships in many professional associations, is a director of numerous corporations, and serves or has served in a leadership capacity on the boards of many charitable organizations and foundations. These include St. John Healthcare Systems, Cornerstone Schools, Inc.,

The Navigators, Promise Keepers, Wayne State University Foundation, and Alpha International. He was the recipient of the Business and Professional Award from Religious Heritage of America, received an honorary doctorate in humane letters degree from the University of Detroit–Mercy in recognition of civic and humanitarian contributions, and received a doctorate from Ave Maria University.

Timmis and his wife, Nancy, are deeply involved in the problems of the poor in the Third World and have developed self-help projects in Africa and Central and South America. They have actively addressed the educational needs of children in Detroit, and Timmis was named one of the leaders of the '90s by *Crain's Detroit Business* magazine.

He is president of the Archdiocese of Detroit Endowment Foundation, Inc., and a founding member of the National Fellowship of Catholic Men. His autobiography, *Between Two Worlds: The Spiritual Journey of an Evangelical Catholic,* was published in 2008 (NavPress). Michael T. Timmis and his wife have two children and five grandchildren and reside in Michigan and Florida.

//

LEADERSHIP IN DEPTH

JERRY WHITE

From his rich and varied background in multiple leadership environments, Jerry challenges us to embrace the essential building blocks of personal and professional effectiveness. Plumbing the scriptural depths of God's calling, he raises our awareness of how privileged we are to be given leadership opportunities. He reminds us that leadership requires a team effort and that we should never forget that no matter how talented and seemingly successful, every leader has fundamental weaknesses and flaws. One of the most important dimensions of Christlike leadership, he suggests, is the attitude of honor and respect for all across our organizations, no matter what their function. Jerry concludes with a poignant and personal reflection on the important place of suffering in refining and molding our leadership vision and practice.

Leaders come and go. Some leave a mark, and others leave a mess. With each leader there are varying degrees of how big a mark and how big a mess. As I reflect on my own life of leadership in the Air Force and in the world of nonprofit Christian ministry, I have done both. It would be arrogant to say I left no messes.

Were there any biblical leaders who did their work perfectly? Except for Jesus—none. We are all fallible. The Scripture is not primarily a manual for leadership. The Bible can be viewed through several lenses—the plan of salvation in Christ, the broad promises of God, the history of Israel and its place in redemption, instructions for living a godly life, and many others. Whatever the theme, people are included—all the way from Adam and Eve to John of Revelation. Many were leaders. Some did well. One example is Jehoida the priest, who deposed the wicked Queen Athaliah and installed the rightful king, Joash (2 Chronicles 23). When Jehoida died, "he was buried with the kings . . . because of the good he had done" (24:16).

Other Bible leaders failed miserably. One of the saddest epitaphs is that of King Jehoram, of whom it was written, "He passed away, to no one's regret, and was buried . . . but not in the tombs of the kings" (2 Chronicles 21:20).

A person can be a leader of godly repute and then blow it in an act of immorality, anger, or disgrace. We want to follow God to the very end.

// GO DEEP //

As I think of my own life and the counsel I would give to younger leaders, one foundational issue rises above all others—be a man or woman who goes deep in the Word of God regularly and persistently. This practice goes far beyond formal training. It is marked by regular study of the Scriptures, a meaningful devotional life, and consistent application of the Word to one's life. Depth in the Word of God is the basis of all leadership. Can a person do well without this? Unfortunately, yes—in the short term. However, we cannot live on yesterday's walk with God. We are playing for the long haul in life and leadership. "Do your best to present yourself to God as one approved, a workman who does not need to be ashamed and who correctly handles the word of truth" (2 Timothy 2:15).

// LEADERSHIP IS A PRIVILEGE //

Leadership is developed in the smaller segments of our ministries (skills and character are nurtured here), as well as at the very senior levels of our organizations. A key principle at every level is that leadership is a responsibility and a privilege—not a right. When a person understands this, there will be no room for pride. The gift of leadership, like all spiritual gifts, brings with it the responsibility to use it well. "If a man's gift is . . . leadership, let him govern diligently" (Romans 12:6, 7).

It is arrogant to become impatient to find leadership opportunities. Calling and vision must always supersede any thoughts of position. Flitting from one organization or opportunity to another evidences a clear lack of calling to a mission or vision. In the secular corporate world, that is often a way of life—one can keep pushing to the top regardless of the industry, product, or company. But this should not be the pattern of Christian organizations.

Even when we know we possess some measure of leadership gifting, we do not have a *right* to lead. It is not something we can demand; it is a responsibility when we are asked and given a task. It is a privilege to lead people. Almost every leader I know has been passed over for some leadership roles or has experienced some failure. God opens the doors, and we respond to his leading. And not every open door for leadership is one we should take.

We also need to remember that all leadership roles are temporary. Whether a four-star general, a corporate CEO, or a ministry leader—that role will come to an end very quickly. If our identity is tied to our role, our identity will soon be crushed. We do not lead out of obligation, pride, or even reluctance, but simply by the call of God.

// THE IMPERATIVE OF A TEAM //

No one leads alone. In my Air Force responsibilities, a number of colonels and generals worked for me. I once told them, "We are overhead. We don't fix or fly airplanes. We don't launch missiles. Our job is to clear the way for the people who do the work so they can do their jobs well." So it is also in ministry. Leaders serve those on the front lines. We have heard the statement that "every leader has followers." I believe a better statement is that "every leader has a team." This should be a team of equals, not a leader with subordinates.

Jesus, who was fully capable of doing anything on his own, still chose to work with a team of ordinary laborers. He ordained (chose) twelve as his apostles, "that they might be with him and that he might send them out to preach" (Mark 3:14). He was divine but still chose to work with and through fallible human beings.

The apostle Paul constantly traveled with a team. In fact, he despaired when he was alone, as we see in 2 Corinthians 7:6: "But God, who comforts the downcast, comforted us by the coming of Titus." Paul also traveled with Barnabas and some whose names are less familiar to us: "He was accompanied by Sopater son of Pyrrhus from Berea, Aristarchus and Secundus from Thessalonica, Gaius from Derbe, Timothy also, and Tychicus and Trophimus from the province of Asia" (Acts 20:4). And of course, the writer of Acts, Luke, accompanied Paul and documented his life.

King David also had his band of men. They were not what you would call the cream of the crop. Rather, "all those who were in distress or in debt or discontented gathered around him, and he became their leader" (1 Samuel 22:2). He praised these "mighty men." He spoke of them often and honored them. And he could not have succeeded without them (see 2 Samuel 23).

I have never seen an effective leader who could not or did not work with a team. A good leader knows that he cannot function without a team. The team is not always of his or her own choosing. Good leaders can work with inherited teams as well as with teams they choose. Individuals on the team may be more gifted and capable than the leader in certain areas. A good leader is comfortable with that. In fact, he knowingly recruits and develops team members who make up for his weaknesses, can do many things better than he, and can easily replace him. Not only must we work with a team, we must always be dependent on them.

// WE'RE ALL MADE OF CLAY //

People are the central focus of leadership. However, not all people are lovable and easy to work with. A great lesson for me was that every leader you know, including yourself, will eventually disappoint you. Paul emphasizes this in 2 Corinthians 4:7: "We have this treasure in jars of clay to show that this all-surpassing power is from God and not from us." We are all "cracked pots." We all have chinks in the armor of character and actions. One of my children insisted, "Dad, no one is perfect!"

Since we all are human, we all have different giftedness, talents, and experience . . . and failings and flaws soon appear. There are no perfect heroes of faith recorded in Scripture. We are no different. People will see our faults and shortcomings. Therefore, we must live with the understanding and tolerance of weaknesses—and even some character deficiencies. When we realize this, we are more likely to act with grace and love in all our relationships. Leadership is *all about* relationships. People are not tools to accomplish a task. Leadership opens the channels of grace to other people's lives.

// HONOR AND RESPECT //

I strongly advise that you treat every person with honor and respect. There is never an excuse for treating someone with harshness and disrespect. That includes children, the elderly, the infirm, the weak, and the less gifted. All are part of our kingdom work, especially inside our organizations. The "least of these" (Matthew 25:40) are God's heroes.

Two stories of real people come to mind. In The Navigators, we had a single woman working in our administrative headquarters. She was physically deformed but mentally sharp. She took the bus to work daily. Often someone would offer her a ride. If it was a man, even another employee, she kindly refused because she did not want to be a single woman in a car alone with a man. She had principles. It was easy to overlook her in a sea of physically capable people.

Tragically, she was struck and killed by a drunk driver one morning as she was crossing a street toward the bus stop. Her funeral was crowded with people honoring her. I am pleased that she was always respected in our organization.

A second incident occurred following my time on the faculty of the U.S. Air Force Academy. It involved a janitor, whom I did not know personally, though I wish I had, since he was there during my tenure. The source of this account is Col. James Moschgat from the USAFA class of 1977[1]:

William "Bill" Crawford certainly was an unimpressive figure, one you could easily overlook during a hectic day at the U.S. Air Force Academy. Mr. Crawford, as most of us referred to him back in the late 1970s, was our squadron janitor. . . . Bill quietly moved about the squadron, mopping and buffing floors, emptying trash cans, cleaning toilets, or just tidying up the mess 100 college-age kids can leave in a dormitory.

Sadly, and for many years, few of us gave him much notice, rendering little more than a passing nod or throwing a curt "G'morning!" in his direction as we hurried off to our daily duties. Why? Perhaps it was because of the way he did his job—he always kept the squadron area spotlessly clean. Even the toilets and showers gleamed. Frankly, he did his job so well, none of us had to notice or get involved. After all, cleaning toilets was his job, not ours. . . .

His gray hair and wrinkled face made him appear ancient to a group of young cadets. And his crooked smile, well, it looked a little funny. Bill was an old man working in a young person's world. What did he have to offer us on a personal level?

That changed one fall Saturday afternoon in 1976. I was reading a book about World War II and the tough Allied ground campaign in Italy, when I stumbled across an incredible story. On September 13, 1943, a Private William Crawford from Colorado, assigned to the 36th Infantry Division, had been involved in some bloody fighting on Hill 424 near Altavilla, Italy. The words on the page leaped out at me: "In the face of intense and overwhelming hostile fire . . . with no regard for personal safety . . . on his own initiative, Private Crawford single-handedly attacked fortified enemy positions." It continued, "For conspicuous gallantry and intrepidity at risk of life above and beyond the call of duty, the President of the United States . . ."

"Holy cow," I said to my roommate, "you're not going to believe this, but I think our janitor is a Medal of Honor winner." We all knew Mr. Crawford was a WW II Army vet, but that didn't keep my friend from looking at me as if I was some sort of alien being. . . .

We met Mr. Crawford bright and early Monday and showed him the page in question from the book, anticipation and doubt on our faces. He stared at it for a few silent moments and then quietly uttered something like, "Yep, that's me." . . .

Almost at once we both stuttered, "Why didn't you ever tell us about it?"

He slowly replied after some thought, "That was one day in my life and it happened a long time ago." . . .

After that brief exchange, things were never again the same around our squadron. Word spread like wildfire among the cadets that we had a hero in our midst— Mr. Crawford, our janitor, had won the Medal! Cadets who had once passed by Bill with hardly a glance now greeted him with a smile and a respectful, "Good morning, Mr. Crawford." Those who had before left a mess for the "janitor" to clean up started taking it upon themselves to put things in order. Most cadets routinely stopped to talk to Bill throughout the day, and we even began inviting him to our formal squadron functions. He'd show up dressed in a conservative dark suit and quietly talk to those who approached him, the only sign of his heroics being a simple blue, star-spangled lapel pin.

Almost overnight, Bill went from being a simple fixture in our squadron to one of our teammates. Mr. Crawford changed too, but you had to look closely to notice the difference. After that fall day in 1976, he seemed to move with more purpose, his shoulders didn't seem to be as stooped, he met our greetings with a direct gaze and a stronger "good morning" in return, and he flashed his crooked smile more often. The squadron gleamed as always, but everyone now seemed to notice it more. . . . While no one ever formally acknowledged the change, I think we became Bill's cadets and his squadron.

Bill Crawford retired from the USAFA to his hometown of Pueblo, Colorado, where he died on March 15, 2000.

How we treat the poor, the less capable, the less educated, and the ordinary person speaks more about our leadership than any set of achievements. All the management techniques and principles fade and fail when people are not treated well. Getting the right people on the bus and in the right seats, for example, is good but does not replace the respect we owe to all who work with us.

Many of us encounter ordinary people—never knowing the story of their lives, never knowing their achievements or heartaches. Sometimes we even "have entertained angels without knowing it" (Hebrews 13:2). But even if people have done nothing of public note, they are worthy of our respect. Others are watching. More importantly, God is watching.

I could share many other suggestions that have helped me. Here are a few:

- Find a coach and mentor. Mine were Lorne Sanny (former president, The Navigators) and J. Oswald Sanders (former president, China Inland Mission).
- Interact and relate to people in other ministries. For eighteen years the CEOs and spouses of five ministries similar to The Navigators met for prayer and fellowship for twenty-four hours twice a year. No one ever missed except for a last-minute emergency.
- Seek out personal training. I was privileged to meet with Peter Drucker, the renowned management expert, along with a few other leaders.
- Learn who you are as a person, using some of the excellent instruments available to assess your personality and skill. I did several of these and found them always helpful, though not always determinative on what I should do.
- Develop the people on your team. They are your work family. Rejoice in their success.

// SUFFERING HAS ITS PLACE //

I would like to expand and reflect on the first point in this chapter, "Go Deep." Our leadership is always a reflection and overflow of our life and walk with God. Consequently, we continually need to nurture this spiritual reservoir of our life. I regret that I did not go deeper earlier in my life of leadership. If you had asked me when I was in my thirties whether I was going deep, I would have said yes. My heart wanted to. I was disciplined in my time with God. But

I was far too busy, too focused, too driven, and too unaware of the needs of my inner life and my marriage and family. God did get my attention through a time of burnout and depression (age forty) and certainly through the death of our only son when he was thirty (I was fifty-three).

The place of suffering and brokenness cannot be understated in the development of character and the deepening of our inner life with God. Almost every leader I know has suffered in some way. We do not seek suffering. In and of itself it does not make us better or more holy. It is what we do in and with the suffering. When our suffering becomes public, we do not parade it as a work of godliness, but we also do not hide it.

Until our son died, I think many of our staff felt that I was distant—perhaps they even feared me. Some of that had to do with my military background and my personality. But that event (what a terrible word for what happened) became a leveling influence in all our relationships. We were on public display. I could not lead on my own. The team had to pick up the pieces and keep the ministry going. The experience knitted our hearts together in ways we could never have imagined.

A significant influence on our lives as a couple, and on me as a leader, has been the influence of a covenant group with three other couples. We have been together (not geographically) for twenty-eight years. It is friendship, but yet it is more. This group goes far beyond the usual accountability group; it's more of a mutual commitment to help each other walk with Christ for a lifetime. We have weathered storms and conflict these many years. As couples, there is almost nothing that is hidden.

In my own walk with God, I have been stimulated by a number of writers. I recently have been rereading Andrew Murray's book *The Inner Life*. Murray focuses the entire book on our walk with God. In his preface he writes:

The Church of Christ and the spiritual life of thousands of its members suffer from root disease—the neglect of secret communion with God. It is the lack of secret prayer, the neglect of the maintenance of a hidden life "rooted and grounded in love" (Ephesians 3:17), that explains the inability of the Christian life to resist the world and its failure to produce fruit abundantly. Nothing can change this except the restoration of the inner chamber in the life of the believer. As Christians learn to daily sink their roots deeper into Christ and to make secret personal fellowship with God their main priority, true godliness will flourish.[2]

The prophetic voice of Alliance pastor A. W. Tozer still rings true: "No one can lead another farther than he himself has gone. For many ministers this explains their failure to lead. They simply do not know where to go."[3] That same book concludes with a "Prayer of a Minor Prophet" written in 1950. In part he prays:

And if in Thy permissive providence honor should come to me from Thy church, let me not forget in that hour that I am unworthy of the least of Thy mercies, and that if men knew me as intimately as I know myself they would withhold their honors or bestow them upon others more worthy to receive them. . . .

Though I am chosen of Thee and honored by a high and holy calling, let me never forget that I am but a man of dust and ashes, a man with all the natural faults and passions that plague the race of men. I pray Thee, therefore, my Lord and Redeemer, save me from myself.[4]

Is leadership important? Certainly. But *followership* is more so. We follow Christ. We serve people. We submit ourselves to other leadership. We give ourselves wholeheartedly to the temporary task assigned to us. But above all, we seek to daily walk with Christ!

MY LEADERSHIP BOOKSHELF

The Inner Life by Andrew Murray (Whitaker House, 1984). This devotional classic speaks powerfully to the importance of developing the inner intimacy with Jesus Christ that is required to walk worthy of his high calling in our lives.

God Tells the Man Who Cares by A. W. Tozer (Christian Publications, 1970, 1992) is a must-read Christian classic for all who desire to know and understand the voice of God.

Leaders: The Strategies for Taking Charge by Warren Bennis and Bert Nanus (HarperBusiness, 1997) is heralded as one of the top fifty leadership books. The authors believe that leadership is about character. In addition, leaders must create an organization that fosters intellectual capital, display a passion to realize their vision, be able to generate and sustain trust, persuade others to sign on to their vision, and display a bias toward action.

////// PERSONAL REFLECTIONS AND APPLICATIONS //////

1. Track your personal devotional life, particularly the focused time in the Scriptures, for the past thirty days. Be honest and accurate about what you find. Were you as disciplined and consistent in this critical leadership support area of your life as you were in your exercise, eating, work, and recreational regimens? What changes can you make? Track these for the *next* thirty days.

2. Are you at peace and fully engaged with your current leadership responsibilities, or are you persistently on the lookout for new opportunities for promotion and advancement? Is your full attention focused on the responsibilities of today's leadership calling—being faithful to what is currently in your hands? If not, why not? Your attitudes and actions, in relationship to your current position, reveal the degree of confidence you have in the Lord to order your days and manage your leadership calling.

3. In your current leadership responsibilities, are you performing out of a sense of duty or positional entitlement, or some other motivation? The unheeded admonition of noblesse oblige (nobility obligates) led to the French Revolution. Leadership is a privilege and a sacred responsibility—given so that we may serve rather than be served. Ask forgiveness for any unholy motivation and thank the Lord for today's privilege to lead by and for him.

4. Have you recognized the gifts God has given you in your leadership team? Have you thanked him for those gifts lately? Consider each member and thank the Lord for the distinctive contributions (personally, professionally, and/or spiritually) they each make that enhance and support your leadership calling, and your organization or ministry.

5. How have you experienced the Lord's strength being made perfect in your weaknesses—particularly during times of pain, distress, and failure? Make a list and refer to it periodically as a reminder that his grace uses even the cracks in our "jars of clay" to enable us to better lead.

6. Pray Tozer's "Prayer of a Minor Prophet" on page 242. What aspects of that prayer do you find most challenging? What confessions most unsettling? Why?

///////// TEAM REFLECTIONS AND APPLICATIONS /////////

1. What are you as an organization doing to help people shine in their areas of individual giftedness? Is your corporate culture one that nourishes or squelches the specific callings of those God has provided to get your work and mission accomplished? What barriers exist? Which one could you remove in the next five days?

2. How is your team discovering the hidden treasures of talents, experiences, and insights of those in your organization? Too many times great gifts and understandings go unrecognized and, as a result, underutilized because individuals are locked into a particular function or structure. Explore some ways to better determine the breadth of contributions your employees might be capable of making. A place to begin is by asking each employee what specific talent or experience he or she has that has not yet been fully utilized in your organization.

3. Is it possible to make your leadership team more of a covenant group to shoulder one another's burdens and celebrate each other's victories? A place to begin is by making time in the team meeting's agenda for prayer about personal as well as professional needs.

4. How can your leadership team better ensure that every employee is honored and respected in your organization? One step is to encourage supervisors to visit employees in their workstations for the purpose of encouraging and thanking rather than monitoring and directing.

JERRY WHITE
INTERNATIONAL PRESIDENT EMERITUS, THE NAVIGATORS
///

Dr. Jerry White is the international president emeritus and chairman of the U.S. board of directors of The Navigators (www.navigators.org). An international Christian organization, The Navigators has over four thousand staff ministering in 105 countries, working with college students, military personnel, business and professional people, and churches.

White was born in Iowa and raised in Washington. He received a BS in electrical engineering from the University of Washington, a master's degree in astronautics from the Air Force Institute of Technology, and his PhD in astronautics from Purdue University.

Following graduation from the University of Washington, White received a commission in the U.S. Air Force. His thirteen and a half years of active duty included an assignment as a mission controller at Cape Kennedy during the height of the American space program. He was an associate professor of astronautics at the U.S. Air Force Academy (CO) and coauthored a nationally recognized textbook on astrodynamics.

White spent twenty-four more years in the Air Force Reserves, retiring as a major general. In his last Reserves assignment, he was mobilization assistant to the commander of Air Force Materiel Command, Wright-Patterson AFB, Ohio. AFMC is responsible for the development, acquisition, and support of all new and existing airplane and space systems in the U.S. Previously he had assignments with the Electronic and Aeronautical Systems Centers, and what is now the Air Force Space Command and the National Security Agency.

Jerry White came into contact with The Navigators as a student at the University of Washington. Throughout his military career he maintained close contact with The Navigators, beginning the organization's ministries at the U.S. Air Force Academy and Purdue University. He served The Navigators as director for three regions and was named executive director in 1983. White then served as international president from 1986 to 2005. He currently serves on the boards of the Lausanne Committee on World Evangelization and Greater Europe Mission. He is past chairman of the Christian Leadership Alliance.

His many awards include the George Washington Honor Medal from the Freedom Foundation, the Legion of Merit Medal, and the Defense Service Medal. He is an associate Fellow of the American Institute of Aeronautics and Astronautics and chaired the Colorado Rhodes Scholarship Selection Committee.

Jerry White and his wife, Mary, have written thirteen books on practical topics such as work, ethics, and parenting adult children, including *Honesty, Morality & Conscience, The Joseph Road,* and *Rules to Live By.* The Whites have four children and eleven grandchildren and live in Colorado Springs.

14

///

PRESCRIPTIONS FOR LEADERSHIP

C. JEFFREY WRIGHT

One of the most beloved titles of Jesus is that of Great Physician. And one of the most powerful prophetic messianic images of Scripture is the portrayal of the Christ as the wounded healer. Jeffrey takes his extensive background in the business of healing and combines it with his current calling in Christian media to develop a powerful metaphor of Christ-honoring leaders as pharmacists—dispensing the essential compounds for organizational and leadership maladies. He uses back-to-basics parallels to help us understand, evaluate, and then prescribe those qualities of character, strengths of giftedness, and attitudes of service that transform organizations and those who lead them into healthy members of the body of Christ. As you read and reflect, think about the "healing ministries" your leadership contributes as you seek to be our Lord's pharmacist—dispensing grace, mercy, hope, and direction.

In Japan during the early eighth century, the government was organized into two branches under the Taiho Code—the Department of Worship and the Department of State. This division into sacred and secular positions and responsibilities included numerous leadership roles in a highly structured administrative system, with the division of the country into provinces and then further subdivisions. This created a system that is similar today in the United States through our state, county, and city governments. Among the most important positions established in this structure was that of the pharmacist—a position and person respected above all the professions in health care, including doctors and acupuncturists. In the 1834 edition of the *Annals of the Emperors of Japan,* pharmacists were ranked above even the personal physicians of the emperor.[1] Recent surveys continue to rate pharmacists as among the most highly respected professions in the United States.[2]

Why could the pharmacist be a metaphor for Christian leadership? And what can we learn from this profession that can lead to exemplary management models in the challenging environments of nonprofits today? These professionals, who compound and fill prescriptions; who advise patients, physicians, and other health-care specialists; and who sometimes create unique preparations for healing provide several examples and approaches instructive for undertaking the critical tasks of leadership today. Using the pharmacist model we will consider seven leadership attributes.

// 1. PREPARATION AND TRAINING //

"Jesus grew in wisdom and stature, and in favor with God and men" (Luke 2:52).

Medical training is commonly understood to be the most rigorous of academic and professional pursuits. Years of education; advanced science courses; and long periods of residency, internships, and study are required even after the formal education is completed. And even more study is needed for board certifications and licensing. Ten-year periods of preparation are common. Yet despite this extensive preparation, much of what physicians do comes down to a fifteen- or twenty-minute encounter with a patient, usually resulting in a prescription being written.

The importance of selecting that drug is critical. Yet for all their preparation, physicians don't necessarily take many courses in pharmacology. They can be uncertain about the appropriate uses of the particular drug they prescribe. This is where pharmacists play a critical role in the health-care system.

A pharmacist's knowledge goes well beyond simply knowing the names of drugs to also knowing what is in them, how they can help, and what they could do that might harm a patient. Pharmacists are required by all states to be licensed; they usually earn a doctor of pharmacy (PharmD) degree from a college of pharmacy and pass several examinations. The degree requires courses in mathematics and the natural sciences, including chemistry, biology, and physics, as well as subjects in the humanities and social sciences. In addition, students learn how to communicate with patients and other health-care providers about drug information and patient care. Courses dealing with professional ethics, concepts of public health, and business management are also commonly included. Most pharmacists have completed three or more years at a college or university before moving on to a PharmD program, which generally takes another four years to complete.

The pharmacist occupies the final checkpoint in assuring that the right prescription has been given to address the issue or illness to be treated. The extensive but focused preparation and training that pharmacists receive provide high levels of assurance that serious consequences will be avoided.

Leaders who lead like pharmacists have the training and education to make wise decisions in the matters that apply to the organization they are leading. Though there is much to be said for leaders being generalists who know much about many things, it is critical in today's knowledge economy and specialist culture that they also have the detailed knowledge and skill sets required to address their organization's unique challenges.

The debate about whether leadership can be *taught* or *caught* is long passed. Leadership skills can and must be learned. For most leaders the specific knowledge of the field of operations of their organization is essential for success. However, having the foundational education and training for a leadership position is just the start. It is important to understand that while there is a difference between professional education and natural intelligence, it is better to have both. And while few would disagree that a formal degree in the fields relevant to your sphere of leadership is a strength, it is equally important to understand that learning must be lifelong in light of the rapid changes occurring in almost every field.

Lifelong learning and continuing education are now well established with the rapid growth of executive education programs and intensives in virtually every discipline and profession. *Mind power* more than *manpower* has become the order of the day. Access to current and relevant information creates a separation between those who know and those who do not. Pharmacists must continually review information on new drugs, as well as understand how they fit in the armamentarium of other prescriptions. Understanding where dangerous interactions could occur, as well as knowing the patient and understanding his particular allergies or sensitivities, is critical to success in carrying out the pharmacist's responsibilities safely and effectively. We must require no less of leaders in all fields—particularly those who steward the organizations that seek kingdom impact.

// 2. POSITIONING AND AUTHORITY //

"During the fourth watch of the night Jesus went out to them" (Matthew 14:25).

Walk into any drugstore, or the many mass merchandisers that now sell prescriptions, and you will see the pharmacist in a white coat, easily identified and usually at the back or some other strategic location in the store where a broad view of the operation is possible. The pharmacy may contain as many different items as the rest of the entire store and usually in small containers. However, size does not matter—these small but powerful substances can improve physical conditions and save lives when given in the correct amounts to the right people.

In the days when pharmacists were usually entrepreneurs and business owners, the position at the back of the operation allowed observation of all store activities. It also was a place of security for dangerous, controlled, and often expensive products. Leading like pharmacists requires knowing where to stand as well as understanding the power of the products dispensed—taking care to ensure that the right amount is given to the right person and at the right time.

The place from which you lead is symbolic and important because of what it communicates. Corner offices are prized because they usually are larger and have more light and windows. However, some leaders position their offices in the center of the organization so that they are more accessible. In the work environment where leadership must operate today, the center is the new "back of the store." Being in the place where most must pass, where the critical issues are being wrestled with, and where people interact provides a strategic place for the exercise of leadership authority. You must be in the center of the action and on the front lines of the operations.

Usually the over-the-counter prescription medicines are directly adjacent to where the pharmacy counter is located. Often a person with a question about which product to choose or specific ailment experienced might step over to the pharmacy counter for advice and guidance from the pharmacist. The pharmacist's position is where the critical decisions are being made.

Leaders who are physically present use their positions to give direction and exercise authority, setting the expectation of and tone for accessibility. For all the talk of servant leadership, it should be clear that it is difficult to be available for service if you are not present regularly and consistently in the place where service is needed. Make sure that you and your key executives are physically positioned to allow access, providing the guidance that is needed at critical decision points.

Jesus made it his business to *be there.* Walking though the regions, from one encounter to another as recorded in the Gospels, his leadership was demonstrated by personally addressing people, problems, and opportunities. He did not desire a corner office in a synagogue with a closed door and rigid office hours. And though in the case of Lazarus (John 11), he may have delayed coming, he usually came to the patient and not the other way around. He was out and among the people needing his ministry—being accessible to children, outcasts, and the disadvantaged where they lived. His model of *being there* is a critical leadership practice that strengthens the authority and impact of the leader. Make deliberate opportunities for communication, for questions and interaction. It is amazing how many leaders undermine their effectiveness simply by not being there. Lead like a pharmacist by being strategically located and accessible.

// 3. PARTNERING AND DELEGATION //

"He called his twelve disciples to him and gave them authority" (Matthew 10:1).

A pharmacist is often the silent partner in medical care. The first contact that many people have with a health-care professional is with the pharmacist. The counseling on medications and physical conditions usually leads to physician referrals and treatment. Once treatment begins, it may be the pharmacist's role to monitor the therapy, provide information on side effects, and assure patient compliance with products dispensed. If, for example, a person requires daily dosing of a thirty-day prescription product and has not returned for a refill of two weeks of medicine at day twenty, it is usually the pharmacist who catches this lapse. In the hospital setting, clinical pharmacists work in teams to care for patients who need multiple medical disciplines for effective recovery—such as in geriatrics, pediatrics, and oncology.

When you lead like a pharmacist, you understand and can articulate your unique gifts and role as a leader. However, you also recognize the power of teams and the importance of specialists. "No one can do it all," the saying goes—and your position of leadership is not a license to try to prove that adage wrong. Christ's example of developing and deploying a diverse team of leaders is evident in those men's occupational specialties, which ranged from fishermen to tax collectors. But even more, it also is evident that their differences in temperament and personality, in turn, shaped the nature and methodologies of Jesus' teachings and ministry. The impulsiveness of Peter and the relationship skills of Andrew, for example, dictated their individual leadership styles. Each led others to lives of effective service in their own unique ways.

Empowered leadership teams, where differences are valued and understood, create unique capacities in an organization. This is the picture of the body of Christ described in 1 Corinthians 12. Vision is improved when multiple points of view are available and given opportunity for expression. The leader with a homogeneous group of yes-persons has much in common with the proverbial carpenter whose only tool is a hammer—everything looks like a nail. God's Word makes it clear that each of us is created for unique purposes, which he "prepared in advance for us to do" (Ephesians 2:10). When you lead like a pharmacist, you use not only your individual gifts but also the skills and dispositions of every person on your team to bring about the best results for your organization. By empowering your team, you empower your ability to lead.

// 4. PROFESSIONAL INTERVENTION AND EXPERT ADVICE //

"This kind can come out only by prayer" (Mark 9:29).

Pharmacists know to call the doctor when needed. Often when a prescription is handed to a pharmacist and he or she looks at a patient record and sees a drug interaction, the next step is a call to the prescribing physician. At times a doctor may have scripted one drug because its name is similar to another drug that actually was intended. Sometimes the doctor is called because the prescription is illegible. Another possibility includes a customer trying to avoid a doctor altogether by asking the pharmacist for an over-the-counter recommendation. The wise pharmacist in this situation may sense something more serious, and in turn refers the customer to a doctor. Pharmacists know when to seek greater expertise and bring other professionals to a decision-making process.

Effective leaders understand this as well.

When Jesus' disciples were unable to drive out the evil spirits in the boy mentioned in Mark 9, the father appealed directly to Jesus—who both handled the problem and explained why the disciples were unsuccessful. Too often pride prevents leaders from turning to more experienced professionals. Sometimes ignorance or misapplication of prior lessons results in leaders not seeking help from others. Whatever the cause, leaders should follow the example of the pharmacist—recognizing that being a part of a healing team often means that the solutions must involve other experts who can uniquely address the issue.

In the nonprofit setting, organizations often struggle with problems and issues that already have been addressed and resolved in secular business settings. Best practices can come from many places. The development of the drug Taxol is a good example of how teams using distinctive and varying expertise can solve major problems.

In 1962, a team of botanists from the U.S. Department of Agriculture collected bark from the Pacific Yew tree. Samples from this tree were then analyzed by a team of chemists at the Research Triangle Institute in North Carolina, under a contract from the National Cancer Institute. The chemists teamed to discover the drug Taxol. This drug was further developed and commercialized by chemists, pharmacologists, physicians, and scientists in the pharmaceutical industry. It has become the most widely used drug for breast and ovarian cancer, both saving and prolonging thousands of lives.[3]

Starting with the bark of a tree, God used botanists, chemists, other scientists, physicians, and clinicians to create a powerful lifesaving compound that is now dispensed by thousands of pharmacists to millions of patients. "There are different kinds of gifts, but the same Spirit. There are different kinds of service, but the same Lord. There are different kinds of working, but the same God works all of them in all [people]" (1 Corinthians 12:4-6). In our leading like a pharmacist, we succeed when we admit what we do not know and then humbly look to those whom God has already prepared, to produce the results he planned in advance. Remember, "it's what you learn after you know it all that counts."[4]

// 5. PRODUCT AND SERVICE KNOWLEDGE //

"[Jesus] did not need man's testimony about man, for he knew what was in a man" (John 2:25).

The drugs that pharmacists prescribe have been through a discovery and approval process that takes many years. Research and development costs millions. Despite this investment, very few of the drugs discovered ever make it to the pharmacy shelves after the rigorous testing and approvals required by the Food and Drug Administration (FDA). These tests begin with laboratory protocols and animal experiments. They usually conclude with a series of human clinical studies in phases, designed to assure that the drug is safe and efficacious—that it produces the desired results when prescribed and administered. Yet even after all these tests, few drugs pass.[5]

This standard of practice is what we have come to expect in a country that has the most well-developed system of pharmaceutical research and production in the world. Sadly, however, the standards that we accept in the areas of ministry and nonprofit practice sometimes fall short of this level of rigor. In some instances, it seems that in Christian ministry and nonprofit management, there is a belief that since the work is "for God" or "about God," mistakes, poor performance, and knowledge gaps will somehow be forgiven because "God is in the plan" or "the intentions of the heart were good."

That road, paved with good intentions and somewhat rash presumptions, usually leads to less than God-honoring outcomes. The psalmist wrote that the Lord's name is excellent (Psalm 8:1, *KJV*). Our work must not dishonor his name because of a lack of knowledge or lack of commitment to the highest quality. Leading like a pharmacist means an uncompromised dedication to excellence and understanding that reflects that others' eternal lives depend on what we do.

A typical challenge to this standard of excellence in product knowledge, service, and results comes from those who point to a lack of resources—people, financial, talent, etc.—that prevents the level of excellence we desire. We are called as leaders to operate with knowledge and wisdom, defining carefully those situations where we should not act because we do not know. It could be that the lack of knowledge or resources is God's indication that we should not act. Pharmacists' knowledge of the drugs prescribed to us includes what the drug is "indicated" for—that is, what it works to heal or cure. Pharmacists also know when a drug is "contraindicated"—when it should *not* be used. Effective leaders know when they have the information and understanding to act and when they do not.

The FDA's standards provide the leader with helpful benchmarks for much of the decision making that is faced in the nonprofit environment. Is it safe? Will it work? Can my organization effectively steward its resources and mission with this decision, or will it damage or impair some aspect of the organization? Is the decision one that will lead to accomplishing the objective? Leading like a pharmacist means that the more you know, the more prepared you are as a godly leader to address the critical issues that will define organizational outcomes. Here are some ancient protocols worth heeding and following as we seek the knowledge to lead:

- "A wise man has great power, and a man of knowledge increases strength" (Proverbs 24:5).
- "Wisdom is supreme; therefore get wisdom. Though it cost all you have, get understanding" (Proverbs 4:7).

The book of Proverbs is full of leadership strategies. Orlando Magic senior vice president Pat Williams has written an entire book devoted to them: *The Leadership Wisdom of Solomon* (Standard Publishing, 2010).

// 6. PRACTICAL SOLUTIONS AND CREATIVE ALTERNATIVES //

"Daniel then said to the guard . . . , 'Please test your servants for ten days: Give us nothing but vegetables to eat and water to drink'" (Daniel 1:11, 12).

An *ethical drug* is a traditional way of describing medicines that are only sold by a pharmacist filling a prescription from a doctor, dentist, or appropriately licensed medical professional. The idea is that a higher level of expertise and understanding is required for the right use of these products as compared to over-the-counter (OTC) products. Historically, a third category of products consisted of pharmaceuticals that did not require a prescription but were available only upon request from a pharmacist. Acetaminophen, most popularly known as Tylenol, a brand from Johnson & Johnson, was such a product in this third category known as *ethical OTC* products.

The still-unsolved crime of the poisoning of this ethical OTC product resulted in major changes in the way products are packaged and sold. Safety seals and protective packaging are now on virtually all drug (and many food) products in an effort to prevent a crime of this type from recurring. The story of the Johnson & Johnson leadership's response to the poisoning and deaths has become a case study in how ethical leaders handle crises—honestly, quickly, and publicly. Doing the right thing cost the company millions in profits as an entire national stock of product was removed from pharmacy shelves and destroyed until protective packaging could be introduced. However, after the poisoning and recall, sales made a comeback far exceeding expectations.[6]

An ethical leader operates according to the moral standards and principles of the Bible. The lessons here for leaders in nonprofits are twofold:

1. Ethical conduct works.
2. Developing a creative alternative in the face of a crisis is a critical and essential leadership skill.

The book of Daniel opens with a very difficult situation that clearly demonstrates these lessons. A hostile enemy held Daniel and his colleagues captive, due to no fault of their own. Forced to learn occult sciences, serve a pagan ruler, and probably suffer other indignities, Daniel came up with a way to survive as well as to serve God. His proposal to the guards that he be allowed to continue a "kosher diet" while in captivity is a model of quick thinking and creative leading in the most difficult of circumstances. Daniel's ethics, integrity, and faithfulness to God became the hallmarks of his leadership.

Many leaders struggle with maintaining this kind of integrity in far less hostile circumstances than Daniel encountered. His willingness to serve and lead responsibly, even in the face of extreme political and theological differences, is an example for Christian leaders today. Leaders need to pray for the wisdom to work creatively and pursue alternatives that will transform the efforts of even their enemies and competitors. Martin Luther King Jr. said, "Love is the only force capable of transforming an enemy into a friend."[7] Christ was even more straightforward in his command, a challenge for all who claim to follow Christ today: "Love your enemies, do good to those who hate you, bless those who curse you, pray for those who mistreat you" (Luke 6:27, 28).

Pharmacists often illustrate this principle in their unique way of handling the selection of generic drugs over more costly brand-name prescriptions. When a drug loses its patent protection, the original manufacturer can face competition from companies that make less expensive versions of the same pharmaceutical compound that they hope will be used by the pharmacist. Sometimes the pharmacist is required by legislation or insurance providers to substitute the product, but often it is their choice to offer the less expensive product—saving the patient money even when it means making less profit. The generic drug industry depends on this process occurring. As a result, many products become affordable for millions because of the pharmacist's commitment to creative alternatives and ethical business practices. Interestingly, the largest generic drug company in the world as of this writing is Teva, an Israeli company[8] that has established a global presence through the same kind of creative alternatives that served Daniel in the courts of Babylon.

Creative alternatives are essential in recessionary environments, resource-constrained leadership settings, and those situations in which the easy and the obvious are elusive and the usual approaches cannot be trusted. Leading like a pharmacist in these situations requires a "what if" mind-set and the encouragement of constructive challenges to teams to tap into new ways of seeing or doing things. It might also mean making sure that when resources are sought or appeals made to those in authority, leaders persist (refusing to take no for an answer) until the right individual steps forward with a creative solution.

// 7. PRESENTATION AND COMMUNICATION SKILLS //

"They read from the Book of the Law of God, making it clear and giving the meaning so that the people could understand what was being read" (Nehemiah 8:8).

"The tongue has the power of life and death" (Proverbs 18:21).

In many pharmacies the counter is a raised platform, making it necessary to look up to the pharmacist when you receive advice or take receipt of your prescription. Pharmacists are on the speaking platform all day! They do their jobs on a stage with a constant flow of strangers to connect to, communicate with, and advise on some of the most important issues of life. If leading like a pharmacist means public speaking, many leaders might cringe—since so many people attest to this as one of their greatest fears.

An effective leader should work to become a confident and poised communicator. If this is a weakness for you, there is almost no other skill that will give you a greater return on the investment of time, coaching, and study than to improve your public speaking ability. Effective communicators can inspire action, motivate extraordinary passion, create an environment for greater results, and transform their organizations. Even poor or evil ideas, effectively communicated, can have dramatic influence on people. The tower of Babel is a striking example of that.

When you powerfully communicate the truth, bringing biblical principles into the lives of others, your leadership is strengthened significantly. Regardless of where you are on the spectrum—poor, fearful communicator or seasoned, expert motivational speaker—the benefit of improving your communication skills is undeniable.

In Illinois two pharmacists demonstrated just how critical communication skills are when they refused to dispense the abortion inducing morning-after pill because of religious objections. Their willingness to speak out publicly, maintaining a principled stance, was a tremendous testimony and encouragement to many who are asked to perform tasks that violate biblical and moral standards. You never know when you, as a Christian leader, may be required to take such a stand or respond to a crisis when God wants you to be his voice against evil and injustice. Make a commitment now to become a better communicator!

This is, however, an area where excuses abound. Moses and the apostle Paul both complained about their communication skills. Moses' self-criticism was rebuked by God as he reminded him, "I will help you speak and will teach you what to say" (Exodus 4:10). In 2 Corinthians 10:7, Paul pointedly critiques the Corinthian focus on the external attributes of speaking ability, demeanor, and oratorical skills—as opposed to the deeper meanings of the communicator. This might seem to give us an excuse for not developing our communication skills. It is true that there are many persuasive but doctrinally deluded communicators in ministry, nonprofit management, and other fields. Despite these abuses and excuses, an effective leader needs to develop and improve communication skills. And you can do it, because the God who promised help to Moses makes that same help and discipline available to you.

// SO STEP UP TO THE COUNTER AND LEAD LIKE A PHARMACIST! //

We as Christian leaders have such important and sacred work to accomplish. We hold in our hands and hearts the spiritual health—both here and for eternity—of multiplied billions of people around the world. We are called to serve those broken and fractured by the congenital effects of sin by filling the prescription of our Great Physician, written in blood on the cross of Calvary. We are dispensing God's love and forgiveness for all who will receive and obey. So let us lead like a pharmacist, employing the fundamental and essential healing business of our gospel, binding up the broken, liberating the afflicted, and declaring that now is the time of the Lord's acceptance!

MY LEADERSHIP BOOKSHELF

Talent Is Overrated by Geoff Colvin (Penguin Group, 2008) discusses the scientific research on the roots of the extraordinary performance we all wish to see in our colleagues and coworkers. Its surprising conclusions have informed how I view performance management in my organization.

Why You Can't Be Anything You Want to Be by Arthur F. Miller Jr. (Zondervan, 1999) explores the biblical basis of giftedness and how understanding our unique God-given strengths can help us achieve in the areas for which we were designed to be successful.

Follow This Path by Curt Coffman and Gabriel Gonzales-Molina (Business Plus, 2002) details the Gallup organization's research on engagement at work. Its subtitle says it all: *How the World's Greatest Organizations Drive Growth by Unleashing Human Potential.*

////// PERSONAL REFLECTIONS AND APPLICATIONS //////

1. Have you completed the educational requirements and degrees that would be foundational for your field of leadership, or are you leaning on experience and intelligence only? What personal knowledge gaps do you have that can be addressed by a seminar or other learning experience that you have been putting off?

2. How are the "prescriptions" you are applying to your organization right for your circumstances and the unique attributes of your operation?

3. How are you available to key personnel? Do you have at least weekly face-to-face meetings with them? If not, how could you build this into your schedule?

4. Can you quickly name your five greatest leadership strengths? your spiritual gift(s)? Do you trust your team's expertise to make final decisions in areas where they have the authority and responsibility, or do all major decisions come to you? What decisions do you never delegate? Why? What examples can you recall when a team member's judgment was better than your own?

5. Do you have an effective board of trustees/directors, as well as access to outside advisers with specialized expertise who may be better prepared than internal staff to assist in critical areas of your operations? If not, why

not, and what can you do about it? Do you understand your own limits and know when to draw on the strengths of others? If not, why not, and what can you do about it?

6. How do you know the will of God in your decision making as a leader? Do you understand why you are not getting the results you want? Think about this: Your system is perfectly designed to produce the results you are getting.

7. Think of two or three effective communicators you admire and respect. What specific attributes make them effective? Have you had media training or been coached in crisis communication? If not, consider investing in this critical preparation for the unexpected interview or presentation.

///////// TEAM REFLECTIONS AND APPLICATIONS /////////

1. Do you have a program of continuing education for yourselves and key employees in order to encourage lifelong learning? If not, how could you begin one? What evidence can you provide that demonstrates that you are continuing to grow in wisdom as well as skill sets in your leadership?

2. Do you as senior leadership meet at least monthly or quarterly (depending on size and locations of organization) in some forum with all associates/ managers? Have you had a personal encounter with every employee of your organization? If the organization is too large for such a commitment, what are you doing to assure your employees that the leadership team is accessible and available? How could you use available technology to extend the visibility of your leadership (video, the Web, blogs, etc.)?

3. What does diversity look like in your organization (age, gender, ethnicity, cultural heritage, church background, marital status, other)? What does it look like in the leadership team? Who has influence and who does not?

4. How are your spiritual, legal, financial, and technical capacities bolstered by strong outside advisory relationships? What keeps you from admitting you need help beyond your own expertise and experiences? Remember, pride always goes before a fall.

5. How often do you go with your gut or go with the available information, even when it is not adequate for the decision? How has that been working out? Are there knowledge gaps in the organization that are not being addressed? If so, what are they?

6. Are you doing things the way you've always done them, or are you doing things the *best* way? Is this true for the most important activities of your organization? How would your team rate the creativity of your organization? your own leadership?

7. Does your team have the ability to present a well thought out and concisely focused "elevator pitch" that describes your organization in two minutes or less? Practice speaking and communicating. We must trust God as Moses did and believe in his ability, even if we do not believe in our own.

C. JEFFREY WRIGHT
CEO, UMI (URBAN MINISTRIES, INC.)
///

Since 1995, C. Jeffrey Wright has been CEO and principal of the largest independent African-American religious media firm, UMI (Urban

Ministries, Inc.), www.urbanministries.com. UMI has been a leader in independent (nondenominationally affiliated) urban Christian and positive media content for forty years.

UMI magazines, books, Sunday school and VBS curriculum, videos, DVDs, music, and crafts have been used in over fifty thousand African-American churches. UMI's unique Sunday school curriculum, which is specifically contextualized for the African-American audience, is used in over twenty thousand churches weekly for Bible study. The company also publishes resources on an exclusive or semi-exclusive basis for a dozen major denominations.

Chicago-based UMI has been a distribution partner as well as content provider for several other firms. As a promotion partner, UMI has worked with McDonald's Corporation on the successful Inspiration Celebration Gospel Tour. Additionally, the organization has produced and distributed video/DVD and film products since the mid-1980s and has Emmy and Angel Award–winning productions to its credit.

Wright's professional background, prior to taking the helm of UMI, includes more than fifteen years in the *Fortune* 500 companies Johnson & Johnson and Bristol-Myers Squibb, where his last position was as vice president of corporate development (mergers, acquisitions, and strategic alliances) for consumer businesses. A minister, lawyer, and graduate of Georgetown University Law Center, Wright is admitted to the Pennsylvania bar and the U.S. Supreme Court bar. He has an MBA in finance from Columbia University Graduate School of Business and graduated with honors from Fisk University. He completed additional study in the Harvard Law School Program of Instruction for Lawyers, the Wharton School in business development, and taught jurisprudence and ethics at the graduate level at the University of Evansville (Indiana).

His leadership in the parachurch community includes serving on the boards of Care Net, the Evangelical Christian Publishers Association, Fuller Theological Seminary, and The Marriage and Family Foundation. He also serves as board president and CEO of Circle Y Ranch in Bangor, Michigan.

C. Jeffrey Wright has four children and is married to Lakita Garth, a media consultant and professional entertainer.

15

//

FINISHING WELL

DAVID J. GYERTSON

A s one of the editors, I have had the privilege of reflecting on the excellent insights and advice contributed for this book. Having been the CEO of several faith-based organizations, and having served as an employee in and a consultant to many others, my own personal journey of discovering and appropriating a Christ-centered leadership model is approaching its final phase. My leadership calling has been deeply influenced by so many of those I followed—most significantly the life and lessons of our Lord Jesus Christ. As you read through these reflections, some of the themes from our contributors are reprised. Hopefully, my thoughts on these themes will motivate you to take all that has been said, pull threads that speak to your unique sense of leadership and calling, and weave a fresh tapestry of insights, convictions, and strategies that build on, or perhaps course-correct, your leadership journey. Most of all, may these insights and reflections bring glory to our Lord.

As Christ-centered ministry leaders, we have a challenging and difficult responsibility to model Christian leadership that is relational, transformational, and operational. To succeed in this calling, I believe we must embrace a whole-person model of disciple making that, at its core, is a process of spiritual awakening and formation. At the very heart of this calling is a commitment to regeneration, restoration, and renewal designed to produce spiritually formed disciples of Jesus Christ who are able to change their world as they work in the ministries that we lead.

Our theology of what it means to be a disciple must be grounded in an understanding of spiritual formation. Then we have to get serious about building this into our methods of leading people to become disciples. It is more than an intellectual or social exercise; it affects the whole person. To that end, we need a profile for spiritually formed leadership that will serve not only our own sense of mission but contribute to God's larger purposes in and through our work. The foundations of my thinking are anchored to a discipleship development process that began when I was an undergraduate student at a Christian college. The initial lessons learned in that setting continue to fuel my passion for and methodologies of Christian leadership.

This chapter describes a personal pilgrimage into the mission, message, and meaning of spiritually formed leadership. It is not my intent to present this model as the final or ultimate answer for our important work. Rather, the goal is to encourage, motivate, and inspire you to take your distinctive understandings, experiences, and applications of the call to Christian leadership to their next levels. I assert that as Christ-centered leaders chosen to lead Christ's redeeming work in the nonprofit world, ours is ultimately a calling to excellent, noble, and sacrificial service.

// STRETCHING MINDS, CRADLING HEARTS, AND EXTENDING HANDS //

In the fall of 1966, I began a journey of discipleship formation that challenged my thinking, touched my heart, and prepared my hands for service at levels I could not have imagined. Lacking a high school diploma, but convinced that I needed an education to fulfill my calling, I came to Spring Arbor College (now University) in Michigan. There I encountered a call to radical whole-person discipleship—I confronted something called the Spring Arbor Concept.

I did not fully appreciate the concept while I was a student. I felt discipleship was more a matter of *doing* rather than of thinking and being. Despite my resistance, an integrated profile of those who serve God's purposes as leaders in their generation began to emerge. I became convinced that I must be a disciple of "the tough mind and the tender heart" (a phrase I gleaned, I believe, from an Elton Trueblood book) if I was to use my hands effectively and contribute meaningfully to the work of God's kingdom. Today my passion for Christ, vision for service, and commitment to let the mind of Christ be in me (Philippians 2:5, *KJV*) and the love of Christ flow through me remains rooted in the images of a lamp, the cross, and a needy world that I first encountered as a student at a Christian college.

// THE LAMP OF LEARNING—STRETCHING THE RENEWED MIND //

In the context of Spring Arbor University's approach to whole-person education, I was challenged to first commit my life to a *head* knowledge understanding. Having come to faith in Jesus Christ out of a troubled and dysfunctional home, I needed to understand that it was necessary to become a mature follower of Christ through the disciplines of the renewed mind. I was challenged to understand that discipleship requires a disciplined commitment to "study to show [myself] approved unto God" (2 Timothy 2:15, *KJV*).

I learned that effective discipleship is driven by the Great Commission mandate to "go and make disciples . . . teaching them to obey everything [Jesus] commanded" (Matthew 28:19, 20). The building blocks of mature leadership rest on the foundation of divine revelation. Those who follow Christ so they can lead effectively see the world differently because they understand it through the mind of Jesus. He is the clearest revelation of all that is ultimately and eternally true. Effective spiritual leaders can define reality only when they have understood ultimate reality in the one who is "the way and the truth and the life" (John 14:6). The need to develop a Christian worldview is ultimately a demand to pursue a Christ-centered perspective of truth, service, and sacrifice.

This relationship with Jesus Christ begins with the revelation that we need a Savior. "'Come now, let us reason together,' says the Lord. 'Though your sins are like scarlet, they shall be as white as snow'" (Isaiah 1:18). Jesus spent more time teaching than in any other single activity. The primary means he used to turn fishermen, tax collectors, harlots, and zealots into revolutionary leaders, able to turn their culture upside down, was the transforming of the mind—guided, guarded, and enabled by the Spirit of truth. While these disciples marveled at our Lord's miracles, they were enlisted by his message—a call to a Christian counterculture delivered with a depth of insight and level of authority they had not experienced previously. And this shaped the thinking of Christian leaders who influenced the intellectual, social, and cultural world for centuries after Christ's death.

The early church fathers did not distinguish between sacred and secular knowledge. They recognized all truth as God's truth. Jesus is "the way and the truth and the life" (John 14:6). In God "we live and move and have our being" (Acts 17:28). These facts necessitate that leaders teach disciples to truly *think* like Christians. Having a transformed mind is more than affirming a list of beliefs. It is replacing secular paradigms with a wholly biblical worldview.

I once read a sermon that Martin Luther delivered to the political leaders of his day, titled "Keeping Children in School." In it he established the central place of education in discipleship formation, championing the renewing of the mind across multiple disciplines. He taught that children needed to study not only languages and history but also singing and music, together with the whole of mathematics. The ancient Greeks trained their children in these disciplines, and as a result, Luther believed, they grew up to be people of wondrous ability, subsequently fit for anything.

I read that John Milton, in his *Tractate on Education,* emphasized the value of broad and comprehensive learning—what we know today as the liberal arts—when he suggested that a complete and generous education is one that fits a person to perform all the offices, both private and public, of peace and of war. He insisted that the goal of learning is to repair the ruins of our first parents by knowing God and, out of that knowledge, to love him, imitate him, and be like him.

I read how John Wesley and missionary leader Francis Asbury called their itinerant preachers to read not only the Bible and theology but also the classic literature, as well as the daily news.

As an emerging Christian leader, I was challenged to know God in every expression of creation and discipline of human learning. To lay Christ as the only foundation challenges us to catch God at work in every place, plan, process, and person so that we can advance his purposes in each for the glory of Jesus Christ. I have discovered a new application of a favorite childhood game. With the belief that God is always up to something somewhere and with someone, I choose to greet each new ministry challenge with the prayer "Come out, come out wherever you are." Each day I give myself to the Christ-centered commitment of stretching the mind, reaching for the highest levels of learning so that I might lead others into a deeper walk with Christ.

As we master the disciplines of the stretched mind, laying hold of the lamp of learning, we honor Paul's command not to be conformed "to the pattern of this world, but be transformed by the renewing of your mind" (Romans 12:2). I challenge you to be a disciple and lifelong learner with a renewed mind. Only as we continue to learn, stretching our minds and thoughts beyond what we currently know, can we be fit to lead with courage, conviction, and clarity.

// THE CROSS—CRADLING THE RESTORED HEART //

One of the great challenges of this kind of discipleship, however, is that learning, left to itself, can lead to arrogance, isolation, and self-preoccupation. The greater the knowledge we acquire, the more critical it is that with the learning we nurture compassion. Knowledge is the blossom of the exercised mind. Compassion is the fruit of the circumcised heart. The cross, the second symbol in the Spring Arbor Concept, is the sobering symbol of the restored heart.

The Great Commission focuses on the head-first calling of teaching them to obey all Jesus commanded. His other "great," the great commandment (Mark 12:30, 31), is the key to employing our knowledge for the ultimate good of humanity. We must embrace Jesus' command to love the Lord our God with our total being—body and spirit as well as mind—and to love our neighbor as ourselves. It is this motivation that restores and renews the hearts of spiritually transformed disciples.

While I hold the lamp of learning in one hand, I must embrace the love of God demonstrated on the cross of Christ with the other. To comprehend Jesus Christ as *the* truth, we must apprehend him as the way and the life in every dimension of learning, living, and serving. Jesus becomes our supreme teacher when we embrace him as our suffering Savior. Loving God and humanity answers the "so what" questions of learning, providing both meaning to and motivation for the pursuit of truth. Our ministry leadership is enlivened when it becomes the means to change both hearts and minds. To embrace the cross is to receive Christ's redeeming work accomplished on the tree, and follow its shadow into sacrificial, risk-taking love for others.

My experiences as a Christ-centered leader are punctuated often by the convicting and conforming presence of our Lord's love in our midst. During my days as a student—and in the years following as a pastor, teacher, and university administrator—my life encountered what I see now as divine appointments that forced me to confront the Lord's redeeming love of Calvary. Often these occurred in scheduled religious services, awakening me to a need for forgiveness or the hunger for a deeper commitment. At other times, it was a sustained knocking disrupting my academic, professional, and social calendar for days until his work was completed. I realize now that he was present in all my activities, lovingly reminding me that in him my intellectual, spiritual, social, and professional life has its ultimate being (Acts 17:28).

In light of the Jesus model of effective spiritual leadership, I believe that good leadership is anchored to good teaching. Good teaching is as much a factor of the heart of the teacher as it is the head. One of the most important resources for me in this quest to embrace the cross in my calling to lead by teaching is Parker J. Palmer's *The Courage to Teach.* Palmer lays out the following premise: "Good teaching cannot be reduced to technique; good teaching comes from the identity and integrity of the teacher."[1] He continues: "In every class I teach, my ability to connect with my students, and to connect them with the subject, depends less on the methods I use than on the degree to which I know and trust my selfhood—and am willing to make it available and vulnerable in the service of learning."[2]

In one of my teaching assignments, a student gave me a plaque whose saying sums up the challenge to embrace the cross perspective in our leadership formation pedagogy: "To learn and never be satisfied is wisdom, to teach and never be weary is love."

I saw the crucified Jesus so often in the lives of those who have sought to lead me. They became his encouragers for embracing the love of the cross. Theirs is a journey of a long obedience in the same direction, willing to embrace, at any cost and consequence, God's call to love unreservedly and lead sacrificially. A few of those living epistles, like my lifelong mentor David McKenna, continue teaching and mentoring me today in the "more excellent way" (1 Corinthians 12:31, *KJV*). So many other models, among them Ted W. Engstrom, now held by the nail-scarred hands of Jesus, lived for me as disciples of both "the tough mind and the tender heart" I mentioned earlier.

Leadership is more than a sterile exercise in passing information to one's followers. It is a relationship with the followers. Thus there needs to be more shared than information; we have to share our hearts as well. Just as Jesus invested his life into his disciples—living, traveling, facing storms and angry Pharisees, and touching the hurting together—so we must invest our lives into the ones who would follow us.

// THE NEEDY WORLD—EXTENDING REDEMPTIVE HANDS //

With the lamp of learning in one hand and the cross of Christ in the other, we have been called to a life of leadership that produces tangible, life-changing, and world-shaping results. Throughout the centuries mature followers of Jesus not only thought clearly and loved deeply—they served nobly, effectively, and sacrificially. Transformed minds and purified hearts are manifested in and validated by the exceptional work they perform and the sacrificial service they render. Spiritually formed leadership, as Dietrich

Bonhoeffer eloquently communicated by both pen and life, is usually a costly one focused on the needs and opportunities of a waiting world.

We are enlightened by learning so that we can do the Father's business as revealed in the life of Christ. Spiritually formed leadership extends capable hands for noble, tangible, and measurable purposes. Like the Master we are called to serve the poor, preaching the good news, binding up the brokenhearted, proclaiming release to captives, recovery of sight to the blind, setting at liberty those who are oppressed, and declaring that now is the time of the Lord's acceptance (Isaiah 61:1, 2; Luke 4:18, 19). It is a call to demonstrate the breadth of our learning and the depth of our loving by stretching out competent, compassionate, redemptive hands to serve a needy world.

Enlightened and enlivened leaders develop a compelling sense of social justice and global responsibility that calls them to touch the least, the left, and the lost. It was on a mission trip to Spanish Harlem in the inner city of New York my junior year of college that I touched the heart of—and was challenged to extend the hands of—Christ. Subsequent opportunities to serve, minister, and teach abroad in Europe, Africa, the Middle East, and the Far East deepened my understanding that wholeness requires a commitment to serve the purposes of God in our generation for every tongue, tribe, and nation. It is in the conflicts and contexts of cross-cultural and multicultural engagement that our ideas are challenged and hearts stretched to serve global discipleship causes larger than just our own.

Redemptive hands, however, not only serve compassionately but also excellently. It's possible to do both. We must do what we do with all our might for the glory of God. This is a call to professional and personal excellence if our loving acts are to be both credible and effective. We must exercise discipline, diligence, and the commitment to achieve our fullest potential. Christ taught with an authority and clarity that exceeded even the most skilled and learned of his day (Mark 1:22). We who lead in his name must do no less if the results of our leadership are to reflect the nobility of our king and Lord.

This cup-of-cold-water service is, as the early church understood in James 2:14-26, the evidence that wisdom is comprehended and love embraced.

// A WORLD-CHANGER'S PROFILE //

Through the proceedings of India's 2004 Kolkata Conference of the International Council for Higher Education, I found a framework that informs this culminating phase of my life and calling. Using the contexts of the conference's purpose statement, I developed a series of affirmations designed to tie the elements of my leadership journey to the hub of Christ-centered learning, loving, and serving. Many of these themes have been reflected in the writings of those who have contributed so generously and transparently to this book. I continually use these insights and affirmations to keep my life on track.

AFFIRMATION ONE

Christ-centered leaders embrace the Christian perspective as reflected in God's Word. They are empowered to appropriate those perspectives by the Holy Spirit's gifts and graces to initiate a positive, practical, and respectful dialogue with the world about the implications of such perspectives. Unfortunately, the harshness of much of our dialogue as intentional and serious-minded Christians often limits the impact of our ideas.

AFFIRMATION TWO

Christ-centered leaders move beyond cognitive learning and skill acquisition to intentional discipleship as their ultimate objective. Through the conscious integration of faith, learning, and living, Christ-centered leaders examine their professional missions and motivations, asking how the fruit of their labor relates to the purposes of God. Christ-centered leaders not only analyze the outcomes of their efforts but also explore their moral implications.

AFFIRMATION THREE

Christ-centered leaders embrace a great-commandment motivation that compels them to address poverty, illness, exploitation, discrimination, and oppression in the world. They possess a burden for those who for reasons of culture, social position, political oppression, economic condition, race, gender, and ethnicity are denied the basics of life's opportunities. Christ-centered leaders are driven by the mission and motivation of Christ—to address and resolve human meaninglessness and suffering by understanding, going, teaching, serving, loving, and if necessary, dying.

AFFIRMATION FOUR

Christ-centered leaders reflect major biblical themes of justice, mercy, and humility in their daily lives. They act justly, love mercy, and walk humbly with their God (Micah 6:8). All three of these provide evidence of the transformation that comes when the mind is challenged to see and serve the world as Christ does.

AFFIRMATION FIVE

Christ-centered leaders think clearly and love deeply—providing noble service distinguished by its excellence, innovation, humility, and self-sacrifice.

By embracing those five affirmations, I believe Christ-centered, spiritually formed leaders can serve the present age and help transform the world's future (responsibly occupying until Jesus returns). In an effort to put all of this together, I conclude with a personal parable.

// A PARABLE FOR MY SERVANT LEADERSHIP CALLING //

As the newly trained chef stood before the door of the manor house, he felt himself overcome with thanksgiving. Long he had hoped and prayed for the opportunity to join the household of the one who rescued him from a life of destruction and distraction. Now nothing was more important than using the culinary skills and talents he had honed so sacrificially for the benefactor who had done so much for him.

The door opened. Standing before him was the lord of the manor and the opportunity to fulfill the dreams of a lifetime.

"Welcome home," the master said. "We have your place ready."

As the chef walked in, the master continued, "I know you are well equipped for the tasks of leading my banquet staff. However, I have great needs in my fields. Will you serve me where I need you most—for as long as necessary, perhaps a lifetime?"

As the chef contemplated these words, he found his initial disappointment disappearing quickly.

"Yes," was his reply.

In that moment, he realized that he had learned an even more significant lesson than any cooking technique during his time of training. He had honed his skills to be a chef but was willing to lay that aside out of love if the master required other service. Serving to meet the needs of the one he loved, however that played out, was more important than serving to meet his own.

That story, which came to me at a crossroads early in my life of service for Jesus Christ, remains a secure anchor point as I seek to be a part of the next chapter of God's kingdom work. Those whose lives are transformed by the saving and filling work of the Master want to use the best of their time, talents, and abilities to advance his purposes. I see a measurable increase in the number of Christians longing to go beyond popular perceptions of success, to completeness. Personal fulfillment is among the most treasured core values for those seeking significance within and beyond the church.

Our understanding of the way to significance, however, is highly influenced by the popular wisdom of our self-driven culture. According to this wisdom, we must use the majority of our talents and time in order to attain personal satisfaction. We are daily confronted with media-made and applauded celebrities who purport to have found this satisfaction by discovering and utilizing their giftedness. As a result, many Western-influenced Christians believe that if they just could find that place of service where their gifts are acknowledged and talents fully utilized, they too could be fulfilled and great in the kingdom.

This "be all that you can be by doing all that you can do" formula often stands in stark contrast to and in conflict with the servant leadership models honored in Scripture.

- God took delight in using the foolish and the weak to confound the wise and the strong (1 Corinthians 1:27).
- Moses found that his inadequacies were the means for accomplishing God's greatest purposes (Exodus 3, 4).
- The psalmist was content to be a doorkeeper in the house of the Lord (Psalm 84:10).
- John the Baptist knew that he had to decrease so that Jesus might increase (Mark 1:7; John 3:30).
- Paul, whose résumé begins with a "chief of sinners" confession (1 Timothy 1:15, *KJV*), knew that his weakness was perfected in Jesus' strength—that "earthen vessels" hold life's greatest treasure so others will realize that the power and the glory are God's alone (2 Corinthians 4:7, *KJV*).

Like a marathoner achieving a personal best, the apostle Paul kept the faith and finished the course (2 Timothy 4:6-8). His words echo across the centuries that we too will receive the crown if we will run and complete the race, not in our own strength but in that of the one who declared, "It is finished" (John 19:30). The marathon Paul references is more like today's Special Olympics for those who are mentally and physically challenged than the single-winner events we often associate with competitions. All who cross the finish line receive the winner's crown, the warm embrace, and the Father's "Well done!"

Christians know, because of the witness of the Holy Spirit, that Jesus is the gold standard for doing the will of the Father. We are challenged by the Master's willingness to wash feet and endure the cross—all because he loved the Father who loved the world. Servant leadership has its ultimate definition and illustration in the life of our Lord.

No portion of Scripture has provided me with deeper insights into the mind, heart, and will of Christ's servant leadership than Philippians 2:1-11. Several of this book's other contributors also referenced this great passage. While reveling in this Pauline hymn, I believe the Holy Spirit asked me a sobering question: "Whose needs are you meeting as you lead—your own or those of the people I entrust to you?" As I seek to finish my earthly service to my Master well, I return often to this query, asking for the Comforter's help to evaluate my progress in serving like Jesus.

Those who desire to serve like Jesus must unite around a commitment to humility, self-denial, and other-centeredness. Actions and attitudes, for those who would be like Jesus, must be without selfish ambition and prideful arrogance.

Paul next turns to the ultimate case study, the core curriculum for the master's degree in servant leadership. The foundation stones of service, as Jesus' life so powerfully illustrates, first must be established in the mind and heart. We can only do as Jesus did when we see as Jesus saw and feel as Jesus felt.

While much of serving and leading often is motivated and evaluated by what we get from the experience, our Lord was driven by the desire to be what we needed so that our greatest good might be apprehended. Laying aside his glory as Lord of all, he humbly moved from his rightful place as Creator to taking on our state in order to identify with those he came to lead. He came to serve, not *be* served (Matthew 20:28). Jesus embraced our deepest longings, endured the pain of sin, and finally paid the price for liberation and regeneration. The Son gave up what he was, identified with what we were, so that we could become all that the Father intended—heirs and joint heirs with him for eternity (Romans 8:17).

Our call to leadership is inextricably bound to the form of Christ's humble incarnation. Though it often grates against our desire to be great and profound, Christ's life presents us with a consistent call to humble service under the direction of our Master.

Tools that assess and describe personality types, skill sets, or spiritual gifts help us realize that we are God's unique and distinctive creation, equipped for a specific purpose. We need to be good stewards of the abilities entrusted to us, utilizing them appropriately as the Holy Spirit directs.

I become concerned, however, when these assessments become the exclusive methodology for determining where, how, and whom we should serve. We may be tempted to accept or reject opportunities to serve based on perceptions of fit. The fact that this opportunity "just isn't me" may be the way God ensures that his Son, rather than you, gets the glory. We need to remember that we are his, and he calls us to who we are to be and how we are to serve.

Strength and gift assessments inadvertently can be used to set conditions on and criteria for service, creating expectations that personal needs should be met, agendas advanced, talents fully utilized, and dreams fulfilled. Too easily we take these things as evidence that we are in the center of God's will. There is some truth in these ideas, but we need to hear the whole truth. God does purpose to give us the desires of our heart (Psalm 37:4), but he is also in the process of reengineering the focus of those desires. To serve as Jesus served is to be confronted regularly with opportunities to deny the self, take up the cross, and follow him (Matthew 16:24).

Our Lord has as much need for utility players as he does stars. Biblical examples like Barnabas, John the Baptist, Aaron, Hur, Caleb, Esther, the two Marys, and a great cloud of witnesses (including the named and unnamed of the Hebrews 11 Faith Hall of Fame) became my inspiration. They willingly served another's mission so that those, in turn, could fulfill God's call on their lives.

I believe an unprecedented spiritual harvest is coming in the twenty-first century. It will be brought in primarily by those who have a clear and compelling vision of service that is committed to God's purposes more than to their own. Many will be asked to use their distinctive gifts to full capacity in the work they are given. Most will be required to pool their talents and availability with others because the work is too great to be entrusted to a select few. All will be asked at some point in that service to work outside their giftedness and beyond personal resources so Jesus gets all the glory.

Are you willing to be one of those serving whomever and wherever with whatever God entrusts to you? If so, let me suggest some steps that can make you available and willing for such a calling.

1. Explore and give thanks for the unique person God is making you. Take advantage of the many tools available to help you better understand your giftedness. However, do not be afraid to acknowledge your limitations—his strength is made perfect in your weakness.

2. Surrender the hurts and disappointments of not being fully utilized or recognized. The wisdom of the statement "they also serve who only stand and wait"[3] has been a great help to me when I was unsure of my next steps of service. I encourage you to use inactive or underutilized times to celebrate God's work in you, examine your driving motivations, and support his work in others.

3. Soak up the character of Jesus. Spend time in Philippians 2, the Beatitudes of the Sermon on the Mount (Matthew 5:1-12), and the fruit of the Holy Spirit (Galatians 5:22, 23). What we do has its greatest value when it plays a primary role in conforming us into the image of Christ.

4. Be prepared to be "benched" from time to time. The *stops,* as well as the *steps,* of the righteous are ordered of the Lord (Isaiah 40:31; Psalm 37:23, 24). It is primarily when we have nothing left but Jesus that he becomes our everything. When Jesus is our only thing, as well as our everything, the excellence of the power seen by all is understood to be of him and not of us. In the end, the only star will be Christ Jesus, "the bright Morning Star" (Revelation 22:16).

If Jesus is the gold standard for how to fulfill our calling, then we will obey him by serving those he has entrusted to us according to his leading. Often we will work within the strengths he has provided. As with Moses, the skills and experiences symbolized by the shepherd's staff can become the "rod of God," rescuing the lost and delivering the bound. However, we must not be surprised or unprepared when the Master asks us to minister out of frailty and discomfort. We must remember that we are operating not by our own power and might, but by the Spirit's (Zechariah 4:6).

// A FINAL CHALLENGE //

With Jesus Christ as the hub, the basic elements of spiritually formed leadership become a creative force. I am experiencing deeper understanding as I examine my calling in the context of the teachings and actions of Christ. As you strive to fulfill your leadership calling, I encourage you to develop an integrated approach that stretches minds, cradles hearts, and extends redemptive hands to serve a waiting world with compassion and excellence.

MY LEADERSHIP BOOKSHELF

A Long Obedience in the Same Direction by Eugene Peterson (IVP Books, 2000) is an applied study of the psalms of ascent that has helped me understand the deeper journey of faith needed to lead persistently and consistently.

Engaging God's World: A Christian Vision of Faith, Learning, and Living by Cornelius Plantinga Jr. (Wm. B. Eerdmans Publishing Company, 2002) is an excellent summary of the nonnegotiable core beliefs of the Christian faith, to anchor what leaders believe about faith and leadership integration to historic orthodoxy.

The Hero's Farewell: What Happens When CEOs Retire by Jeffrey Sonnenfeld (Oxford University Press, 1991) is an insightful and well-researched examination of leadership styles and their implications for leadership transitions and succession. He provides a helpful "look in the mirror" to help leaders see themselves more accurately.

Leadership, Greatness & Servanthood by Philip Greenslade (Bethany House Publishers, 1986). While primarily written for pastoral leadership, the focus on the importance of character rather than on leadership techniques and methods makes this a helpful reminder that who we are as leaders outlasts what we do as leaders.

A Tale of Three Kings: A Study in Brokenness by Gene Edwards (Tyndale House Publishers, 1992). This character study of David, Saul, and Absalom provides some invaluable insights and sobering warnings for those who take on leadership roles in ministry contexts.

Nehemiah and the Dynamics of Effective Leadership by Cyril Barber (Loizeaux Brothers, 1999). No other book has been as important in helping me anchor my leadership theories, motivations, strategies, and character. I consider this a must-read for all in or anticipating leadership. It is one I require of my leadership students and coaching clients.

////// PERSONAL REFLECTIONS AND APPLICATIONS /////

1. What were the major themes and insights of the various authors in this book that you found to be the most enlightening as you assess and develop your own sense of leadership calling? Why did you choose those themes?

2. What insights in the book were the most convicting to you personally? What specific changes in your attitude and approaches to leadership will you make as a result?

3. Which of the contributors did you find related best to your personal leadership journey? How and why?

4. As you have the opportunity to mentor the next generation of Christian leaders, what do you believe will be the most important lessons to emphasize? Why?

5. What leadership legacy would you like to pass on? Can you summarize this goal in several sentences?

you identified those within your organization with the gifts, integrity, proper predispositions to help develop the next generation of leader- for your mission and vision? If not, why not? If so, in what practi- ways are you implementing a plan to develop the next generation of ers?

at practical resources do those potential mentors need in order to be ective in equipping the next generation of leaders?

hat insights have you gained as a leadership team as a result of those sources that will help reshape the priorities and leadership culture of our organization for the future?

Vhat are the top three insights gleaned from the contributors to this book that you feel must be addressed quickly in your organization? Why? How?

What are the top three leadership strategies gleaned from the contributors to this book that you feel must be implemented quickly in your organiza- tion? Why? How?

DAVID J. GYERTSON
SENIOR FELLOW, ENGSTROM INSTITUTE
///

David J. Gyertson is the distinguished professor of leadership forma- ion and renewal at Regent University in Virginia. In addition he is a Fellow with the Engstrom Institute of the Christian Leadership Alliance (www.christianleadershipalliance.org), with a special research and consulting focus in executive leadership for nonprofit organizations.

He holds a PhD from Michigan State University with a major in higher education administration and management. He pursued his undergraduate studies at Spring Arbor University (Michigan), graduating with a BA in philosophy-religion and psychology. He completed additional graduate work in comparative higher education at the University of Toronto.

David J. Gyertson served a combined twelve years as the president of Taylor University (Indiana) and Asbury College (Kentucky). Prior to this he was a founding administrator and then president of Regent University. His extensive experience in higher education also includes student development, enrollment management, advancement, and being a faculty member in several disciplines.

Gyertson was the general editor of *Living by the Book,* a twenty-volume biblical and contemporary Christian issues study curriculum published in cooperation with Zondervan by CBN Publishing. He was editor of *Salt & Light: A Christian Response to Contemporary Issues* (Word Publishers) and the revised edition of *One Divine Moment: The Story of the Asbury Revival.*

From 1985 to 1992, Gyertson served the Christian Broadcasting Network in management, leadership, publishing, and broadcasting roles. He presently hosts *Canadian Edition,* a weekly television news, information, and ministry program broadcast coast to coast on Canada's Vision Television Network.

He has served on the boards of the Christian College Consortium and Christian University GlobalNet, and he was featured in the *2000 Templeton Guide: Colleges That Encourage Character Development.* He holds ordination credentials with the Free Methodist Church and has served in senior ministry roles for the Free Methodist Church and the Presbyterian Church, both the PC(USA) and the EPCA.

David J. Gyertson and his wife, Nancy, reside in Virginia and have a married daughter and two grandchildren.

ıg

er
e
-
n

///////////////////////// NOTES /////////////////////////

CHAPTER 1

1. These materials are compiled from several articles on the Engstrom Institute resources Web site and are used under the permissions granted to the Engstrom Institute of the Christian Leadership Alliance.

2. This material was excerpted and adapted from a biographical sketch of Dr. Ted W. Engstrom at www.worldvision.org.

CHAPTER 2

1. Ruth Haley Barton, *Strengthening the Soul of Your Leadership* (Downers Grove, IL: InterVarsity Press, 2008), 131–132.

2. Amy Carmichael, *Edges of His Ways* (Fort Washington, PA: Christian Literature Crusade, 1992), 82. Copied here from: http://youmockmypain.blogspot.com/2009_06_01_archive.html (accessed November 9, 2010).

3. Oswald Chambers, *My Utmost for His Highest* (New York: Dodd, Mead & Company, Inc., 1935), 58.

4. MentorLink, http://www.mentorlink.org/thecall/transformed.html (accessed November 9, 2010).

5. Bruce Wilkinson, *The Prayer of Jabez* (Sisters, OR: Multnomah Publishers, Inc., 2000), 47.

CHAPTER 4

1. *Strong's Exhaustive Concordance* online, http://www.biblestudytools.com/lexicons/greek/kjv/doulos.html (accessed November 3, 2010).

2. http://www.usmra.com/saxsewell/crandallcanyon.htm (accessed November 4, 2010).

3. Alexis de Tocqueville, quoted at http://www.sermonillustrations.com/a-z/f/fourth_of_july.htm (accessed November 4, 2010).

CHAPTER 5

1. Max De Pree, *Leadership Jazz* (New York: Doubleday, 1992). Page 3 at http://books.google.com (accessed November 8, 2010).

2. Larry R. Smeltzer, "An Analysis of Strategies for Announcing Organization-Wide Change," *Group Organization Management*, March 1991, vol. 16, no. 1. Abstract seen at http://gom.sagepub.com/content/16/1/5.short (accessed November 8, 2010).

3. Best Christian Workplaces Institute. http://www.bcwinstitute.com.

CHAPTER 6

1. Daniel Goleman, *Working with Emotional Intelligence* (New York: Bantam, 2000), 26.

2. Arnold Palmer, quoted at http://www.globalsportscoaching.com/documents/FREE_QUOTES_eBook_2_001.pdf, 15 (accessed November 8, 2010).

3. Malcolm Gladwell, *Outliers: The Story of Success* (New York: Little, Brown and Company, 2008), 39.

4. Christopher Parkening with Kathy Tyers, *Grace Like a River* (Carol Stream, IL: Tyndale House Publishers, Inc., 2006), 19–20.

5. I suspect the threshold talent for potential leaders may be lower than most of us might think. Take intelligence using IQ as a crude indicator. Sure, IQ above, say, 120 is probably necessary to lead complex organizations. But there is no evidence that IQ above that threshold makes much difference. Daniel Goleman suggests that there is little correlation between intelligence (above some threshold) and degree of leadership success. See chapter 2 in Goleman's book *Working with Emotional Intelligence* (cited earlier).

6. Not many ministries or small organizations feel they can afford an executive coach. Consider discussing with your board how the benefits of executive coaching could help you and your organization become more effective. As an alternative, there may be qualified individuals who might consider this role on a voluntary basis.

7. Not all 360-degree assessments are created equal. Do your homework to make sure you are using a proven assessment tool. A good coach may edit personal comments made by respondents and will sort out what feedback will be truly helpful.

8. www.m-w.com.

9. Max De Pree, *Leadership Jazz* (New York: Doubleday, 1992), 7.

CHAPTER 7

1. http://www.slo-business.com/tech-talk/2.html.

2. www.salvationarmyusa.org.

CHAPTER 8

1. www.imdb.com/title/tt0047203/quotes (accessed October 20, 2010).

2. Dag Hammarskjold, *Markings,* quoted at www.quotestar.com.

3. Albert Schweitzer, quoted at www.answers.com/topic/albert-schweitzer.

4. David L. McKenna, *A Concept to Keep: Featuring the Concept for a Christian College,* edited by Gayle D. Beebe and Jon S. Kulago (Spring Arbor, MI: Spring Arbor University Press, 2003), vii.

5. Ibid.

6. Charles Wesley hymn line from http://www.ms-umf.org/index.php?q=news.html.

7. John Wesley, www.thinkexist.com.

CHAPTER 10

1. www.dictionary.com.

2. http://oxforddictionaries.com, www.answerbag.com, and www.thefreedictionary.com.

3. James Kouzes and Barry Posner, *The Leadership Challenge* (San Francisco: Jossey-Bass, 2007), 9. Seen at www.mindsetmattersgroup.com/Portals/0/.../Five_Fundamental_Practices.pdf.

CHAPTER 11

1. John Ortberg, *If You Want to Walk on Water, You've Got to Get Out of the Boat* (Grand Rapids, MI: Zondervan, 2001). Page 71 at www.books.google.com (accessed November 15, 2010).

2. 2001 Barna Research Group poll, reported in "Bono Tells Christians: Don't Neglect Africa" by Sheryl Henderson, *Christianity Today,* http://www.christianitytoday.com/ct/2002/april22/14.18.html (accessed November 15, 2010).

3. UNICEF, "Child Mortality Rate Drops by a Third Since 1990," http://www.unicefusa.org/news/releases/child-mortality-rate-drops.html (accessed November 15, 2010).

4. *Chariots of Fire* quote, www.imdb.com/title/tt0082158/quotes.

5. William Sloane Coffin, http://www.williamsloanecoffin.org/ (accessed November 15, 2010).

6. Some material contained in this chapter is excerpted from *The Hole in Our Gospel* by Richard Stearns, © 2009, and reprinted by permission of Thomas Nelson, Inc., Nashville, Tennessee.

CHAPTER 13

1. Information in this section condensed from James Moschgat, "A Janitor's Ten Lessons in Leadership," http://www.homeofheroes.com/profiles/profiles_crawford_10lessons.html (accessed 11/29/10). Used with permission.

2. Andrew Murray, *The Inner Life* (Springdale, PA: Whitaker House, 1984), 6.

3. A. W. Tozer, *God Tells the Man Who Cares* (Harrisburg, PA: Christian Publications, Inc., 1970), 55.

4. Ibid., 88–89.

CHAPTER 14

1. en.wikipedia.org/wiki/Taihō_Code and http://pharmacist.askdefine.com.

2. www.pharmacytimes.com and www.medicalnewstoday.com/articles/210470.php, for example.

3. http://www.research.vt.edu/resmag/1999resmag/taxol.html, http://www.rosswalker.co.uk/taxol/history.htm, and http://ohioline.osu.edu/sc150/sc150_3.html.

4. Variously attributed to both Harry Truman and John Wooden.

5. http://www.fda.gov/drugs/resourcesforyou/consumers/ucm143534.htm and http://www.duke.edu/web/soc142/team2/political.html.

6. http://www.nytimes.com/1982/12/25/business/tylenol-posts-an-apparent-recovery.html and http://articles.cnn.com/2009-02-04/justice/tylenol.murders_1_tylenol-case-tylenol-murders-james-w-lewis?_s=PM:CRIME.

7. www.answers.yahoo.com.

8. http://www.nytimes.com/2010/05/09/business/09teva.html.

CHAPTER 15

1. Parker J. Palmer, *The Courage to Teach: Exploring the Inner Landscape of a Teacher's Life* (San Francisco: Jossey-Bass, 2007). Quote found at http://search.barnesandnoble.com.

2. Ibid., found at http://www.newhorizons.org/strategies/character/palmer.htm.

3. John Milton, www.sonnets.org/milton.htm.

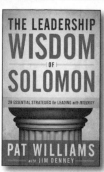